VIRGINIA

DONATED

VIRGINIA FOLK LEGENDS

Edited by
THOMAS E. BARDEN

UNIVERSITY OF VIRGINIA PRESS

Charlottesville and London

Publications of the American Folklore Society, New Series

General Editor, Patrick B. Mullen

Art by Leslie Evans

UNIVERSITY OF VIRGINIA PRESS
Copyright © 1991 by the Rector and Visitors
of the University of Virginia

9 11 13 14 12 10 8

Library of Congress Cataloging-in-Publication Data
Virginia folk legends/ edited by Thomas E. Barden.
    p.   cm. —(Publications of the American Folklore Society. New series)
    ISBN 0-8139-1331-4 (cloth). — ISBN 0-8139-1335-7 (paper)
    1. Legends—Virginia. 2. Tales—Virginia. 3. Virginia Writers' Project.
I. Barden, Thomas E. II. Series: Publications of the American Folklore
Society.   New series (Unnumbered)
GR 110.V8V57   1991
398.23'2755—dc20   91-12422
                                                                  CIP

Printed in the United States of America

ISBN-13: 978-0-8139-1335-3

CONTENTS

CONTENTS

ACKNOWLEDGMENTS

The making of this book has spanned half a century. The first to labor on it were the people acknowledged in the dedication, the WPA field-workers on the Virginia Writers' Project. Every week from mid–1937 to mid–1942 they found informants, interviewed them, and sent the resulting folklore in to the Richmond office. But for all their efforts, they received no recognition. The project shut down, and it must have seemed to them that all traces of what they had done simply disappeared forever. They were on this job first, so to a large extent the book is theirs.

Behind the VWP workers' efforts were those of another group of people who must be acknowledged, the informants themselves. They were the carriers of the great tradition that does not reside in a book. They bore it as invisibly as they did their accents and dialect, which the project workers struggled to translate into writing. They didn't think of themselves as doing anything exceptional, and they probably thought the field-workers were crazy to be going to so much trouble. But, whatever they thought of them, they let them in their homes, talked to them, understood what they wanted, and gave it. The book is also theirs.

But it might never have become a book at all. In 1943 the entire WPA Virginia Writers' Project Folklore Collection was deposited in the manuscript room of the University of Virginia Library. And there it sat, waiting in file boxes through the 1940s, the 1950s, and the 1960s. My part in the story began in 1972. Thanks to Charles L. Perdue, Jr., our folklore professor when we were graduate students at the University of Virginia, Robert K. Phillips and I got summer work/study employment that year indexing and annotating the collection. In 1976 Perdue, Phillips, and I published the ex-slave narratives from the WPA collection (and other locations) as *Weevils in the Wheat: Interviews with Virginia Ex-slaves*, and in 1979 Norwood Editions printed the index we had compiled in 1972. With this index available as a guide, scholars finally had access to this massive body of folklore. So acknowledgment for resuscitating the collection must go to our mentor, Chuck Perdue, to my colleague Bob Phillips, and to a much younger me.

Bringing things into the present, I would like to express my appreciation to my home institution, the University of Toledo, for granting me sabbatical leave so that I could finally turn my attention to this project. I would also like to thank Robert Vaughan and the Virginia Foundation for the Humanities and Public Policy for the summer 1990 residency at the Virginia Center for the Humanities that gave me time and ideal conditions to write the introduction. I want to acknowledge the courteous assistance of Michael Plunkett and the staff of the Manuscript Division, Special Collections Department, University of Virginia Library. And I want to thank Garry Barrow, the Virginia State Folklife Program Coordinator, both for his support and encouragement of my work and for his invaluable insights as we discussed it. His loan of his paper on legend scholarship and recent legend theory was especially helpful. Director Grayson B. Miller, Jr., M.D., and his staff at the Epidemiology Office of the Virginia Department of Health went beyond the call of duty in helping me locate information about Norfolk's 1855 yellow fever epidemic.

To my dear friend Dr. F. J. Lockman—Jay, thank you for the time you took from radio astronomy to read the manuscript and offer such cogent comments and feedback. You are my ideal nonspecialist reader. To John McGuigan, my editor at the University Press of Virginia—thank you for your help, for your excellent advice, and for believing in this project from the beginning. To Chuck and Nan Perdue—a special salute for your continuous friendship over so many years; it has been a great pleasure to return to Charlottesville and pick up our conversations on folklore, the New Deal in Virginia, and things in general. And, finally, my main thanks go to my family—to my wife and dear companion Rayna Zacharias for the steady encouragement and our good talks about everything and to our sons Zacharias, Matthias, and Daniel, my erstwhile editorial assistants and ever-enthusiastic auditors of Virginia's folk legends.

VIRGINIA
FOLK
LEGENDS

INTRODUCTION

On September 9, 1939, in Wise County, Virginia, a man named Samuel Simpson Adams told Virginia Writers' Project folklore collector James Taylor Adams a story about a man who was attacked by a panther as he carried a sack of pork across the mountain on his way home from helping a neighbor butcher hogs. As he raced homeward, he dropped pieces of meat in the path to stall the panther and gain distance. When the meat was gone, he threw down the sack, too; and the big cat stopped to eat that as well. The story, in Samuel Adams's own words, is printed here as legend 6, "A Race with a Panther." The incident burns in the mind—the blood-freezing sound of the panther's cry, its tail patting the ground as it lopes into view, the sight of it mauling the empty meat sack, and the palpable feeling of relief when it stops at the edge of the field, turns, and disappears. We identify with the nameless man walking at dusk in solitude and empathize with his sudden terror, his quick thinking, and his survival. And the story's power is intensified by the thought that it actually happened.

Somewhere in the Florida Panhandle in 1974, Carol Ann Turner's mother told her another story about a panther. John Burrison printed in it *Storytellers: Folktales and Legends from the South.* Carol Turner's mother said she'd heard about a young couple who got married and settled down to farm in a remote area where panthers still roamed the woods. She said people who knew the area told the girl if she ever heard a noise like a woman screaming that it would be a panther. They said she should "pull off her clothes one piece at a time and run as hard as she could, because the panther would stop and tear whatever you put down to shreds."[1] One day when she was coming back from taking water to her husband in the field she heard a scream and knew it was a panther. She started to run and pulled her clothes off—first her bonnet, then her coat, her apron, her skirt, her blouse—all the time running as hard as she could. By the time she got home she was completely naked. But she outran the panther and saved her life.

This panther story, like the Virginia one, was supposedly an account of something that really happened. But, as the notes to "A Race with a Panther" (legend 6) indicate, numerous versions of both the meat-throwing and the clothes-stripping forms of this "true" story have been found from Maine to Florida and from Ireland to the Ozarks. Questions arise. The most immediate one, naturally, is whether the incident really happened in Wise County as Samuel Simpson Adams said (and believed) it did. In a sense, the story is ruined. The first impression—that it is a true account of an actual event—collapses under the weight of the new information that it exists in many forms in many places. Loss of belief in the story coincides with the recognition of what it actually is. It is a legend.

The definition of the word *legend* has been debated and quibbled over, but one is generally accepted: A legend is a traditional prose narrative, set in this world, in the past, involving human characters, which is regarded as fact by its teller and its audience.[2] This definition needs one qualifier: legends may be told when they are not believed, simply as good stories; but the issue of their truth usually still comes up. We may account for this case by saying legends have the rhetorical quality of being true, a quality which is part of their aesthetic appeal. The questions Is this true? Did it really happen? are hard to answer about any particular legend. It may have happened. Or something may have happened and later been conformed in the telling to a traditional narrative pattern. Or it may never have happened at all. The Florida version of the panther story indicates that people knew what to do when a panther appeared, so the events of that story may have occurred many times in many places. Or it may simply have been a pioneer safety lesson, a way of passing on a traditional procedure to use in "the panther situation."

The question of whether the events of a legend actually occurred is inevitable once the spell of belief is broken and the genre recognized. The question is inevitable, primary, and overriding. But I would like to give it up. Besides often being unanswerable, it can overshadow other questions, some of which are more interesting—Why did this story circulate in tradition and thrive in so many ways in so many places? Why did the people who told it give it a local habitation and situate it in their group so that it became true? Why do some stories strike us as powerful, haunting, disturbing, or significant? And what does that reveal about the people who tell them, listen to them, and bring them up when folklore field-workers come asking for stories?

The stories in this book are legends. They range in mood from gory to funny, from frightening to inspiring, but they all hang heavy with an atmosphere of hidden meaning and complexity, the feeling that there is more to them than meets the ear. It is the purpose of this introduction to explore these meanings and messages. But first some background information about them is needed.

Employees of the Virginia Writers' Project (VWP), a subsidiary of the Work Projects Administration (WPA), collected these stories between mid–1937 and mid–1942. Their collecting was part of a general folklore-gathering effort which altogether amassed over 3,850 items of oral, customary, and material folklore from sixty-two counties around the state. Over seventy workers submitted items, but the bulk of the collection was the work of twelve individuals: James Taylor Adams, Gertrude Blair, John W. Garrett, Susan K. Gordon, Emory L. Hamilton, James M. Hylton, Roscoe E. Lewis, Pearl Morrissett, Susan R. Morton, Bessie A. Scales, Raymond Sloan, and Isaiah Volley.[3] They were not searching for legends in particular. The Washington, D.C., office of the Federal Writers' Project (FWP), under Henry G. Alsberg, and its folklore unit, under John A. Lomax and later Benjamin A. Botkin, told the state offices to have their workers collect a wide variety of local customs and lore. To Alsberg, the main purpose of the collecting was to get colorful copy for the state guidebooks, the publication series that he saw as the FWP's main work. But he recognized that the folklore was valuable in its own right. In 1937 he and Lomax wrote a letter to the state directors saying that "such an opportunity to collect this material may never recur."[4]

Their instructions reflected a somewhat disorganized sense of what should be collected. Borrowing the phrase from a 1937 FWP literary publication called *American Stuff*, they suggested the states collect "American Folk Stuff," a title they had in mind for a future FWP folklore book. They provided an almost random list of suggested topics that included "stories of animals and of relations between animals and people, peculiarities of table service or dining routine, special religious customs, such as public denunciations of wrongdoing, blessings of crops or of rivers, tall tales, drinking toasts peculiar to a locality, unusual epitaphs in old graveyards, and stories of persons with psychic or supernatural powers."[5] When Benjamin Botkin took over the folklore program in 1938, he tried to give the field-workers a more scholarly idea of folklore categories. In August 1938 he sent out a mimeographed *Manual for Folklore Studies* which included an "index to folklore subjects." This manual gave an orderly presentation of the major genres of folklore, although its conception of the legend genre was still not clear. In the category "legend" it gave only two subheadings, "local and Indian." It listed "place name stories" in the category "tales." Under the subheading "tall tale," it listed "tales of American legendary heroes (especially little-known local heroes)." And under a catchall subheading of the "tales" category, it listed "stories of lost mines, treasure, ghost towns, and outlaws."[6] While these vague categories may have caused problems, they had a positive effect, too. For one thing, personal experiences, anecdotes, accounts of dreams and visions, and character sketches, which academic folklorists of the 1930s ignored, were dutifully recorded and preserved. The item titles in the Virginia collection show that the category "American Folk Stuff" was used extensively. The idea seems to have been to collect everything, send it in, and let the state office worry about what to call it. Worker Raymond Sloan, for example, sent in a narrative about a man who carried a hundred-dollar bill around in his pocket all his life. In a preface to the story, he wrote: "This is not exactly in the category of tall tale, but still, it is remarkable. Maybe it is just one we could add to Mr. Ripley's 'Believe It or Not' collection."[7]

As the collecting progressed, reactions to it were varied. The national efforts were not very well received among academic folklorists. At its 1937 annual meeting, the American Folklore Society, the official American scholarly folklore organization, formally rejected the writers' project as a legitimate instrument for gathering folklore. The members passed a resolution declaring that only a scientifically trained folklorist was qualified to collect dependable folklore. In some instances FWP staff workers themselves had their doubts. The director of the Wyoming project stated that "when we received the index of folklore subjects . . . we thought it was the biggest piece of malarkey we'd ever seen."[8] And detractors of the Roosevelt administration were quick to use the program as an example of the make-work excesses of the WPA in general, which they said stood for "We Piddle Around." A conservative newspaper editorial, after citing the folklore project, said: "There is no end to the work to be done—there is no limit to the money it will cost. The Boondoggling must go on and on and you must pay the bill."[9]

These negative attitudes might have been overcome in time. When Botkin replaced Lomax as head of the program, the American Folklore Society softened its objection to the FWP's folklore work. Its leaders saw him as more academic and less publicity conscious than Lomax; also, his inclusion of American Folklore Society members on his WPA Joint Committee on the Folk Arts was a well-received gesture to the scholars. The few folklore books and pamphlets that were published from the FWP's collecting gained critical and popular approval.[10] But World War II disrupted the whole enterprise, and most of the FWP folklore was never published.

By the spring of 1943 the Virginia Writers' Project office in Richmond was in the final stages of closing down. Its files were supposed to be dispersed to Washington, D.C., and various places around the state. In June 1943 Professor Arthur Kyle Davis, Jr., a folklorist at the University of Virginia, convinced Eudora Ramsay Richardson, then director of the Virginia project, to send the bulk of the folklore, thirty file boxes, to the University of Virginia Library in Charlottesville.[11] Fifteen of the boxes contained folksongs, four held administrative paperwork, and eleven contained the nonmusical folklore materials from which the legends in this book were selected. These eleven boxes were divided into two completely separate collections, the first two containing the black lore and the next nine the white material. There is no indication as to who suggested this arrangement; there is, in fact, no indication as to who provided any of the final organization of the collection as it was deposited. But it reflects a more rigorous conception of folklore genres than either Lomax's or Botkin's guidance had suggested. The items go from such complex verbal forms as tales and legends, through short-item verbal forms such as jokes, riddles, and rhymes, then on to customs, beliefs, and behavior, and finally to material culture forms such as quilt patterns, recipes, folk art, and house and cabin information.

Altogether the WPA Virginia Writers' Project's Folklore Collection is, as Bruce Rosenberg described it, "one of the richest unpublished holdings in the country."[12] It is certainly rich in sheer number of items, in geographic spread, and in intriguing titles, such as "Live Chicken Cures Snakebite," "A Lost Mine," and "John's Pass to Sally's———." But the question remains as to how valuable all this "American Folk Stuff" is as a collection of folklore. As far as the qualifications of the workers goes, one thing is clear; they were amateurs. The correspondence files indicate that they were students, bank tellers, teachers, clerks, newspaper reporters, and aspiring writers. What folklore training they got was on the job, from the written guidelines of the Washington and Richmond offices, from their own experience discovering what worked in the field, and from each other. One worker, James Taylor Adams, wrote two papers he called "finders"—"A Field Worker's Finder for Traditional Tales" and "Folklore Finders: Song"—which he used as memory jogs to himself and his informants. Copies of these were widely requested when word got out about them, near the end of the project's work.[13]

Some of the collectors initially sent in material copied verbatim from books, newspaper clippings, and court records, but the Richmond office soon set them straight. A few VWP workers attempted to elevate their own ideas and prejudices to the level of folklore theory. For example, a worker named Aubrey Boyd (who fortunately did no fieldwork for the program) made the following pronouncement in an essay about some of the folk superstitions collected from around the state: "The wild gibberish of the savage Africans imported into Virginia soon vanished, as did their crude music and voodoo practices. Today the Negroes of Virginia are said to be among the best-mannered and most cultivated in the South. They have, it is true, a folk lore of their own, but it is probably based in large part on the superstitions and traditions of the whites."[14] And Susan R. Morton, who collected Simon Kenton legends in Prince William County, faulted her informants for telling stories that did not conform to printed histories of Kenton. But, in general, though not professionals, the workers deserve high marks as fast learners, energetic interviewers, and conscientious researchers.

Their manual told them that with each item of folklore, they were to record "as much as possible about [its] source, history, and use, in addition to the past and present experience of the people who keep it alive." Their guidance also required that as well as coming strictly from oral sources, the folklore must be "recorded precisely as heard, have a clear purpose and reason for existence, and be submitted in the form of full, unedited notes of the interview sessions."[15] The manual also suggested that the writers include a short description of the circumstances of their collecting with each item they submitted. Since most of the workers (especially the prolific twelve) did so faithfully, a relatively good idea of how they went about their collecting can be ascertained.

These descriptions reveal that the workers employed good field techniques and had excellent rapport with their informants, many of whom they had known for years. In the "circumstances of interview" sheet he filed with a set of stories by C. W. Renfro, for example, James M. Hylton stated that he had sat with his informant under the big maple tree on the lawn at the Wise County courthouse throughout the afternoon and that Renfro "had had a nip or two and was enjoying it very much at the time. He was really in the mood to reel off some of the old yarns."[16]

In some cases the folklore collection sheet itself reveals contextual information. A ghost tale titled "The Quilt Pulling Ghost," for instance, begins with a short framework paragraph in which a former informant gives the collector a new lead. "'Are ye still huntin' haint tales?' asked Si Craft, as I [James Taylor Adams] greeted him July 14, 1941, on State Road 626 where he is employed. . . . 'Well, Noah Hamilton can shore tell ye a good'un. I've heard him tell hit to the boys. Hit's a good'un, an' true too. He's right up yonder where they're loadin' that truck.' Walking on up the road about three hundred yards I met Bill Green, another road worker. 'If you're lookin' for haint tales, Noah Hamilton knows a good'un,' he greeted me. 'That's him leanin' 'gainst the truck with them white lookin' britches on.'"[17]

It is important to remember that the VWP was a public government program. The storytellers who talked to the workers knew that their words were going to be sent in to Richmond, and then perhaps on to Washington, D.C. They knew they would have no control over them once they were written down. And, knowing the interviews would have their names on them for all posterity, they were aware that what they said would reflect long and widely on themselves and their community. This surely influenced the stories they told. I am sure it is the reason, for instance, that there is so little obscene or even mildly risqué material in the collection. It is also likely that it diminished the amount of religious, political, and racial material the workers got.

The fact that much of the black folklore was gathered by black workers was an influence, too, but in this case a positive one. Black informants found some things presentable to the black workers which they would not have shared with whites in the segregated Virginia of the 1930s. This is most apparent in the VWP's oral histories of ex-slaves. Informant Jennie Patterson, for example, told black worker Susie R. C. Byrd: "Some of us slaves had ole mean an' wicked marsters an' mistess dat would beat 'em unmerciful. I don[e] tole you I was feared to tell all I done see in my lifetime, an' I ain' tellin' white folks but so much even now in dis new day an' time."[18] This same attitude shows up in the legends too. Comparing the legends collected from blacks by whites with those told to blacks reveals differences in tone, texture, and what they chose to tell. The story of James Bowser, for example, which was collected by black workers Emmy Wilson and Claude Anderson, rings with dignity and pride that are absent from such narratives as "Why Butterflies Was Made" (legend 15) or "The Old Negro That Flagged the Train" (legend 140), which were collected by white workers Bessie Scales and John W. Garrett, respectively. And the local legends of colorful and sometimes antisocial black characters such as Peacock Wydeman, Henry Armstrong (de Forgin' Man), or Bad Bill Cabell, which were related to Claude Anderson, Roscoe Lewis, and Jessie Williams, in my opinion, would not have been told to white workers at all.

In assessing this collection, then, we have to consider the field-work that generated it—the amateur status of the workers, their biases and those of their informants, and its shaping by their sense of what was presentable. The artificial circumstances of its collection must be acknowledged as well. How, for example, could Adams's gathering of a ghost story in the blazing sun on a public road-work site possibly reflect a natural performance context for such a tale? Also, it surely would have helped if there had been more versions of items and more specifics about the context of their performance. These factors limit the value of the collection, and field-workers on this side of the 1960s obviously would do things differently. But the fact remains that the WPA collection is the most extensive folklore fieldwork ever done in Virginia, either in the thirties or any other time. The alternative to accepting and working within its limitations is not to use it at all, and that would be a great loss. Since care in selecting and editing materials from the collection can minimize its limitations, we should now turn to my editorial procedures in this regard.

The first task in making a book titled *Virginia Folk Legends* is to qualify the terms. The VWP's "Virginia" question was resolved in the thirties by the working proposition that anything collected in Virginia was Virginia folklore. Numerous items from the western part of the state came from or were set in Kentucky, and some from Danville crossed the line into North Carolina. But, since this was a national effort, these things were collected and submitted. My "Virginia" question was that of distribution. A Virginia collection should include all regions of the state. But only sixty-two of the one hundred Virginia counties were represented in the WPA collection, and folk legends were gathered in only fifty of those. I attempted to include as many counties as possible in my selection, although that was not the primary consideration. Thirty-eight counties survived the final winnowing, and fortunately they do represent all of Virginia's major geographical zones. There is a regional skew in the collection toward the southwest. Workers in that area submitted much more folklore than those in any other; they also produced the best work, the most accurate texts, and the most complete contextual data. Due largely to the energy and skills of James Taylor Adams, Emory L. Hamilton, and James M. Hylton, but also because it is an especially isolated and folklore-rich region, Wise County is the most heavily represented county in the book.

The second word of the book's title, *folk*, refers to the goal of including only legends taken from active oral circulation. Previous collections of Virginia legends have been literary and popular texts gleaned from newspaper human interest stories and old commonplace books. Such books as Charles A. Mills's *Treasure Legends of Virginia*, Robert F. Nelson's *25 Thrilling Legends of Virginia*, and George Holbert Tucker's *Virginia Supernatural Tales*[19] give no sources and yet suggest, based on no fieldwork, that such figures as Pocahontas, Grace Sherwood (the Virginia witch), William Byrd, and George Washington populate the active repertoires of Virginia storytellers. My aim was for *Virginia Folk Legends* to contain only narratives that actually circulated in tradition and were subjected to the shaping forces of the folk process. Sometimes it was easy to tell these from literary texts. Who could miss the smell of the writer's lamp surrounding a story about Grace Sherwood, the Chesapeake Bay witch, which begins: "Grace Sherwood was the daughter of John White, a carpenter who owned his small farm in the flat country bordering on the bay. In 1680 she married James Sherwood, who was also, like her father, a yeoman who combined carpentering with tilling a few sandy acres. Sherwood seems to have been an inoffensive citizen."[20] The literary syntax, noun clauses, and essentially nonoral vocabulary (try saying "combined carpentering" aloud) give this away immediately as a written tale. Of course, not all determinations were so easy to make, but looking closely at linguistic and stylistic details and confirming established folk motifs in the texts gave me concrete specifics to add to my subjective judgments.

In most cases I excluded texts that failed to meet my folk stylistic and folk motif criteria no matter how fascinating the subject matter (as with Grace Sherwood, the witch) or how much the workers insisted the story was "widely told." The few exceptions are cases in which workers acted as their own informants and submitted items from their personal recollection. Emory L. Hamilton's "Legend of the Dogwood Tree" (legend 22) is an example. He wrote: "Anyone who has ever studied the dogwood flower can readily see the symbols in the flower that are mentioned in this legend. Whether the legend be true or false, one is lead [*sic*] to believe that it is pretty near the truth." It seemed inequitable to me to exclude this story from a native Virginian who had heard it all his life solely because he chose a writerly rather than a conversational way to tell his story. He was, after all, a writer in the employ of a government writers' project.

The categories for *Virginia Folk Legends* were not taken from any preexisting list of folk legend types. They emerged organically from the categories of the WPA collection itself. Some are standard—place-name stories, treasure, the supernatural, and legendary people. Others, such as Indian legends, Civil War legends, tales of Daniel Boone and Simon Kenton, and slavery and race stories, reflect the collection's distinct regional and Virginia flavor. After some consideration I decided to include legends that circulated only within a family. These do have an oral tradition, even though their group life was circumscribed. The texts of forty family legends are included in this volume; but twelve of these had both family and wider existence, as evidenced in statements like "I heard Tom Evans tell this, and I believe I heard mother talk about it too," from Martha Shupe.[21]

One final selection principle should be explained. *Virginia Folk Legends* contains only fully developed narratives. It is a book of stories. Numerous items that met all other criteria were excluded on this basis. In a long narrative by ex-slave Fanny Berry, for example, she said her master told her that "on his way to de gallows Ole John [Brown] stopped an' kissed a little nigger child."[22] It is a gripping moment in the life of a man who is legendary to both black and white Virginians. But it is only that, a moment. It is not an elaborated story. Of the subject categories, place-name legends were most affected by this restriction. Although clearly legendary, many of these were simply too short and undeveloped. In Wise County, for example, Emory Hamilton reported that "old folks say 'Devil's Marble Ground' was named because the Devil had his apron full of these little white rocks and the string broke, and the marble-like pebbles rolled all over the uneven ground." In the same submission he gave the following name origin for the village of Donkey: "A pioneer family, pushing their way from Virginia to Kentucky around 1810, camped there. Their belongings were packed on a mule and a donkey. The donkey died that night and left the family stranded. The place and later the village became known as Donkey."[23]

In editing the individual texts, my rule was to leave them alone as much as possible. When garbled, clichéd, or patently unrealistic dialect renderings made a text incoherent or suspect, I did not try to fix it; instead, I looked for a different item to represent the same legend type or subject. I have added paragraphing when it is called for, regularized quotation marks and ellipses, and glossed some words and information in brackets. Other than that, the texts are as I found them.

Having looked at how the legends were collected, their limitations and value, and my editorial methods, we can now return to our initial search for their meaning and significance. That search must begin with the fact that they were told as true. While this may or may not have diminished their entertainment value (numerous informants spoke of hearing the tales around fires in evening tale-telling sessions), it vouches for their cultural importance. As Jan Harold Brunvand put it, "Legend study is a most revealing area of research because the stories that people believe to be true hold an important place in their worldview. 'If it's true, it's important' is an axiom to be trusted."[24] Such weight has always been a feature of the legend genre; it is even revealed in the etymology of the word. The word *legend* comes from the Latin *legenda*, meaning "that which is to be read." It refers to medieval stories of the lives of saints that were taken from oral tradition and written down by the church. The often miraculous events in the stories were believed to have occurred. They were considered important narratives, to be read and contemplated for the moral instruction and edification of Christian laymen.

While it is no longer their main intention, the presence of some moral lesson remains an important feature of legends. Folklorist Polly Stewart found that both the surface style and the deep structural features of the legends she studied supported the moral order of their narrators' society. She said:

Though on the surface legends may be told without any open claim to instructiveness, most are informed by a powerful moral message couched in ironic terms: seekers of hidden gold mines, intruding in forbidden places, meet with unknown terror, with inexplicable death, or, at the very least, with frustration. Greedy people get their just desserts by losing money where they had contrived to gain money. Young people going places they should not go, to abandoned buildings, to lovers' lane, are confronted with sometimes horrifying events that defy logical explanation. Whether the events in the stories can be rationally accounted for or not (and in many cases they can), they illustrate the dangers inherent in behavior that is inimical to collective order and to personal well-being.[25]

Her list fits the Virginia texts well. The treasure tales, for example, have numerous ironic moral messages. "The Beverly Diamonds" (legend 132) and "The Old Woman Who Found the Silver" (legend 135) imply that seekers waste their time and find nothing for their trouble, but "A Spirit Dog Guards Swift's Mine" (legend 134) contains the stronger moral warning—that the wife's obsessive greed actually caused her husband's death. Warnings about greed appear in other kinds of legends, too. Murder tales, for example, often cite greed as the motive of the crimes they depict. Guilty parties may be punished by chance or unintentionally by their intended victims, as in "Scaring the Widow" (legend 91). But supernatural agents often avenge crimes as well, as in "A Strange Light at a Murder Site" (legend 88) and "How Bloody Branch Got Its Name" (legend 96). Or the retribution may be left ambiguous; supernatural forces may have been at work, or the criminals may have died later merely by chance. Not all the moral issues are so violent or grave as these. But even minor sins may have drastic consequences, as in "The Man in the Moon" (legend 17) and "How Dragon Run Got Its Name" (legend 95), in which people die for merely working or fishing on Sunday.

The danger of alcohol is a common theme in the stories. In "How Bloody Branch Got Its Name," drinking is given as the context of violence and murder; and in "A Devil Dog in the Path" (legend 113), two men on their way to a drinking bout meet a huge ghostly dog in the road, which the informant interpreted as the devil, "there to turn 'em back from goin' after liquor." Warnings against meanness and cruelty are frequent, too, again usually in ironic form as examples of the fate of mean and cruel people. Both natural and supernatural forces often intervene on the behalf of weak and/or oppressed individuals. While this is most common in the African American legends, with a diversity of intervening agents—horned snakes, boats, ghost dogs, or even God directly—it also occurs in the material. "The Warning Dog" (legend 111), for example, tells of a large black dog which threatened and growled at a young girl's father and cruel stepmother. The dog would appear and disappear at random and intervene when they beat or overworked the defenseless girl. The legend ends: "It soon got to be the general talk of the section of town where they lived and everybody has heard about the dog at Sizemore's. Anyway, that lasted 'till the girl grew up and it like to worried the man and woman to death. The woman was ill and the man a nervous wreck during the time. Later, Stella got married to a man and moved away, but everybody knew of the dog they had seen which seemed to be a warning to them not to be so mean to the little motherless girl. After she married and moved they claim they never saw the dog any more."

The particulars of these messages vary across the state's regions and subgroups, of course. In the former plantation region of Northumberland County, Mrs. Robert Edward told worker Cornelia Berry the legend of "The Old Plantation Master's Ghost" (legend 49). In this narrative the ghost of a plantation master (an ancestor of Mrs. Edwards) returns to decry the neglect and demise of his formerly glorious estate. He terrorizes the former slaves who are sitting on the porch of the big house enjoying their new status. The moral of this story is one that the former slaves would hardly agree with.

The messages of the witch tales vary, too. In Appalachia, where belief in them was strong, they typically carry forceful warnings against getting involved with such evil forces. Those who do are usually burned, killed, or at least run out of the community. In contrast, Shenandoah Valley and Tidewater witch tales seem light, almost comic. In "A Witch Gets Caught in a Store" (legend 43), for example, a group of witches break into a store through the keyhole to drink whiskey and have "a big ol' time." The African American stories of conjure present a thoroughly sympathetic view of its practitioners: in "The Conjuror's Beck" (legend 32), the magician resorts to using his power only when pushed into it; and in "A Slave with a Magic Hoe" (legend 31), he uses it to trick his master, get out of work, and avoid a beating. But for the most part, in the white materials at least, the moral of legends involving the supernatural is clear: do not mess around with such powers. Even attempting to find out who one will marry constitutes a violation of this rule. "Caught in the Graveyard" (legend 149) tells the story of one girl who tried: "And the people told her, if you will go to the graveyard some night all by yourself, and not tell nobody where you are going, and take a table fork with you and stick it down in a grave, you will see the man who you will marry. . . . So after a while she decided to go. So she went, and as she stooped down to stick the fork in the grave she stuck it through her dress. And she thought it was something pulling her down, and it scared her to death, and she died right there." Here again is a punishment that is completely out of proportion to the crime; this innocent young girl meets the same fate as the thief and grave robber in the second version of the story.

As both versions of the above story show, respecting the graves and the remains of the dead is a strong corollary of the axiom of avoiding supernatural matters. It is especially common in the ghost and haunted house tales. Often their disturbed or unburied bones provide the motivation for the ghosts' appearances. The pioneer tales of the Appalachian region, which typically have the mind-set of "the only good Indian is a dead Indian," even include Indian graves and remains in this interdiction. "Disturbing Indian Graves" (legend 64) shows how strongly the taboo was regarded.

Even when there is little rationale for a moral, one may be supplied. Mrs. Rebecca Ashby ended her telling of how Simon Kenton was forced to leave home when he thought he had killed a man in a fistfight by saying, "otherwise he might never have started his travels what made him such a great man, what shows [how a] little thing can work out t' do th' Lord's will as He had a planned things." Usually the moral intention is graphic and unmistakable. This is certainly the case in "The Black Cat" (legend 127), the story of a woman who was thought to have killed her infant children.

> She'd stuck pins right in the tops of their heads to kill 'em, but they couldn't prove she done it. So it went on and it wasn't long 'till she took down sick. She got worse and worse and one night they knew she was dying. All of the neighbors was there setting up with her. About midnight they heard a cat squalling up the hollow from the house. They didn't pay much attention at the start, but [it] kept coming closer and closer. . . . All at once it come right through the door. It was a big black cat, bigger than any cat they'd ever seen and its eyes shone like balls of fire. It squalled and walked to the bed and rared up on it and looked the sick woman square in the face. She screamed out that it was the devil come to get her for killing her children, and she she wheeled over with her face to the wall and never drawed another breath. The cat slid out through the closed door and went squalling back up the hollow.

But in other instances the message is more subtly encoded, as in "Killing an Unwanted Infant" (legend 90), a horrible narrative of cruelty and murder. "There was a certain family that had a child they didn't want. I don't remember if it was their child or a grandchild, but anyway they wanted to get rid of it. One night they took it to the stable and put it in with the horses. They thought sure they'd tramp it to death that night. But they didn't. They said the horses would step over it. Well, they saw that wasn't going to work and they put it in the hog pen for the hogs to eat. Next morning they got up and the hogs hadn't touched it. They got it and went to the house and the old man heated a red hot poker and stuck [it] up its rectum and killed it." The teller of this tale appears to take no moral position on its content; her disengagement and neutrality in relating the ghastly crime are reminiscent of the narrator's attitude in a Child ballad. But the narrative itself has much to say. The act is so abhorrent that even the animals rise up against it. The image of the horses stepping carefully to avoid the baby, when juxtaposed to the acts of the human beings, is the moral point. Perhaps with more impact because it is unstated, a powerful message of disapproval is conveyed.

Strategically, folk narratives may direct emotions toward values of which the narrator approves or disapproves. Both tactics appear in these legends, although negatives predominate. Perhaps this is simply because (as the writers of grocery-line tabloid headlines know) lurid, grizzly, and bizarre stories are attention grabbing. The positive messages are most often given through tales of exemplary individuals, models of approved behavior. Thomas Jefferson's politeness and egalitarian kindness to an old slave are an obvious example. So are Molly Mulhollun's spunk and gumption in disguising herself as a man and building thirty cabins in the Shenandoah Valley. So are Johnny Gilliam's entrepreneurial energy and vision in starting the town of Hickory Gap. So are Johnny Appleseed's piety and determination in his mission of planting trees. And, although less high-minded, so are Gowl James's skill and single-minded pursuit of his calling as a ratter.

The African American legends have positive messages and role models, too, but they advocate different behavior and different morals. When the Anglo-American legends validate moral and social norms, they reinforce white society as it is. They uphold the status quo. The black narratives, on the other hand, typically describe protest (usually veiled) and rebellion (usually failed) against the white over-class and its treatment of blacks. A few of the African American tales ignore whites and white society altogether; "The Ficklin Field Haunted House" (legend 54) and "Midnight Annie" (legend 45) come to mind. But most involve interaction and/or conflict with the white world in some way. The Civil War, of course, brought the two groups' interests into direct, active conflict, so legends about it have wholly different points of view; the white tales typically glorify brave rebel soldiers, Southern belles, and loyal house servants, while black ones celebrate men like Henry ("Box") Brown, who had himself shipped out of slavery in a crate, or James Bowser, a spy for the Northern army who gave his life for freedom.

African American local legends depict smaller heroics than

those called for by the Civil War, but most uphold the same values of resistance and struggle. Unlike white legends, which, in Polly Stewart's words, "illustrate the dangers inherent in behavior that is inimical to collective order and to personal well-being," a black legend such as "William Wydeman: Peacock and the Soldiers" (legend 77) approves of and applauds its subject's futile but heroic gesture of seizing the rifles of two Fort Monroe soldiers who harass him and forcing them to do military drill up and down all-white Buckroe Beach. He may have gone to jail for it, the tale implies, but didn't he have a glorious moment! "The Old Negro That Flagged the Train" (legend 140) is another local legend which advocates resistance. The man is cursed and yelled at, but he stops the train, and he gets to ride. This tale is as clear a metaphor for confronting the power of white society in order to reap its benefits as one is likely to find. But the old man is more in the tradition of the African trickster than a straightforward hero. As Lawrence Levine has noted, the trickster is concerned "with manipulating the strong and reversing the normal structure of power and prestige."[26] Unlike the heroic but ill-fated Wydeman, the old man in this narrative manipulates his more powerful adversaries and gets away with his exploit. The character in "A Slave with a Magic Hoe" (legend 31) is also a relative of the African trickster; his shrewdness and magic allow him to escape both work and punishment. Conjure was less objectionable to black narrators than witchcraft was to whites. A subtext of conjure stories is often that blacks needed all the power they could call upon to survive in Virginia's slaveholding and later Jim Crow society.

These should be enough examples to show that while the specifics vary, the legends reinforce moral and social values; they illustrate how to be good or bad, whatever that meant to the groups circulating them. Related to this, but working unconsciously, is the fact that they also bring up individual and group anxieties and allow people to come to terms with them. This connection is logical since moral and social codes address precisely those areas of culture with the greatest potential for stress—death and dying, wealth and poverty, violence, cruelty, sexuality, incest, lawlessness, jealousy, racial animosities, fear of nudity, etc. So the question to pose next in the search for the meaning of the legends is, What anxieties do the Virginia WPA folk legends reveal?

The most common one is about "loss of control." Human beings have a deep need for order; our civilization is based on efforts to assert order through laws, manners, customs, social hierarchies, moral codes, and empirical and scientific attitudes. Events which bring on the feeling of losing that order and control, and even narrative accounts of such things happening to others, generate stress. Having one's naked body exposed publicly is an example. Since clothes are a large part of a person's social power and legitimacy, being nude in front of others is a loss of control. This is the source of the humiliation it invokes. "The Naked Bull Ride" (legend 148) is a "nudity anxiety" story. It is a predecessor of the whole cluster of modern urban legends such as "The Nude in the RV" and "The Nude Surprise Party" that involve people caught naked in embarrassing situations.[27] It tells of a boy who decides to go swimming on Sunday instead of going to church. We can expect that something bad will follow from such a violation of the group's moral code. But it is not only beestings and a wild ride on a raging bull that the boy is subjected to; he is dumped naked in front of the local church just as all the well-dressed people of his community emerge from morning worship service. He is stripped (literally) of his dignity and his status in the group. We get the moral to this story, but we also get a whole range of complex responses—this really happened; well, it could happen; it could happen to me; it is hilarious; he deserved it; imagine it; all those people looking at him, etc. To perceive the moral is to interpret the story (it happened because he broke a taboo); to interpret the story is to lessen its stress (if I don't break the taboo it won't happen to me); and finally, to contemplate and consider the story is to feel a sense of catharsis. The fearful thing has happened; we have (imaginatively) confronted it; we are purged and calmed.

If my use here of Aristotle's terms from the criticism of classical Greek drama appears to aggrandize this comical narrative, consider another legend, "A Scar Identifies a Slave Woman's Husband as Her Son" (legend 139). Both the critical terminology and the commentary, from Aristotle to Freud, about the basic plot and conflict of this story are clearly relevant and applicable. The source of anxiety in the text, Oedipal incest, is a stronger taboo than nudity, but the same conscious and unconscious mechanisms are operating. There is the moral level involving the evils of slavery; there is the fearful, anxiety-inducing mother-son incest; and there is a believable, supposedly true story for our contemplation and interpretation. Just as ancient Athenians once heard Sophocles' version of a famous old story, so people in Portsmouth, Virginia, in the 1930s heard Georgiana Gibbs's tale of incest and were filled with pity and terror.

Anxiety about wildness, the wilderness, and human beings reverting to a feral state is more common in the legends than sexual stress. As one might expect, these fears were greatest in the western reaches of the state. The stories depict what happens when the boundary between wilderness and civilization is crossed, and in places like Wise County it was easy to cross. Two from Wise County, "The Wild Girl" (legend 145) and "The Boy Who Turned Wild in the Woods" (legend 144), arc explicitly about people who revert to wildness. They lose their clothing and power of speech and live on roots and berries. The girl, after she is caught and brought back to the settlement, is said to have stripped off her clothes as fast as they were put on her. And the boy is described as having grown hair all over, "just like a varmit." The reference to transforming into an animal is significant, because, along with the fear generated by the presence of real wild animals such as bears and panthers, a number of the texts reveal anxiety about the fragility of people's status as human beings. "The Cat Woman" (legend 121) is an obvious example. This is a story about a crossing of the boundary line between humans and animals. In it a man marries and has children by a woman who is later revealed to be a cat in human form. The legends of Devil Bill Boggs and Railroad Bill contain transformations into animals as well. And several tales attribute human traits such as mercy and kindness (and even speech) to animals, in juxtaposition with people at their cruelest and least human.

The presence of Indians in the state's frontier region generated particular stress in this regard. Here were creatures who, while obviously human in many ways, resembled wild animals to the settlers. They lived in the woods and posed a greater threat to them than the panther and bear combined. That the legend tellers mentally equated Indians with animals is demonstrated by the fact that they often substituted one for the other in the motifs of their narratives. Also, the Indian narratives contain the same double tension as the animal stories—they describe real dangers from Indian attacks on the settlers in gory detail, but they also divulge psychological stress about the settlers themselves, especially the women, losing control, "going native," and joining the Indians in the woods. The conscious message, or moral, of the Indian legends is of the need to be constantly vigilant and on guard. "The Ten Indians" (legend 62), for instance, begins: "One time a man went off from home and just left his wife right by herself. They lived away off from anybody else." But "The Two Women Who Married Indians" (legend 63) adds to warnings of the need to protect civilized white women the anxiety-inducing thought that they might defect. One of the pioneer women in this legend likes her Indian life and her Indian husband and is almost induced to stay with him. Her choice is negated, however, and the Indians are confirmed as total savages when her husband attempts to kill her rather than let her return to white society.

While the pioneer tales of animals and Indians paint a disquieting picture of an "out there" in the wilderness, the narratives of murder and violence depict an equally frightening territory "within." These tales generate anxiety over a thing more fearful, and yet more fascinating, than nature at its wildest, the out-of-control human being. As Nathaniel Hawthorne put it in his story "Young Goodman Brown," "The fiend in his own shape is less hideous than when he rages in the breast of man." The stories may have conscious moral points, such as "crime does not pay," or they may not. They do not necessarily end with their villains' defeat either. Sometimes, as in the tales of the baby killers or "The Murderous Tavern Keepers" (legend 89), the capture and punishment of the wrongdoers do not even come up. When the human institutions of law and order fail, as they do in "A Murder Belief Solves a Crime" (legend 93) and "A Strange Light at a Murder Site" (legend 88), supernatural forces may solve the crimes and mete out justice. But justice is not inevitable. The narrator of the strange light tale says of the ax murderer who bribed his judges and got off free, "Dallas Wright may be still living somewhere."

The moral messages of murder and violence stories are peripheral; it is the anxiety they invoke that is central. What holds us spellbound is their graphic proof that violence and cruelty dwell in our fellow human beings and, therefore, potentially in us. The shock of this recognition may even work against a story's intended purpose. The message of "A Strange Funeral" (legend 94), for instance, seems to be that "uppity" black males should be careful, docile, and under no circumstances go near white women. But this account of a lynching reveals great unconscious anxiety, especially about black male sexuality ("They found him holed up next day under a store porch an' snaked him outten there right fast lick [like]"). It depicts mob hysteria, an orgy of brutality, intimidation ("Niggers, though, wus sca[r]ce atter thet"), and a community cover-up. No doubt, this story meant various things to a variety of audiences in different situations and performances, but its subtext of psychosocial anxiety, like its visceral emotional impact, is undeniable.

Like violations of the boundary between nature (or human nature) and culture, crossings of the line between normal everyday life and the supernatural world elicit strong loss-of-control anxieties. Ghosts, witches, and unexplained phenomena frighten us because they shake our assumptions about the world and reveal how little we truly know about reality. Folktale scholar Max Lüthi offered the following explanation: "In the [supernatural] local legend, one senses the anxiety of man, who, though apparently a part of the community of his fellow men, finds himself ultimately confronted with an uncanny world which he finds hard to comprehend and which threatens him with death. . . . The local legend expresses a basic human condition: although deeply entrenched in human institutions, man feels abandoned, cast into a threatening world which he can neither understand nor view as a whole."[28]

Supernatural legends in the WPA collection concern ghosts, haunted houses, ghost animals, witchcraft and conjure, and such unexplained occurrences as premonitions, the appearance of a huge fireball in the sky, a mysterious cave where music from a long dead fiddler is heard, and a shower of stones raining out the sky onto a man's house. As in the other instances of loss of control, imaginatively confronting the supernatural event and interpreting it relieve the anxiety. In most of the ghost tales the revenant has some business with or message for the living; while this does not explain the ghost, it does connect it to our world and give a reason for its appearance. In the shower of stones story, the narrator says a slave girl had insulted an old black woman who was thought to be a witch. When the girl is sold south, the supernatural events stop. Though we may not understand what happened, this fact in some way explains the event and connects it to our world and our sense of order—we are purged and calmed.

Reading the stories as moral lessons or psychological stress relievers is not the only way to interpret them. Structural analysis approaches them as narrative diagrams of personal and group problems, conflicts, and ambiguities.[29] One of the major concepts underlying structural analysis is that certain basic human conflicts and tensions recur in narratives as diametrically opposed elements. These oppositions, such as male-female, live-dead, wild-civilized, night-day, and good-bad, are mediated by the events of the story. Generally the mediation does not resolve the problems that the story poses, nor is it a dialectic from which a synthesis emerges; it simply invokes and engages deep structural oppositions as a way of asserting some degree of imaginative control over them.

Structural analysis of the pioneer legends of western Virginia reveals a basic ambivalence about the wilderness. So far I have described the wilderness only as a source of anxiety. But it was more than that. The settlers depended on the wilderness for survival. While it could dispense death, with some effort it could also offer meat, fruits and berries, fuel for heating, material for housing, and land for grazing and farming. In other words, it was simultaneously bad and good. "A Race with a Panther" (legend 6) mediates this conflict about the wilderness in terms of a tame versus wild polar opposition. It has several attendant oppositional structures as well, such as life-death, communal-solitary, human-animal, eating-being eaten, and taking-giving. There are two zones in the story, the woods and the clearing. There are two principal agents, a man and a panther. As the story begins the man is properly with his neighbors (tame and communal) and the panther in its place in the forest (wild and solitary). But when the man slaughters hogs (tame and animal) and crosses into the panther's domain (wild and animal), the basic dichotomy is revealed. He has taken from the animal realm. The score, so to speak, is: domestic + 1, wild −1. The mediation begins when the (solitary) man must pass through the (wild) woods to get back to his (tame and communal) home with the (tame and animal) pork. Once he enters the panther's solitary domain, he becomes the food rather than the eater. He has been the taker from, and the killer of, animals; now he becomes the giver to an animal, to save his life. In a patently systematic way, he moves through the wild animal's zone back toward civilization and his community in direct proportion to his giving back the meat he has taken from the animal. The pork runs out precisely at the boundary of the two realms, and the tale concludes with the score settled—the panther "followed him to the edge of the field and then turned back." The panther remains where he belongs; the man returns where he belongs. The panther eats the man's pork; the man is allowed to live. There is no moral to the story, unless it is that we must have our priorities straight and know when to let something go. There is no easing of anxiety either; the panther will still be there waiting the next time. The resolution is only one of balancing "bundles of relations" and showing (literally) the give-and-take of man and nature.

Supernatural legends of ghosts structurally invoke our inherent uncertainty about death. Their primary opposition is alive versus dead. The deep emotional conflict behind them is summed up in the folk saying "Everybody wants to go to heaven, but nobody wants to die." The presence of a ghost is frightening because it belongs to the world of the dead, but it is also comforting because it vouches for the reality of life after death. A ghost is by definition a mediational figure, dead-but-not-dead, from the afterworld; but in these legends, a ghost is also a boundary crosser who demonstrates that the dead have a stake in the world of the living. The stories typically involve ghosts returning to set something right which is out of joint on this side; they may come to avenge a wrong, to reveal a treasure, or to resolve a problem involving their burial or remains. Or, as in the case of "Converted by a Ghost" (legend 50), they may come to mediate a religious conflict. In this story the live versus dead opposition is superseded by that of saved versus damned. Some secondary dichotomies are believer-unbeliever, young-old, house-grave, house-church, and community-individual. The young son of an old man dies and is buried on the hill above their house. The boy was a singer in the church choir and a pious individual. The old man has denied religion and refused to go to church despite the pleading of a revival preacher and the other members of his saved family. He stands in danger of eternal damnation. At this point the boy's ghost returns to mediate the conflict; through singing, shaking the man's bed, and various other proofs of his presence, he convinces the man to reconsider his stand. Members of the church come to the man's house in the course of the narrative's transactions, and finally, on the sixth night of the revival, he goes to church. On the seventh night he is converted and welcomed into the religious community. The ghost never appears again after that. The narrative concludes by offering the man's current status as a saved Christian as proof of the events of the story.

This introduction began with some questions—why were these stories told, what was their function for the people who told them, and what are their messages and meanings? At this point I am ready to offer some answers. In discussing folk legends Max Lüthi once quoted the German folk saying "He who takes a trip has something to tell" and suggested that legends are travel reports from beyond life's everyday reality.[30] He was referring to supernatural stories, but his metaphor applies to all kinds of legends. They may report on the natural world, the supernatural world, the social world, or the world within the human psyche, but the perspective they give extends and expands the experience of those who tell and hear them. Some are the folk equivalent of sermons in that they reinforce moral and social codes. Some are the equivalent of philosophical treatises in that they posit and question definitions of reality. Others are folk therapy in that they relieve personal and social stresses and anxieties. But these are such practical uses. We must remember they have an aesthetic side, too. They are all the folk equivalent of literature in that they create imaginative order and significance out of the events of people's lives.

Until I was almost seven years old, I used to listen to Virginia folk legends after supper on summer evenings in my grandparents' backyard. At least a few of my grandmother's ten brothers and sisters and their wives and husbands would come over every night and sit on lawn chairs and talk while it got dark. They all had moved to Richmond from King and Queen County at about the same time, and by the 1920s they had settled in Richmond's West End within a few blocks of each other. They would talk about work, housekeeping, church, and their gardens at first, but by the time the lightning bugs and cigarettes tips were the only lights left, the talk would always turn to the country and old times.

One night my uncle Everett told about a boy who got separated from his family somehow and got lost in the woods. They searched for him, but they never found him. Then years later they saw a man in the woods. He couldn't talk and he acted like a wild animal. Maybe he kept tearing off clothes they tried to put on him; I can't keep his story separate from the one I have put in this book. It is hard to sort many of my memories from those times, and that particular story was just part of the ebb and flow of talk that was putting me to sleep on a soft Richmond night. But it struck something in me that woke me bolt upright. I clearly remember the jolt of uncertainty I felt about the size of the world. Where it usually fit nicely with the cut grass, the streets all named for trees (Maplewood, Parkwood, Idlewood), and the almost fifty relatives I knew within a bike ride around the block, it suddenly occurred to me that the world was really very large and very strange, much larger and stranger than I knew. That night was the first time I couldn't sleep all night. I just lay there, adjusting myself, I suppose, to the expanding of my horizon.

Sometime that summer of 1953, they bought a television set. My grandmother's brothers and sisters still came over, but they went inside to watch it. They still talked, but it was never the same. They watched the shows—Boston Blackie, Garry Moore (maybe he was later), "The Hit Parade," Sid Caesar. These people were professionals, and they shamed my uncles and aunts into silence. They were backyard amateurs who only knew their own lives, the old days, and some old stories. I went inside and watched television, too. I didn't think about their stories again until the summer of 1972 when I saw them in writing on aging, yellowed paper in the Virginia WPA folklore archive. Then, as I sat reading them in the University of Virginia Library, the wrenching feeling of that sleepless night from my childhood came rushing back. I realized I was finding something I hadn't even known I had lost. There on those pages, because of politics, economics, chance, Franklin Delano Roosevelt, and the vision and work of more people than I could begin to name, something of irreplaceable value was preserved.

NOTES

1. John A. Burrison, ed., *Storytellers: Folktales and Legends from the South* (Athens: Univ. of Georgia Press, 1989), p. 226.

2. The wording here is from the introduction to Ronald Baker's *Hoosier Folk Legends* (Bloomington: Indiana Univ. Press, 1982), p. 2. It is taken from the work of anthropologist William Bascom; Baker's essay is a good basic orientation to the subject of folk legends. For further background on legend definitions, types, problems, and scholarly issues and debates, two good sources are Wayland D. Hand's "Status of European and American Legend Study," *Current Anthropology* 6 (1965): 439–46, and the fourteen conference papers he edited as *American Folk Legend: A Symposium* (Berkeley and Los Angeles: Univ. of California Press, 1971). Linda Dégh and Andrew Vázsonyi's "Legend and Belief," pp. 93–123 in *Folklore Genres*, ed. Dan Ben-Amos (Austin: Univ. of Texas Press, 1976), is the best discussion of the issue of the believed nature of legend narratives.

3. Charles L. Perdue, Jr., Thomas E. Barden, Robert K. Phillips, eds., *An Annotated Listings* [sic] *of Folklore Collected by Workers of the Virginia Writers' Project, Works Projects Administration—Held in the Manuscripts Department at Alderman Library of the University of Virginia* (Norwood, Pa.: Norwood Editions, 1979). An appendix to this guide gives a listing of the collection by the worker who collected each item.

4. Jerre Mangione, *The Dream and the Deal: The Federal Writers' Project, 1935–1943* (Boston: Little, Brown, 1972), p. 265. This history of the writers' project is invaluable not only for specific details of the operation of the national and state offices but for a good overview of the political and intellectual circumstances of the FWP, the WPA, and the Roosevelt era in general.

5. Ibid., pp. 265–66. In his article "WPA and Folklore Research," *Southern Folklore Quarterly* 3 (1939): 6–14, Benjamin Botkin said the FWP's publication was going to be titled *American Folk Stuff: A National Collection of Folk and Local Tales*. He also listed the various government agencies that were involved in folklore research, their administrators, and their principal projects.

6. A copy of the manual is in box 14, folder 4, of the WPA Virginia Writers' Project Folklore Collection, accession no. 1547, University of Virginia Library

(hereafter cited as the WPA collection). According to Susan Dwyer-Schick in "The Development of Folklore and Folklife Research in the Federal Writers' Project, 1935–1943," *Keystone Folklore Quarterly* 20 (1975): 11, the FWP published several manuals for field-workers and the Botkin one quoted here was the best. Her article and pp. 19–29 of Lorin W. Brown, Charles L. Briggs, and Marta Weigle's *Hispanic Folklife in New Mexico: The Lorin W. Brown Federal Writers' Project Manuscripts* (Albuquerque: Univ. of New Mexico Press, 1978) are the best available studies of the FWP's folklore work.

7. Note to "Norman Sigurd's $100 Bill," box 5, folder 1, item 531, WPA collection.

8. Mangione, *The Dream and the Deal*, p. 266. On p. 276 Mangione mentioned the American Folklore Society's rejection of the FWP's work; for details and clarification of the event, see Susan Dwyer-Schick's "Folklore and Government Support," *Journal of American Folklore* 89 (1976): 476–86.

9. Mangione, *The Dream and the Deal*, p. 266; the newspaper was the *Wyoming Tribune*.

10. Mangione devoted the final chapter of *The Dream and the Deal* to an evaluation of the FWP. In it he quoted reviews from across the American spectrum of opinion from the *Nation* and the *New Republic* to the *Saturday Review of Literature* and the *New York Herald Tribune* praising the various books, guidebooks, and pamphlets published by the project. He also quoted H. G. Nichols, a British critic from the *Contemporary Review*, who felt the overall work of the FWP was likely "to prime the pump of American national self-awareness to a degree not unlike that which attended the War of Independence" (p. 365).

11. See app. 9, "Present Disposition of Virginia WPA Materials," in *Weevils in the Wheat: Interviews with Virginia Ex-slaves*, ed. Charles L. Perdue, Jr., Thomas E. Barden, and Robert K. Phillips (Charlottesville: Univ. Press of Virginia, 1976), p. 389.

12. Bruce Rosenberg, *The Folksongs of Virginia* (Cambridge: Harvard Univ. Press, 1969), p. 18.

13. A copy of the tales "finder," no date, is in box 14 of the WPA collection; a copy of the song "finder," dated April 20, 1942, is in box 15.

14. A copy of Boyd's essay is in box 15 of the WPA collection.

15. Botkin's *Manual for Folklore Studies*, p. 1.

16. Box 6, folder 4, item 915, WPA collection.

17. Box 3, folder 4, item 233, ibid.

18. Perdue, Barden, and Phillips, *Weevils in the Wheat*, pp. 219–20. See pp. xl-xliv for further discussion of the issue.

19. Charles A. Mills, *Treasure Legends of Virginia* (Nokesville, Va.: Apple Cheeks Press, 1984); Robert F. Nelson, *25 Thrilling Legends of Virginia* (Richmond, 1971); and George Holbert Tucker, *Virginia Supernatural Tales* (Norfolk: Donning, 1977).

20. Box 3, folder 1, item 56, WPA collection.

21. "Killing an Unwanted Infant," legend 90.

22. Box 1, folder 8, item 85, WPA collection.

23. Box 6, folder 2, item 844, ibid.

24. Jan Harold Brunvand, *The Vanishing Hitchhiker: American Urban Legends and Their Meanings* (New York: Norton, 1981), p. 2.

25. Polly Stewart, "Style in the Anglo-American Legend," *Motif: International Newsletter of Research in Folklore and Literature* 6 (1988): 6.

26. Lawrence W. Levine, *Black Culture and Black Consciousness: Afro-American Folk Thought from Slavery to Freedom* (New York: Oxford Univ. Press, 1977), p. 105.

27. See chap. 6, "Dalliance, Nudity, and Nightmares," in Brunvand's *The Vanishing Hitchhiker*, pp. 125–52, for a thorough discussion of the moral and psychological aspects of the nudity theme in modern urban legends.

28. Max Lüthi, *Once Upon a Time: On the Nature of Fairy Tales* (Bloomington: Indiana Univ. Press, 1976), pp. 142–43.

29. Pierre and Elli Köngäs Maranda's *Structural Analysis of Oral Tradition* (Philadelphia: Univ. of Pennsylvania Press, 1971) provides a good introduction to the methods of structural analysis by bringing together eleven essays by leading folklorists using the approach to examine myths, rituals, riddles, folktales, and folksongs. While structuralism recently has languished in literary critical circles in lieu of variations on the "deconstructive" methods expounded by Jacques Derrida and others, it remains a viable and valuable tool for analyzing folk narratives.

30. Lüthi, *Once Upon a Time*, p. 85.

ANIMALS

Over 130 stories in the WPA folklore files concern animals, making them one of the major topics of the collection. Most of the stories concern animals as animals (rather than animals talking and acting in human ways), but they inevitably involve people, too, and refer to human behavior. The ones that feature wild animals usually depict people up against nature at its most unpredictable and fearsome. Many critics and commentators have noted that nature has long been seen as a threat and challenge to the American mind.[1] "Conquering" the continent of North America put pioneer Americans in conflict with nature in a primal way. The wilderness was not to be left alone, observed, lived with, and learned from; it was to be met, struggled with, and overcome. "The Child and the Snake" (legend 2), a local version of an international migratory legend popularized by the Grimm brothers, shows this conflict.[2] It symbolically pits man (the adults) against nature (the snake); the girl is too young to join the fray. The story's theme is that nature can suspend its battle with humans if they are innocent and without prejudice against it. The Freudian implication of the snake as a sexual symbol looms in the background as well; the girl attracts and tames the wild (phallic) reptile, much to her parents' dismay. In the Grimms' version of this tale the reptile is a toad, that much analyzed companion of and receiver of kisses from adolescent girls.

In the African American legend "A Horn Snake Kills a Cruel Mistress" (legend 1), the agent of wildness comes out of its natural habitat and attacks a morally offensive adult. It is interesting how the topic of slavery and its cruelty is subtly broached here, and how aggressive feelings toward the slave owner are indirectly vented. As in the previous story, the snake emerges from the wild into civilized space. In the first case the girl (it is never a little boy) tempts the snake out. In the second, the snake arrives voluntarily as an agent of retribution for the mistress's cruelty. The mistress eats the fruit of a tree and dies; justice is provided by nature. In both cases the snake's positive interaction is with the weak and/or defenseless. The cruelty of the human adults suggests that nature may be superior to culture.

"A Black Snake Chokes an Infant" (legend 3) depicts the war between the cultivating humans and hostile nature in a more straightforward way. Nature attacks a helpless infant and tries to pass the last line of defense between self and other, an orifice of the body. And "The Eagle and the Baby" (legend 8), which has an agricultural setting, too, also depicts the humans in the basic cultural act of farming. Here again nature attacks ruthlessly and without warning.

If wild animal stories highlight our conflict with nature, domestic animals and pets concern the peace we have negotiated with it. These animals have symbolic meanings, too, most of which correspond to human traits and values. Dogs, for example, symbolize faithfulness. But since they are also carnivores, the legends about them often reflect ambivalence. The tale of the dog saving its master's baby, for example, shows how quickly it is assumed that the beast has become vicious. The narrative's surface moral is simply that we should trust "man's best friend" better. But it also invokes the inversion that the animal is more faithful than, and morally superior to, the man. This inversion also appears in the tale of the guard dog that turns on its master. Though perhaps too behaviorally focused, the dog is clearly morally superior to a man who would rob his own widowed mother. Like the horn snake, the dog is the agent of human justice.

If we have qualms about our dogs' domestication, we have none about horses'. They are not carnivores that could conceivably turn on us. The horse, especially before the car prevailed in American society, was viewed as an extension of the self. And more than any other animal, except perhaps the shepherd dog, it has been a willing tool for our use. The WPA legend narratives about horses brag of their speed, strength, devotion, and/or intelligence. The horse legend given here (legend 13) is a good example, as is "The Horse That Came Home to Die,"[3] which tells of a horse on loan to a neighbor which comes back to its own stable in order to die at home. This pioneer legend which James Taylor Adams collected demonstrates not only how smart but also what a helpmate the horse can be. A man who had been drinking late into the night fell off his horse on the way home and decided to stay on the ground and sleep until he sobered up a bit. He knew his horse wouldn't leave him. As Adams's informant told him: "The man didn't know how long he'd been asleep when he suddenly waked up with that horse, jes' a-lickin' him in the face. He got up an' looked aroun' an' there comin' down the trail about a hundred yards up the branch was a big bear. He didn't have a gun or anything to fight it with. So he got on that horse jes' as fast as he could an' they lit out towards home."[4]

Other sections have narratives that involve animals to an extent. In the Unusual Events section there is a legend of a slave boy who was chased by wolves. And the entire section Spirit Dogs could be said to be animal tales. But the animal legends here have animals as their central focus, and they involve actual animals. While it is debatable whether horn snakes, hoop snakes, walking rattlers, and bears that say "O-o-o Lor-r-d" when they die are actual, the distinction between supernatural and supernormal clarifies the issue. Ghost dogs are clearly supernatural, but the unusual legendary animals in this section could exist in nature; they (like the Loch Ness monster) simply have not been verified. Stories of these creatures do not bring up the question of the existence of a supernatural world.

NOTES

1. R. W. B. Lewis, *The American Adam: Innocence, Tragedy, and Tradition in the Nineteenth Century* (Chicago: Univ. of Chicago Press, 1955); Leo Marx, *The Machine in the Garden: Technology and the Pastoral Ideal in America* (New York: Oxford Univ. Press, 1964); Henry Nash Smith, *Virgin Land: The American West as Symbol and Myth* (Cambridge: Harvard Univ. Press, 1950).

2. *The Complete Fairy Tales of the Brothers Grimm*, trans. and ed. Jack Zipes (New York: Bantam, 1987), pp. 380–81.

3. Box 5, folder 2, item 705, WPA collection.

4. Item 707, ibid.

A HORN SNAKE
KILLS A
CRUEL MISTRESS

Eliza Gunther, interviewer unknown,
in an unknown location in Bedford County, no date given

Pa told me how in slavery time on his plantation his ole missus had a strawberry patch in a garden jes' a little piece from de big house. Dis was over in here Franklin Junction near Danville. So one day de ole' missus tells one of de little slave gals dat worked 'round de house to git de basket an' go down to de garden an' git some strawberries. De gal didn't go right den, so de ol' missus gits mad, grabs a big bull whip an' starts hidin' de gal fo' life. After while an ole' horn snake come runnin' outen de strawberry patch, makin' straight fo' de missus. He didn' pay no 'tention a tall to de little nigger gal but kept coming straight to ole missus. Missus saw him an' broke an' run toward de house but de ole snake was pushin' her so close dat she took up a big cherry tree dar in de yard. Jes' as she got up de tree de snake stuck his horn in de tree. Adder [after] missus got up de tree she didn't pay de snake no mind. Der was some mighty big cherries on de tree, so Pa said, and missus started eatin' de cherries. She stayed up dere right smart time eating de cherries. But after while ole missus fell outen de tree, dead. Yes sir, dem horn snakes is some mo' pissen. Dat quick de pissen had run all through dat tree an' into de cherries what ole' missus was eatin'. Pa said his marster cut down dat tree so dat nobody else would git pissoned wid de cherries offen dat tree. Well sir, Pa said all de niggers on dat plantation was some mo' glad when ol' missus got pisoned to death.

—————— 2 ——————

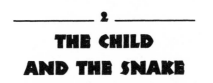

THE CHILD
AND THE SNAKE

Mary Ross, interviewed by Pearl Morrisett
in Danville, on January 16, 1941

Mary Ross told the visitor the following remarkable story which she (Mary) vouches for: My cousin livin' out in Pittsylvania County had a little girl and sometimes when they gived her a cup of milk she'd go off out doors and set down on a log to drink it. One day they saw her holdin' the cup down and was skeered to death when they saw she was feedin' milk to a snake from her cup. Watching for a second or two, they saw her take the cup back up in her lap, tellin' the snake "You can't have any more of my milk now." Somebody run to the house and got a gun and when the snake moved off far enough from the child, they shot it.

They told it that this little girl was born with snake charmin' blood, and that was why the snake didn't hurt her. It liked her. You have to be born that way to get by like that.

3

A BLACK SNAKE CHOKES AN INFANT

Mrs. Nellie Hamilton, interviewed by Emory L. Hamilton
in Wise, Wise County, on November 25, 1940

I've heard my grandma tell about, one time there was a woman that had a suckling baby and went to the field to hoe corn. She made the baby a pallet in a sinkhole and left it there while she hoed her row through the corn field. She'd hoed her row to one end and then start back to the end where the baby was laying. She'd let it nurse and see that it was alright every time she'd hoe a round. Well, she hoed a round once, and when she got back she went to look at the baby. There it laid as black in the face as tar, and part of a black snake sticking out of its mouth. The snake had tried to crawl down the baby's throat and had choked it to death.

4

A BLACK SNAKE SQUEEZES A GIRL'S BODY

Mrs. Charlotte Collins, interviewed by Emory L. Hamilton
in Hawthorne, Wise County, on November 19, 1940

I've heard my grandmother tell this many a time. She said one time a lot of people was coming from church and a boy and girl in the bunch who was sweethearts had walked on before, you know, just like sweethearts will. They got on ahead of the crowd a ways and sit down. He noticed that she was getting pale as death. He watched her a few minutes and saw that something had to be done. He unloosened her clothes and found that a black-snake had wropped her body. He couldn't pull it loose and finally he took his knife and cut it loose. She got alright in a few minutes after the boy cut the snake loose.

————— 5 —————

THE WALKING RATTLESNAKE

Silas Craft, interviewed by James Taylor Adams
in Wise, Wise County, on June 19, 1941

I can tell ye a tale that none of ye'll believe, but hit's true, as God's my judge. Brother Johnny lived on what ye call Bear Creek, an' he loved likker then. He wrote for me to come over an' bring some whiskey one Saturday night an' we'd have some music and a good ol' time. He played a fiddle a lot then. So I told my wife to git ready for Saturday an' we'd go over to Johnny's an' have a lot of music. We started out an' come down the Pound [River] an' turned up the branch at the Mack Sturgill place. Got way up there an' my horse was gittin' mighty hot an' I said, "Let's stop here in the shade an' I'll take off the saddle an' let his back cool."

Now what I'm tellin' ye I could prove by Henny Gilliam 'f he was alive today, an' old Uncle John Gilliam will tell ye hit's the truth an' Henny's wife, she's livin' right out here at Wise. They was draggin' wheat off the hill to a thrashin' floor an' was goin' to flail hit out. You've seed thrashin' floors an' flails, I know. Made a thrashin' floor by cleanin' off a level place an' beatin' hit 'till hit was hard as a rock. Made flails out o' hickory poles an' beat 'em an' twisted 'em 'till you could come round an' round with him. Then they fanned hit out by pourin' the wheat an' somebody shakin' a sheet.

Some of the Gilliams had three awful fine bars [*JTA note:* barrows] in a pen jes out tother side of the thrashin' floor, an' my wife said she'd step out an' look at the hogs while I was lettin' the horse rest an' cool. She'uz a fool about hogs.

She hadn't been gone but a minute an' I pulled a gallon jug out o' my saddle pockets, sort o' shook hit, watched the bead, an' was thinkin' o' takin' a drink. I hadn't drunk a drop so far. When all at once I heard her scream an' looked an' seed her a comin'. Her hat flew off and her hair come down. I jes' dropped everything an' run to meet her. Couldn't think what in the world was the matter. I looked an' seed a big rattle snake runnin' right behin' her. Hit was standin' straight up like a person, not more than six inches of hits tail on the ground. An' hit was usin' part of that to sing with. Hit was singin' as hit come an' its head was right up on a level with her hair.

I grabbed up a flail that was lyin' thar an' knowin' they sometimes broke I thought, what if it breaks an' the head flies off an' hits her. But I didn't have no time to lose, so I cut loose an' that snake's head flew fifteen feet the first lick. Well, hit was the biggest snake I ever seed. Hit was nearly as big around as this pole we're sittin' on [*JTA note:* about four inches through].

Miss Gilliam [*JTA note:* Henny's wife] come down thar in a run an' my wife run on to the horse an' fainted. Well, I'd allus heard hit said 'f one fainted an' ye'd put likker on their breast, they'd come to. So I poured out some likker on a han'kercher an' unbuttoned her waist an' laid it on her breast an' she come to.

They told us after that that that [*JTA note:* his own words, three "thats" in a row] rattlesnake had been seed there for several years, an' had eat up all their young pigs, chickens and geese. Couldn't raise nothin' for hit an' they'd offered a reward of twenty-five dollars for anybody that'd kill hit. But they never paid me anything.

I axed my wife where she first seed hit. She said hit come out of an old snag that stood out there near the hog pen. We went out there an' looked, an' somebody, I believe it was Henny Gilliam, cut in there an' found twenty-one little rattlesnakes all the way from six inches to that long [*JTA note:* he measured about fourteen inches on his arm]. When I hit the rattlesnake a lot of the rattles flew off. They hunted around an' found twenty-three of 'em, I believe hit was. That's the truth, if I ever told it in my life.

———— 6 ————

A RACE
WITH A PANTHER

Samuel Simpson Adams, interviewed by James Taylor Adams
in Big Laurel, Wise County, on September 9, 1940

I used to hear the old people tell a tale about a man who had been helping his neighbor on the other side of the hill kill hogs and had started home just about dusk with a sack full of meat that the other feller had give him for helping him.

He was a-going along through the woods and all at once he heard what he thought was a woman screaming back up on the ridge. "He-ee-eee!" it went, just plimeblank [exactly—perhaps from "plumb like" or "point blank"] like a woman hollering. He stopped and listened. He thought some woman might have got lost and was hollering to try to get somebody to answer. "He-ee-e-e!" He heard it again, closer this time than before. He eased his load off'n his shoulder and answered, asking her who she was and what was the matter. Then he heard it again. "He-ee-e-e!" This time it was right close to him. It was nearly dark there under the trees, but in a minute or two he heard something coming through the leaves, "pitty-pat, pitty-pat, pitty-pat," and seed a big panther coming right straight towards him, pattin' hits tail on the ground as it come.

He knew then it had smelt the fresh meat in his sack, and he reached in the sack and pulled out a piece and threw it towards it and hit out down the mountain towards home just as hard as he could go. He hadn't got far 'till he heard it scream again right behind him.

He throwed down another piece of meat and run again. Soon it was nearly up with him again, and he throwed down another piece of meat. It wasn't long 'till he had throwed down all the meat, and he was still a right smart piece from home. So he throwed down the sack, and he looked back as he run and seed it come up and grab the sack and start just riddling it. While it was doing that he got out of the woods and it followed him to the edge of the field and turned back.

———— 7 ————

THE BEAR
AND THE PANTHER

Samuel Simpson Adams, interviewed by James Taylor Adams
in Big Laurel, Wise County, on August 20, 1940

Mother told this tale to me. Many times I remember hearing her set around the fire of a night and tell it to us children. She said that one time when she was about twelve years old that her father, old Joel Church, and his wife, her step-mother, went off one night to stay a while at one of the neighbors' and her and the rest of the children was playing whoop-hide around the house. The moon was shining just as bright as day, and she run around behind the house to hide and hunkered down in the chimley corner. Just as she was scrooching up in the corner she heard something going "pat, pat, pat" and she looked out about ten feet and there set the biggest panther she'd ever laid eyes on. It was just sort of stretched out on the ground, its forefeet in front of it, and looking right at her. Just plimeblank like a cat you've seed about to jump on a mouse. And it was pattin' its tail against the ground just like a cat does when it's about to jump on somethin' or 'nother. She said she screamed and run just as hard as she could go and got all the children in the house and barred the door. They watched it through a crack and seed it go off after while right up the branch in back of the house and ever now and then [it] would turn around and look back at the house.

When her pap and step-mother come in she told them about what she'd seed, and her pap wouldn't hardly believe her. He said, "Now, Julia, if you're telling me the truth I'll see if I can find it in the morning, for if it come that close to the house, it's bound to have young'ns right here close somewheres."

The next morning they got out and looked and sure enough there was signs of where it had laid and there was its tracks where it went off up the holler. It had rained just before that and the ground was soft.

So her pap got his gun and started out after it. He kept seeing its tracks ever' now and then up the holler. After while he got in a leafy place and couldn't track it any furder. But he went on and was getting right up next to the head of the holler. There was a big log across the holler where a tree had fell. He was standing sort of resting when all at once he seed a bear walk up on one end of the log and start across it. And at the same time a panther hopped up on the other end and started meeting it. They met about the middle of the log and the bear just up with its forepaw and "slap!," it knocked the panther off into the holler. But it hadn't no more'n hit the ground 'till it sprang right back up. "Ker-slap!," and the bear knocked it off again. And again it didn't more'n hit the ground 'till it give a quick spring and right back on the log it come. And this time it seemed to light right on its back [legs] and, catching the bear right about the throat with its forepaws, it just "Ri-i-ip!" and tore every gut the bear had in it out. The bear hollered, "O-o-o Lor-r-d," just as plain as you ever heard in your life and fell off the log dead.

The panther walked over to the other end of the log and set down and begin licking its paws. He watched it for a minute and then he up with his gun and, taking level aim, he shot it right smack center between the eyes. It rolled off the log and down the bank and right square on top of the bear. So there he had them both together.

He followed the bear's tracks where it tore up the leaves and found its den up on the hill under a cliff, and it had four little cubs in it. He caught them and tied 'em up and come back down and looked around and seed where the panther had slid down the other hill side, and he went up there and found its den with six little panthers in it. He couldn't catch them; I don't think he even tried. But he killed them and took the cubs on home. He petted one of them and sold the others to other people for pets.

8

THE EAGLE
AND THE BABY

Royce Cress, interviewed by James Taylor Adams
in Big Laurel, Wise County, on February 2, 1942

Mother told me that one time there was a man an' woman an' they had a little baby. The man an' woman had to go out in the meadow and cut hay an' rake it up, an' they laid the baby in the shade. They kept noticing a big eagle sailin' around and around. Hit come down lower an' lower. They never thought of anything. Then all at once the eagle come down with a swoop an' carried the baby off. The woman started screamin' an' the man he started hollerin', an' they both started runnin'. They seen the old eagle flyin' way back in the mountain to where there was a big high cliff. The man an' woman run to the foot of the mountain and then they clomb an' clomb an clomb. At last they got to the cliff an' the man told the woman to wait there, an' he climb hand over hand up the side of the cliff. They seen the old eagle fly off again an' when the man got to the nest, there laid their baby in the nest with the young eagles. They hadn't bothered hit, an' the man just got it an' clomb back down the cliff with it.

9

A CAT FEEDS
ON A CORPSE

Mrs. Lenore Kilgore, interviewed by James Taylor Adams
in Big Laurel, Wise County, on April 15, 1941

I heard Mary Mullins tell just a while before she died about set-tin' up with a corpse when she was a girl. She said that they kept the woman up for two nights after she died. The first night, she said, the old folks all set up and sung songs and talked and the young folks mostly laid down and slept. The second night the old folks went to bed and the young people stayed up to watch the corpse. Mary Mullins said that one of the old women told her that she waked up a way long in the night and heard something making a queer noise, just "ooh, ooh, ooh," like a cat growling when it was eating something. She said she listened and it seemed to be right over where they had the dead woman laid out. She heard the young folks out on the porch talking and laughing under their breath. She got up and stirred up a light, and as she did so a cat jumped off the corpse and went skidding out of the house. She went over to look at the dead woman and found that the cat had eat one whole side of her face off. Mary didn't say whether she was one of the young folks on the porch, but I think she was. She told who the woman was that was dead, but I've forgot the name.

——— 10 ———

DANIEL BOONE'S
DOG THRASHER

Taylor Nash, interviewed by James M. Hylton
in Wise, Wise County, on May 15, 1941

My mother Margaret Ramey and her sister Polly Ramey told me this story and said they heard their father, old Uncle Jesse Ramey tell it to them many a time by the fireside at their home and that it had been handed down to him through a very truthful source, otherwise he would not have let them hear it in his household. He was one of the early settler[s] from the Carolinas into this country and was very much interested in the goings on of the early men before him and his day. He said that he was told this tale by a man by the name of Johnson who was older than

ANIMALS

he and who hailed from Kentucky and who knew the Boones at one time.

He said that Boone had a dog by the name of "Thrasher" that was a cross from the collie and some other kind that he knew nothing about and that he had gotten him from one of the early settlers from the west that he had come into contact with in his travels. He had the dog trained so that it would go on the trail ahead of him and if it smelled the scent of man or beast it would make a long howling sound and quietly go back toward the master and go up to him on the trail. If the pathway was clear of the Indians and beasts it would go on ahead.

Most of the time it was over some [of] the old trails they had both been over before together and they both knew an' understood the other's movements. But one time they were both almost fooled into a trap while some Indians were in behind them on their trail. They were both upwind and the scent was going in the other direction. Thrasher the dog was ahead of Boone on the trail a good distance and had made no sound for some time, when he let out one of his usual howls of warning and quickly and quietly made his way back to his master. Boone hid in the bushes and soon saw his dog coming back the trail to him. About this time Boone heard a sound behind him so he lay perfectly still in the bushes, and the dog heard it too and seemed to understand and hid and lay still too. The Indians were behind them. The Indians were as good as the dog on scenting man and beast, and they scented something up the trail the same as Boone and his dog had. Soon they soon passed them on by and went on up there. In a short time Boone heard loud talking sounds, and after some time they went on away up the trail.

Hours after, when he felt safe to come out, Boone and Thrasher went on up the trail to the spot and found an old deer that looked as though it had been bitten by a snake; it was swelling up all around on its body, but was not quiet [quite] dead. The deer had fooled the dog and Boone, but it had also fooled the Indians and put them off their trail and saved their lives. Boone could not have outdone the four of them by any means and it would have been death for both [of] them.

11

THE FAITHFUL DOG

C. Wentz Carter, interviewed by James Taylor Adams
in Wise, Wise County, on September 24, 1940

There was a man lived away back in the woods one time. They just had one little baby. They had a big dog an' the dog wouldn't let any thing come near the baby. His wife worked out an' they would leave the baby in a box in the house an' the dog would lay right by it and mind it.

One day they was a-hoein' corn up in the field a right smart piece from the house an' the baby had been left at the house with the dog. That day when they come in, the dog met 'em in the door and he was just a-growlin' and actin' like he was goin' to jump on 'em. He was just as bloody as he could be, an' he was a-lickin' his lips.

They was scared nearly to death. And the man, he kicked the dog out of his way an' run in an' there lay the baby, killed an' nearly eat up. He jus' reached up over the door an' picked up his gun an' shot the dog's brains out. They looked under the bed and there laid the biggest panther they'd ever seed in their life, tore all into pieces. The panther had killed the baby an' the dog had killed it.

They made two coffins, one for the baby an' one for the dog. An' they buried him by the baby and put up a tombstone for him, just like they did for the baby.

12

THE GOOD WATCHDOG

C. Wentz Carter, interviewed by James Taylor Adams
in Big Laurel, Wise County, on September 10, 1941

One time they'uz an old woman that lived right lone by herse'f. Her man had got killed or died an' her only child was a boy an' he had married an' lived on the place, but in a different house. She couldn't git along with his wife, so she jis stayed on by herse'f.

This old woman had a whole heap o' money. Oh, thousands o' dollars they said. She was afraid of banks, 'f they was any banks back then. Hit's been a long time ago. So the ol' woman kep' 'er money locked up in a big safe that set by the door in the front room. She felt she'uz safe in keepin' her money that a-way. All her neighbors seemed hones' an' her boy lived right close by her.

But one evenin' her boy come over an' said to her, says he, "Mother, I heard this mornin' that a certain feller round here had been talkin' about you stayin' by yorese'f here with all that money in the house. I'm afeard," he said, "that he's a-goin' to try to rob ye. 'F'n I'uz you, I'd tie ol' Bull right by the door tonight an' ever' night hereafter, for a while anyhow. You never know what might happen."

So the old woman took 'is advice an' got him to come over that night an' catch the bulldog, ol' Bull, an' tie him right by the door nex' to where the safe set. She went to bed an' axley [actually] didn't think much of what her boy had said. She soon drapped off to sleep. Didn't know how long she'd been asleep when she waked up an' heard sumpin' on the porch like somebody'uz slippin' along across the puncheons [floorboards]. Old Bull growled low an' she heard somebody speak to 'im sorty low. Mutchin' [soothing] 'im. "Take 'im, Bull!," she hissed, an' she heard the dog make a lunge an' heard the chain creak an' somebody holler. No better'n nor worse she kep' sicking the dog. Wudn't long 'till the racket hushed, but she didn't go out. Soon's daylight she got up an' slipped to the door an' opened it an' peeked out. An' thar layed her own boy, dead, chewed all to pieces.

————— **13** —————

SOLOMON THE WISE HORSE

Walter Kennedy, interviewed by James M. Hylton
in Wise, Wise County, on November 21, 1941

The owner of this horse named him Solomon because he was such a wise old horse and knew so much. One time a blacksmith put a new shoe on one of his front feet over at the smithy. Several days later the son of the man that owned the horse came runnin in to him an' said that old Solomon had run off, either that or somebody had stolen him. The owner went to the pasture field where he kept him and looked at the fence and gate and found it was down on the ground. He saw Solomon's teeth prints on the gate so he knew the horse had gotten away by himself.

While he and his son was there lookin' at the gate, the local blacksmith come down the road where they were at and said old Solomon had paid him a visit not long before. He said the horse had come on in to his shop and put his front foot up on the block where the anvil was bolted and looked at him kinda hurt-like. He said he looked at the shoe he'd had put on a few days before that and he saw he'd put it on wrong. No doubt it was hurtin' him awful. He held the hoof up for him to take the shoe off. Then the smith put it back on right, an' Solomon made a happy snort-like and cantered on off down the road. The owner and his son went over a rise o' ground in the field and there was old Solomon eating just as contentedly as ever before.

BEGINNINGS

Stories about the beginnings of things are set in the past, but they usually concern the present. The real question of John Robson's Gypsy legend (legend 18) was not where Gypsies came from, but why they are the way they are now. Why do they roam the earth and never settle in one place? Why were they so different from ordinary citizens of Danville, Virginia, in the 1930s? Robson's story, which he believed, gave him an intriguing and satisfying answer. Like belief legends in general, tales of beginnings tend to have either obvious or concealed moral themes.[1] Robson's Gypsy tale not only explains a group of people who were strange and unknown to him, it also suggests that their freewheeling lifestyle may be a punishment for laziness and overindulgence. The moral of Simpson Randolph Adams's "Disobedient Sammy" (legend 19) is obvious too. The natural phenomenon that is explained in this tale, why black gum wood is hard to split, only comes up in the last sentence. It is much less emphasized than the punishment of the willful child. Similarly, "The Man in the Moon" (legend 17) is less an explanation of the features on the moon's face than a warning not to break the cultural taboo against working on Sunday.

Besides this moral dimension, legends about beginnings explore the limits of daily reality. Like imaginative folktales, they connect the everyday world to the realm of magic and fantasy. But unlike them, they don't break from reality entirely.[2] They don't announce their unreality with openings such as "Once upon a time" but refer solidly to the actual world, usually offering a proof of the interaction of the two realms. Black gum, after all, is hard to split. The dogwood bract is shaped like a cross with bloody nail holes. And there is what appears to be a man (and maybe a rabbit) in the face of the moon. These things, when placed beside a talking fish, a mysterious voice from a tree, or a man being sucked up from the earth into the moon, expand the imagination by mingling the fantastic and the real. John Robson's imagination as well as his moral sensibility was surely struck by the idea that the shadowy vagabonds in their camps on the outskirts of Danville were once birds.

But though they mix realism and fantasy, etiological tales (the

scholarly term for origin stories) do not work the way other legends do about their actuality. Assertions of the truth of the events
they depict, which are so characteristic of most legends, are usually absent. Because of this, they are often categorized as myths.
And, depending on their time setting and atmosphere, they may
be. Myths are sacred narratives. They are regarded as true, as
legends usually are; but while legends are about historical events,
myths are about timeless sacred events. As such, their actuality
does not come up when they are told. The anthropologist William
Bascom clarified this difference by saying that myths deal with
events before the creation of the world as we know it; legends deal
with the period after the creation.[3] This prehistoric, even ahis-
toric, setting gives mythic stories a special mood and atmosphere—"Why Butterflies Was Made" (legend 15) and "The Legend of the Dogwood Tree" (legend 22) are examples. They are
clearly mythic. Within the A (Mythological Motifs) category, they
have the designations A2041, "Creation of butterflies," and
A2711.2, "Tree blessed that made the cross." And they involve
God, the creator or the savior, directly making or involved in the
world.

But etiological tales, even mythic ones, are not always told as
true. In his writings on belief legends among Texas Gulf Coast
fisherman, which are based on extensive fieldwork, Patrick Mullen noted two relevant facts: (1) just because a legend is told does
not mean it is believed; and (2) when a legend does cease to be
believed, it does not necessarily drop out of a teller's repertoire.
In discussing narratives that support folk beliefs and superstitions, Mullen said: "If a superstition is believed, the legend sup-
ports the belief and it is a true belief legend. If the basis of a belief
narrative is not believed, then the story functions as entertainment and is a fabulate. Of course there are many degrees of belief
between these extremes."[4] The two narratives included here in
which the workers gave indications of their informants' beliefs
about their stories go to both extremes. The tale of the origin of
Gypsies was noted as completely believed, and the one recounting
the origin of the buzzard's baldness was noted as an entertainment
for children and nothing more. Although many of the texts lack

any notation about their informants' beliefs, the WPA collection beginnings tales seem by and large to have been told more to entertain than to reinforce strongly held beliefs.

African American beginning tales concerning the issue of race are common in the WPA collection. Interestingly, a main theme of these from the 1930s is the same one Daryl Dance found to be prominent in her field collections of black materials, both in America and Jamaica, in the 1970s. Dance noted that many black tales of the origins of things portray "the Negro as messed up"; she listed the following common themes: "why he is black, why he has big, ugly feet and hands, why his hair is so kinky, and why he must remain a poor laborer in a rich society."[5] She said that the underlying causes of these inferior traits usually turn out to be some character defect of the protagonist—his tardiness, his ignorance, his greed, or his laziness. These stories are so common that she devoted an entire large section of *Shuckin' and Jivin'* to them, calling them "Self-degrading Tales."[6] She brought up several points that clarify this curious attitude. First she substantiated it by noting a survey published in 1959 which found more antiblack jokes among black than white college students. Then she noted that self-derogatory tales are also popular in other ethnic groups, such as Jews, Puerto Ricans, and the Irish. Her main argument, though, was that when blacks tell narratives which portray bigoted attitudes, and even give them "mythic atmosphere," they are consciously parodying those attitudes and revealing how ludicrous they are.[7] This fits the strategy of protest by indirection that commentators from Zora Neale Hurston to Lawrence Levine have noted as a predominant feature of black folk culture.[8] The rhymed couplet at the end of "Why Colored People Work for the Whites" (legend 16) shows it too. It is an ironic evocation of a patently unfair social situation. It is subtle and careful as it negotiates the territory between protest and resignation to an unalterable fact of life, but it makes its point.

NOTES

1. Donald Ward's "American and European Narratives as Socio-Psychological Indicators," *Studia Fennica* 20 (1976): 348–53, contains a good discussion of the moral function of belief narratives, as does Patrick Mullen's *I Heard the Old*

Fishermen Say: Folklore of the Texas Gulf Coast (Logan: Utah State Univ. Press, 1988), pp. 23–42.

2. Max Lüthi's *Once Upon a Time*, pp. 35–46, devotes a chapter to comparing the märchen and the belief legend's relation to realism. My thinking here about reality and fantasy in etiological legends is indebted to his formulations in that discussion.

3. William Bascom, "The Forms of Folklore: Prose Narratives," *Journal of American Folklore* 78 (1965): 18.

4. Patrick Mullen, "The Relationship of Legend and Folk Belief," ibid., 84 (1971): 413.

5. Daryl Dance discusses these issues in her introduction to *Shuckin' and Jivin': Folklore from Contemporary Black Americans* (Bloomington: Indiana Univ. Press, 1978), and more thoroughly in "In the Beginning: A New Look at Black American Etiological Tales," *Southern Folklore Quarterly* 41 (1977): 53–64.

6. *Shuckin' and Jivin'*, pp. 89–134.

7. "In the Beginning," pp. 55–56.

8. Zora Neale Hurston, *Mules and Men* (rpt. Bloomington: Indiana Univ. Press, 1978), pp. 4–5; Levine, *Black Culture and Black Consciousness*, pp. 81–135.

WHY NEGROES' HANDS
HAVE WHITE PALMS

Levi Pollard, interviewer unknown,
in Richmond, on May 15, 1939

Was back yonder in dem times dey say ev'ybody was niggers an' dey won't nobody else but niggers. But news got roun' dat dar was [a] pond of water, or a lake or something somewhere an' dat if you went into dat pond or whatever hit was, an' washed in hit, why you come out white. Well, I don't reckon de niggers was gettin' long no worse dan de niggers an' white folks now, but dey want to change deyselves den, like dey always has. Anyway, de niggers started a flockin' to dis here place an' dem dat git dar fust was washed jus' as white an' de kinks was washed out of dey hair. Den de niggers started comin' so fast dat de water started goin' down, an' de news gits 'round dat niggers been made into white folks, an' if you wanta git white to hurry, 'cause de water was goin' down fast. Den de niggers dat had put it off gits out an' went in de water. It was gittin' cloudy an' almost gone so dey was comin' out kinda yellow an' dey named 'em mulatters. Some of de kinks was washed out of dey hair.

Den news come dat de water was almost gone, so dat time all de niggers got dere, an' dey was so many dat hit won' 'nough water fo' 'em all to wash in, so dey gits down on dey hands an feets an' walked dis way tryin' to git white. But de water ain't ever cover dey hands an' feets so dey come out wid de inside of dey hands white, an' 'neath dey feets white an' de rest of 'em black, an' dat's de way hit is today, ceptin' when de whites has chillun by de blacks an' den dey might be any color from noon to midnight.

——————— 15 ———————

WHY BUTTERFLIES WAS MADE

Bettie Stevens, interviewed by Bessie A. Scales
in Danville, on February 24, 1941

De lawd made butterflies after de world wuz all fashioned and through. You know de Lawd seen so much bare ground 'till he got sick and tired lookin' at it. So de Lawd told me to fetch him his prunin' shears and trimmed up de trees and made grass and flowers and throwed 'em all over de clearin's and dey growed dere from memorial days. Way after while de flowers said, "We'se put here to keep de world company, but we'se lonesome ourselves." So de Lawd said, "A world is somethin' ain't never finished. Soon's you make one thing you got to make somethin' else to go wid it. Gimme dem li'l shears." So he went 'round clippin' li'l pieces off everything—de sky, de trees, de flowers, de earth. An' every one of dem little clippin' flew off. When folks seen all dem li'l scraps fallin' from de Lawd's scissors and flutterin' dey called 'em flutter-bys. But you know how it is wid de black folks—who is got a big mouf and a stamblin' tongue. So dey got it all mixed up and said butter-fly, and folks been callin' 'em dat ever since. Dat's how come we got butterflies of every color an' kind, and dat's why de hangs 'round de flowers. Dey was made to keep de flowers company.

———— **16** ————

WHY COLORED PEOPLE WORK FOR THE WHITES

Elizabeth Kilgore Carter, interviewed by James Taylor Adams
in Norton, Wise County, on July 31, 1941

I've heard father tell why colored people were slaves and had to work for white people. He said that way back in the beginning that a white man and a colored man were going along a road one day when they looked on ahead of 'em an' saw two pokes lying' in the road. One was a big poke and the other was a little poke. They both wanted the big poke, so they started runnin' jes' as hard as they could, an' the colored man outran the white man an' grabbed the big poke. The white man had to be satisfied with the little poke. So they opened their pokes an' the big poke had a pick, shovel, plow, an' axe in it. So the colored man had to work hard with sech things all his life. In the little poke there was nothin' but a pen, piece of paper an' bottle of ink. So the white man put in his time figurin' out how to git what the colored man worked and made. Father would allus end up by sayin',

> *"Ought for an ought, an' ought for a figure*
> *Two for the white folks an' none for the nigger."*

———— **17** ————

THE MAN IN THE MOON

Lemuel Hamilton, interviewed by Emory L. Hamilton
in Wise, Wise County, on January 6, 1940

I've heard about the man in the moon ever since I can remember. He was sucked up because he burned brush on Sunday. He went out with his dog and fired a brush pile and a rabbit jumped out of it. The dog started chasing the rabbit and the moon sucked them all three up. You can look at the moon when it's full and it looks like the picture of a man and a dog and a rabbit on the face of it. I've heard it told another way where the man was burning brush on Sunday and fell into the moon. It don't say anything about the dog or the rabbit in this last way of telling it.

I've heard my mother tell about this dozens of time[s]. When I was a child I used to be afraid to burn brush on Sunday thinking I'd fall into the moon.

—— 18 ——

THE ORIGIN OF GYPSIES

John Robson, interviewed by Bessie A. Scales
in Danville, on March 3, 1941

In the beginning Gypsies were all birds. They had wings. They flew high over the trees and mountains to gather their daily food. And they were birds that always flew towards warm countries when the weather begun to get cold. They always left one region for another, knowing when the season was about to change. When the leaves on the trees began to turn yellow and red, and the worms and other crawling things were beginning to burrow their holes, there was a great hunger among the birds. Because for a long season they could find nothing to eat. They flew in every direction hunting food.

Finally they came upon a field of ripe grain—the like of which they had never seen. They swooped down and ate themselves so full of this grain that they were too heavy to rise on their wings again. So they had to stay on the ground that night among the grain-straw and grass. In the morning instead of flying away they decided to eat just a little bit more and rest in that field of grain one more night. The next morning and the next day they decided to eat a little more again and stay another day. So the birds got heavier and heavier, hopping instead of flying.

Then the leaves on the trees began to turn yellow and red. The worms and other creatures of the earth crawled into their holes and the cold winter winds began to blow. But the birds could not fly away. The grain-straw was getting dry and the grass was thinning and dying. After watching the crawling things, the birds too began to shake the grain from the blades of grass and gather it into heaps with their wings and shape it into bales. The fluff of the birds' wings crusted, glued, and thickened. Their wings took the shape of arms and hands, and as the birds were no longer able to fly, they had to dig holes in the sides of mountains and along the shores of the rivers.

But Gypsies are birds. Their arms are two stilted wings. They never see a mountain without wanting to get to the top. But they cannot fly; they have to crawl up there. But the Gypsies will get their wings back. They will be birds again.

—————— 19 ——————

DISOBEDIENT SAMMY

Simpson Randolph Adams, interviewed by James Taylor Adams
in Big Laurel, Wise County, on August 28, 1940

One time there was a woman and she had a little boy named Sammy. One day Sammy slipped off and went a-fishin' with some other boys and caught a big fish. He brought it home and him and his mammy had fish for several days. But he hadn't come back when he told his mammy he would and she forbid him to go a-fishin' any more.

So one day his mammy went to town and he got his hook and went to the river. He hadn't more'n got there when he heard something in the river saying, "Throw your hook in, Sammy, throw your hook in, Sammy." He throwed his hook in and he heard something say, "Jerk your hook and catch me, Sammy." And he jerked his hook and there was the finest fish he ever seen. It said "Build a fire and fry me, Sammy." And there was sticks to build a fire and coals to start it with. And he looked around and there was a frying pan setting there by him. So he cut up the fish and fried it. And when he got it fried he heard a voice in the frying pan saying "Eat me, Sammy." And he eat the fish.

Just about the time he got done eating the fish it begin to thunder and there came up an awful storm. He heard the voice in a big black gum tree saying, "Come in out of the rain, Sammy." He went over to the big black gum tree and it split open and there was a sheltering place in it. He got in the tree and it closed back on him and from that day 'till this a black gum tree won't split.

———— 20 ————

HOW VOTE BUYING STARTED IN WISE COUNTY

Judge J. T. Hamilton, interviewed by James Taylor Adams
in Wise, Wise County, on August 11, 1941

They don't buy votes like they used to. I have heard it said that the first vote buying ever done in Wise County was old Creed Flanary buyin' 'em with gingerbread. His wife, who was an excellent cook, would bake up a lot of gingercakes a few days before the election and he would give 'em to certain people to vote the way he wanted them to vote. It was from this vote buying started here. Next, he would mark off a small store account they owed him to vote his way, and from that to a certain amount of money, one or two dollars, until it got to where they paid as much as ninety dollars for a single vote. So you see it was quite a jump from gingercake to ninety dollars, but it's a fact.

I can remember one time when Stuart and Slemp were running for Congress that a certain fellow on the Guests River held out for more money to vote. Each side had offered him a good price for his vote and he wouldn't take it. So the two leaders got together and decided to play a trick on him. So they began to bid for his vote. It was getting late, and one would nudge him and take him to one side and tell him he'd give him twenty-five dollars. The other fellow would call him off and offer him thirty. Then the other one would offer thirty-five, the other forty, and so on. They got up to about a hundred dollars when all at once the people came out and hollered, "The polls are closed!" and the fellow had to go home without getting anything for his vote. They said he was so mad he wanted to whip somebody.

Another time when Creed Flanary and Cam Slemp were running for the legislature, Abe Wells was for Flanary, the Democrat. And old Abe was hard to beat in an election. Well, it looked like Slemp was a sure winner. The county was pretty strong Republican then. All of the Roaring Fork country had to come to Wise to vote then, and they were all Republicans. So the evening before the election Abe Wells sent a fellow they wouldn't suspicion up Roaring Fork telling everybody that the smallpox had broke out in Wise and that they were putting everybody that come to town in the pest house. So not a voter from Roaring Fork showed up, and Flanary was elected.

—— 21 ——

WHY THE BUZZARD IS BALD

Harriet G. Miller, from her own recollection
in North, Mathews County, on July 24, 1939

The buzzard will eat all kinds of carrion, thus helping to prevent odors and the spread of some diseases.

One day a buzzard found a dead horse and ate all he wanted. Then he stuffed the horse full of straw and lightwood knots. Along came Mr. 'Possum and asked the buzzard if he knew where he could get anything to eat. The buzzard told him he'd lead him right over in the field where he'd find a dead horse an' he could eat all he wanted. The 'possum thanked him and went over to look at the horse. The buzzard flew to a tree nearby to watch him.

The old 'possum started in, but he couldn't find anything in the horse to eat but a lightwood knot and straw. He was so mad that he picked up the lightwood knot and threw it at the buzzard and knocked all the feathers off his head.

22

THE LEGEND OF
THE DOGWOOD TREE

Emory L. Hamilton, from his own recollection
in Wise, Wise County, on December 10, 1938

The legend about the dogwood tree is quite widely known in the Cumberlands, as elsewhere in the state of Virginia. Since the dogwood is our state flower and we have begun to have Dogwood Festivals around us, the legend is perhaps just now in the cradle of its infancy and is due much more popularity in the future. Anyone who has ever studied the dogwood flower can readily see the symbols in the flower that are mentioned in this legend. Whether the legend be true or false, one is lead [led] to believe that it is pretty near the truth. This legend runs that during and before the time of Christ, the dogwood tree grew to the height and dimensions of the oak, maple, and other larger forest trees. The wood was so firm and strong that it was the chosen tree to make the cross of crucifixion of the Savior. The trees were greatly distressed at having been chosen for such a cruel purpose, and Jesus, sensing their regret for his great suffering, gave them this promise:

"Never again shall the dogwood grow large enough for a cross. Henceforth it shall be slender, bent, and twisted; and its blooms shall be in the form a cross, two long and two short petals, and in the center of the outer edge of each petal there shall be nail prints, brown with rust and stained by blood. And in the center of the flower will be a crown of thorns, so that all those who see it shall know that it was on a dogwood tree that I was crucified. It shall not be mutilated or destroyed, but protected and cherished as a reminder of my agony and death upon the cross."

THE
CIVIL WAR
AND
EMANCIPATION

Virginia was scarred by the Civil War more deeply than any other state in the South, both because it was the scene of so much of the fighting and because no other state so clearly represented the entire Confederacy and its culture. The WPA collection contains over seventy Civil War stories, revealing what a lively topic it remained in Virginia into the 1930s. An informant in Wise County singled it out it as a major subject of folk legends when he placed his story of a ghostly fiddler "before there was the Civil War to talk about and after the Indian tales had grown stale."[1] But it should be noted that stories of the war per se are mostly from white informants. I have included emancipation tales in this section because the Civil War was in fact two simultaneous events, a national civil conflict and the end of the institution of slavery. And, while "the Old War" was important to many white informants, the emancipation aspect of it was the signal historical event in the minds of most black narrators. As Lawrence Levine noted, "The South's lost cause was the fulfillment of a prophecy the slaves had been singing for more than half a century."[2]

Most stories by blacks in the WPA collection that concern the Civil War and emancipation are passages out of lengthy oral history narratives collected from ex-slaves. These, which give a detailed composite picture of Virginia slave life, are published in *Weevils in the Wheat: Interviews with Virginia Ex-slaves*.[3] The war and emancipation are major subjects in these interviews, even though only twenty-one questions from the list of over three hundred that the VWP workers were given to ask pertain to these topics.[4] Most are personal accounts with no legendary elements, such as the following from Charles Grandy of Norfolk: "I was in de army, but I warn' neah no fightin'. I was a cook fer a white army. Didn' see but one er two colored sojers durin' de whole war. I don' 'member many battles. Ole Beauragard was ascrimagin' 'round Suffolk in '62. I was a cook wid de sojers den. Den I gits tired o' de fiel'. Always a runnin' an' never git no res'; so I list in de Navy one yeah. I was made fust class boy in de third cutter. De cutter is de boat what rows de officers f'om de big boat to de shore. De name o' our big boat was de *U. S. Lawrence*."[5]

Parts of the ex-slave narratives which appear elsewhere in this book, especially "A Smallpox Epidemic: A Curse on Whites" (legend 137) in the Unusual Events section, provide similar descriptions of life in wartime and immediate postwar Virginia. The two narratives from black informants printed here, while they tell of historical events as oral histories and personal accounts do, have a discernible narrative pattern, are told in what is clearly real belief, are about people other than their narrators, and have evident themes and purposes beyond their informational and entertainment values. They are local legends; a local legend is one "in which the proper nouns used belong to the community . . . or in which the material narrated belongs to that same community."[6]

These two narratives about legendary figures reflect distinctly different, but both distinctly heroic, responses to "the peculiar institution" before emancipation—fight and flight. The ambiguous status of free blacks in the slave South and the ambivalent attitudes of both blacks and whites toward them are vividly captured in the legend of James Bowser, the spy and martyr, as is the extent to which the Northern military forces depended on Southern blacks for intelligence and logistical support. And the story of Henry ("Box") Brown distills the longing of slaves to escape to the North, the great lengths to which they were willing to go to make the attempt, and the subtlety and ingenuity of the blacks and whites who made up the loose confederation known as the Underground Railroad.

A few comments on negative effects of emancipation are scattered through the ex-slave narratives, such as this one from Archie Booker of Hampton: "Sometimes ah think slavery wuz bettuh den freedom in one sense. Ef ye wuz sick, ye hadda doctuh. Den ye git food too. But now ef ye git sick an' ye hain' got no money, ye jis die. Dat's all!"[7] But by and large the commentary and stories of the black informants depict struggle, resistance to slavery, and great joy over freedom. When Union soldiers are mentioned, they are usually cast as saviors and liberators. This is strikingly different from the welcome the northern soldiers receive from a house servant in "A Yankee Drinks from a 'Poisoned' Well" (legend 28), which was told by Mrs. Fannie Wilson, a wealthy white Roanoke matron. This situation, the invading Northern army coming to the big house, was one of the most commonly related episodes in the white Civil War tales. In Mrs. Wilson's legend a house slave

displays the indignation and grit that are typically the role rele-
gated to Southern women, children, old folks, and preachers—in
other words, the supporters of the Southern cause who could not
be actively in the war. Giving this role to a slave is significant; an
important but indirect point of Mrs. Wilson's story is that the
house slave makes it clear which side she is on. The vehemence
of her anger at the Yankees equals her contentment with the status quo. And the contentment of slaves was always a part of
Southern attempts to justify slavery.

Some other legends of the Yankee occupation of Virginia in the
WPA collection have titles such as "Bond's Dishes," "Buried Bacon," "The Preacher Who Wouldn't Preach," and "Yankee Raids
on Homes."[8] These have a set pattern in which Yankee soldiers
arrive at a Confederate home, much to the fear and loathing of
the inhabitants. In the interactions that follow, the Northern soldiers are either made fools of, shown to be cruel and uncivilized,
or simply shot, as in "A Young Girl Shoots a Yankee" (legend 29),
the typical "Yankees at the big house" legend printed here.
"Bond's Dishes" is the only such narrative in which a Southern
character is shown in a comic light; Bond was in such a hurry to
hide his household items from the invaders that he dropped his
box of dishes over a cliff.

Most of the white stories reflect a commitment to the cause of
the Confederacy mixed with a middle-class sense of the material
hardships and losses it caused. Tales that were maintained by
other groups typically lack these elements; those from the poor
and the mountaineers have little ideological component. They emphasize the viewpoint of the common soldier, which stresses the
horror and gore of combat. The bloody fighting itself left an impression which endured through the seventy years between the
war and the arrival of the VWP folklore collectors. "A Premonition of Death" (legend 26) and "The Curse of the Carbine" (legend 27) are examples of these war legends. The impact of the
fighting itself can be seen in other genres of folklore as well. In a
listing of Wise County place-names, the location Horse Gap is
noted as being named "because during the Civil War a troop of
Union Soldiers were returning from a raid on Gladeville (now
Wise) and a bunch of Pound River settlers fired upon them killing

all their horses, and a number of men. The bones of the decaying horses lay in the gap until the building of the new road a few years ago. Hence the name Horse Gap."[9] And several versions of a legend about a black ghost dog which appears to travelers along an isolated mountain road give the death of a group of Civil War soldiers at that location as the cause of the apparition (see the Spirit Dogs section).

William Jansen, upon finding the Civil War still a common subject of narratives in a Kentucky legend collection he analyzed in the 1960s, suggested that "ambivalent attitudes keep the Civil War prominent in legends in the region."[10] I believe this is as true for the western part of Virginia as for Kentucky. The ambivalence arose from the split loyalties the war wrought in the region. In the Tidewater and Piedmont, Civil War narratives from whites reveal anxiety over losing the war, being occupied by a foreign force, and having the culture and the land itself devastated. But there is little evidence of ambivalent feelings about the correctness of the Southern cause. To the west there is ample evidence of ambivalence. It should be remembered that the war literally split the Old Dominion, resulting in the organization of the state of West Virginia by the counties sympathetic to the Union. As far east as Culpeper County, a folksinger named Isaiah Wallace stated in an interview that he was "very proud of the fact that not but one of my family [went] off with the Yankees."[11]

Nowhere is this tension so clear as it is in the western counties' legends of the Home Guard. The Home Guards were local militias formed to protect the women and children from attacks and pillaging by soldiers. They were made up of boys and old men who were not able-bodied enough for the war itself. Cornelia Berry, in a piece she submitted on the Southern Home Guards, reported that they were "very hard on their own men who did not believe in war and refused to fight. Several had to leave their homes and go to Maryland to live. One man came back to visit his family and the Home Guard caught him and tied him to a barrel in the river. He was left there for several days and when he was set free he was in such a weakened condition that a serious illness developed from the exposure. As a result of such treatment several men sold their homes and took their families to Maryland for the duration of the war. In many cases these men received better treatment from the Yankees than from their own Home Guards."[12] In the Home Guard legend given here, "The Curse of the Carbine" (legend 27), Bates, the Yankee soldier who shot John Dick Adams, the Confederate Home Guard captain, was known by name and clearly came back after the war to live in the same community he previously shared with Adams. Similar proximity and familiarity among the opposing forces is revealed in a WPA collection legend not given here titled "The Killings on Roaring Fork."[13] Three different versions of this narrative indicate that Southern militiamen killed members of their own community who were returning home after being discharged from the triumphant Union army.

One thing which is clear from the Civil War legends in the WPA collection is that no region of the state was exempted from the powerful impact of the conflict. To suggest, as Mandel Sherman and Thomas Henry do in their book *Hollow Folk*, that the Civil War had no effect on the isolated mountain regions of Virginia, reveals their lack of research. If they had checked the muster books in the county courthouses or if they had listened to the tellers of local legends, they could not have concluded, as they did, that the "hollow folk" of western Virginia "scarcely knew that a war was in progress."[14]

NOTES

1. "The Fiddler of Peter Cave," box 5, folder 2, item 734, WPA collection.
2. Levine, *Black Culture and Black Consciousness*, p. 137.
3. Perdue, Barden, and Phillips, *Weevils in the Wheat*.
4. Ibid., pp. 367–76. The entire set of questions is given as app. 6.
5. Ibid., pp. 117–18.
6. William Hugh Jansen, "A Content-Classification of a Random Sample of Legends, Mostly Local," *Keystone Folklore Quarterly* 16 (1971): 81.
7. Perdue, Barden, and Phillips, *Weevils in the Wheat*, p. 54.
8. Box 10, folder 4, items 1552, 1569, 1571, 1572, WPA collection.
9. Box 6, folder 2, item 844, ibid.
10. Jansen, "A Content-Classification of a Random Sample of Legends, Mostly Local," p. 89.
11. Box 12, folder 1, WPA collection.
12. Box 10, folder 4, item 1563, ibid.
13. Item 1561, ibid.
14. Mandel Sherman and Thomas R. Henry, *Hollow Folk* (rpt. Berryville: Virginia Book Company, 1973), p. 122.

23

JAMES BOWSER,
EMANCIPATION HERO

Virginia Hayes Shepherd, interviewed by Emmy Wilson and Claude Anderson
in Norfolk, on May 18, 1937

I want to tell you about undertaker Hale's grandfather. I'll bet he doesn't know this about his grandfather. This man's name was James Bowser. James Bowser was a free Negro who lived in Nansemond County during slavery times. Now you know free Negroes had to be very careful of mixing with slaves or white folks in those days because both races were always watching them, especially the whites. Some white folks watched all the time, to keep them from mixing with the slaves. Consequently Bowser did his best to avoid trouble in any shape or form. He had five daughters who were in the courting stage. He wouldn't let them entertain any male slave company and allowed very few female slaves to come visiting. His policy was no slaves in his home any longer than possible. If he came in the house and a strange Negro was sitting there, he would ask, "Who are you? Are you your own man?" Generally the conversation would run, "No sir." "Well, then whom do you belong to?" "I belong to so and so." "I'm sorry, you'll have to go home. I can't entertain you. I got enough trouble of my own." When he finished, another young lovesick buck slave was sent back to his master's plantation. Such attitude and action made Bowser very unpopular among the slaves. Bowser hated the fact that his own people despised him, but there was nothing else to do to protect himself from the white man's wrath. He had no redress in court. He owned property which they desired and he knew association with slaves could be used as an excuse for attacking him by jealous white neighbors, one Phelps especially. The slave had protection; Bowser had none. He detested slavery because it kept him bound. As long as slavery existed, Bowser knew he could never be absolutely free; so whenever he could, he threw a monkey wrench in the machinery of slavery.

He did it once too often however. The Civil War began and the Yankees came down to free the Negroes. Because they were in strange country the Yankees needed information. Free Negroes aided them a great deal. Bowser began to act as a spy for the Yankees and give them all the information he knew about his section of the country. He gave it gladly. He saw his chance to deliver a telling blow at slavery and took it.

Soon the news leaked out to the whites. That was all the cause they wanted. Led by Phelps, an envious white man, a band of white planters attacked the Bowser home one night and demanded that Bowser and his son come forth. They came out, were seized by the mob and carried into the woods between Driver and Suffolk. After severely beating both father and son, the horde made Bowser lie on the ground and stretch his neck over a log like a chicken on a chopping block. Then someone cut his head off. The plan was to kill the boy in the same manner, but the more thoughtful ones disagreed. They suggested that he be left to carry the news of this ghastly example back to the other Negroes. The mob gave in. The boy went home, got a cart, and returned for his father's body. The family was stunned by the news and remained as meek as lambs. A quiet funeral was held and the body of James Bowser was laid to rest in the family plot while a few miles away slaves chuckled gleefully in their quarters. Big hat Bowser had got what he deserved at last.

After the war the daughters, all five of them, Ruth, Mary, Evaline and the other two married. The Bowser family was one family that never felt the blight of disgrace on their fair name. Their father had reared them too well. Colored spies were common during the rebellion, but very few of them are credited in today's history. Bowser should be ranked with [Nathan] Hale.

————— 24 —————

HENRY ("BOX") BROWN: MAILED TO FREEDOM

Rev. Norman B. Wood, interviewed by Louise G. Harris
in Newport News, on February 18, 1937

enry Box Brown was boxed up in Richmond, Virginia, by his friend James A. Smith. The exact size of the box was two feet eight inches deep, two feet wide, and three feet long. Having been supplied with a large gimlet, a bladder of water, and a few biscuits, he got inside, was nailed up, and five hickory hoops were put around the box. It was now marked "Wm. H. Johnson, Arch Street, Philadelphia. This side up with care" and sent by Adams Express. Sometimes the notice "This side up with care" did not avail; for miles he was on his head. At last, after twenty-six long weary hours the box and contents arrived at its destination.

In the afternoon of the same day, Mr. McKim, a member of the vigilance committee in Philadelphia, received the following telegram: "Your case of goods is shipped and will arrive tomorrow morning early." The box was brought at once to the anti-slavery office, where William Still, Professor C. D. Cleveland, and Lewis Thompson were invited to be present at the "opening." When all was ready Mr. McKim rapped quietly on the lid of the box and called out, "All right?" Instantly came the answer, "All right sir." Soon the hickory hoops were cut, the top of the box removed. When he arose, [w]ringing wet with perspiration, he said "How do you do, gentlemen?"

After resting a few moments he remarked that before leaving Richmond he had selected for his arrival hymn, if he lived, the psalm beginning "I Waited Patiently for the Lord and He Heard My Prayer." Most feelingly did he sing the hymn, to the delight of his small audience. After spending some time resting and straightening his limbs at the hospitable home of James and Lucretia Mott, and remaining two days with William Still, he left for Boston.

Mr. Samuel A. Smith, the shoe dealer who boxed him up in Richmond, did the same thing for two others, but was detected and spent seven years in the Virginia penitentiary, a martyr to the cause of freedom.

——— 25 ———

A CONFEDERATE SPY

Mary Smith, interviewed by Harriet G. Miller
in an unknown location in Mathews County, no date given

In an old home situated on the Bay, I heard an interesting tale of Civil War days. During the war a Confederate spy by the name of Bell came to the home of Mr. William Hudgins near Fitchett's Wharf and asked for refuge. While he was there some Yankee soldiers prowling through that section of the county came upon a Confederate cap in the vicinity of the Hudgins' home. They immediately started to the house to search, but in the meantime Bell had gone out into a dense woods nearby to hide.

The mistress of the house saw the soldiers coming and ran up to Bell's room to see if any of his belongings had been left there. Nothing seemed to be in the room which would reveal his presence in the house except some letters, which she grabbed quickly and just had time to slip them inside of the dress of a doll which her little girl was holding. She put the child on the porch telling her to sit there and hold the doll tight in her arms.

As soon as the soldiers reached the porch, one of them picked the little girl up in his arms to talk to her. But she remembered her mother's warning and held her doll baby close to her side. So the letters were not discovered.

Mr. Hudgins took Bell in a sail boat at night to Gwynne's Island, where he hid in the woods. At times the Yankees were so near that they could hear them breathing. Later Mr. Hudgins took Bell to Eastern Shore, Virginia, where he remained for a while. His mother was living in New York and he was very anxious to see her. It was during a visit to her that he was finally captured.

[John Wilkes] Booth, who was an old friend and school-mate of Bell's, sent word to Lincoln that if Bell were hung, he (Lincoln) would die. Bell was hung, but before he died he wrote a beautiful letter to the man in Virginia who had befriended him. In this letter Bell wrote about the beauty of the morning of the day before he died, and of how much he wanted to live. He also expressed beautifully his appreciation of the great kindness of Mr. Hudgins and his family. This letter was destroyed by mistake, greatly to the distress of the present members of the family, who would have liked to have preserved it.

Many people believed that the hanging of Bell was one of the causes of the assassination of President Lincoln.

26

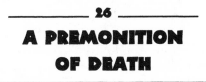

A PREMONITION OF DEATH

Lemuel Hamilton, interviewed by Emory L. Hamilton
in Wise, Wise County, on September 17, 1940

Grandma told one that happened during the Civil War. I don't recollect where it happened. One of her uncles was in the bunch that saw this happen. It was a bunch of Civil War soldiers that saw it happen. She said her uncle said one day they were going along and passing a place [and] they suddenly saw a man with his eyeballs popped out and falling down on his face. He disappeared almost as suddenly as he appeared. Next day one of the men out of the bunch that saw this, I believe there was two or three men, maybe more, got killed. They said his eyeballs popped out on his face when he got killed, just exactly like the man (apparition) they had all seen the day before.

27

THE CURSE OF
THE CARBINE

Findlay Adams, interviewed by James Taylor Adams
in Big Laurel, Wise County, on May 7, 1941

You've heard of John Dick Adams, ol' Uncle Jess Adams boy, Grandpa Spencer's nephew. He was a dangerous man. When the Civil War broke out he got up a company an' was a captain. Some sort o' home guards. They raided around. He owned a fine carbine gun. One time he was at Grandpa's an' told him if he was to be killed that he wanted him to see that his carbine was buried with him. He was on the rebel side.

One day his company and a company of Yankee home guards got into a fight somewhere on Kentucky River I think it was. John Dick, he got shot through one arm. After while he was shot through one leg. He couldn't walk or use but one arm, but he kept shootin' his carbine rifle. At last they shot 'im through the other arm. He was helpless then. They charged up on him an' he said, "Well, men, I've allus said I'd never surrender, but I'm helpless now an' will have to beg for my life." One of [the] Bates' I think it was, said "I'll give you your life!" an' just up an' shot him through the heart. Then he took his gun.

Well, they say that that fellow never rested after that. He would holler out all times of the night—"Take John Dick Adams away from here. He's come to kill me." He even got so he would see John Dick in his cup o' coffee when he set down to the table to eat. He heard about the request that John Dick had made about his gun bein' buried with 'im an' he sent word to Grandpa to come an' git it. Grandpa went an' got the gun, but hit had been several months an' he didn't bury the gun with John Dick then, of course.

But him gittin' the gun didn't do any good. That feller just kept seein' John Dick wherever he went. He didn't live long. Got so he couldn't eat. Said John Dick Adams was in every bite he tried to swallow. So he jes dwindled away. Died in about a year after he killed John Dick.

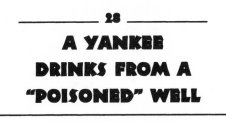

28

A YANKEE DRINKS FROM A "POISONED" WELL

Mrs. Fannie C. Wilson, interviewed by I. M. Warren
in Roanoke, on May 4, 1938

When I was about fourteen the entire south was thrown into a panic by the war. So that ended my school days, and for four long years we lived in mortal terror and suspense. The first years everybody was confident of the outcome; fortunately it was that way, for it kept hope and courage alive in the homes, while sacrifices were being made and growing greater daily as provisions became scarcer and harder to get. The federal soldiers under General Hunter, for some reason, did not take any of my father's horses or destroy property and food as they did in many places. My mother had food cooked for them, and received very courteous treatment from the captain. He gave me a beautiful beaded collar, perhaps taken from some home nearby. I have that collar yet. He also found that some of his men had taken a lot of our flat silver, so he brought that back and gave it to mother.

At Mrs. Moore's in Liberty, news had reached them that Hunter was on his way, so they tried to hide everything they could and put their meat down in a deep well. Well, the soldiers come rushing in, tired and thirsty, and went straight to the well and drew up a bucket of fresh water and one of them gulped down a gourd full.

Just about that time the old black cook appeared, with her red bandanna kerchief wrapped tight around her head; the soldier spied her and called out, "What kind of damn water is this, old woman?" With a terrified look on her face she said, "'Fore God, you ain't done drinked dat water, has yer? We'se been drappin' dead cats and ebery old thing down in dat well. We neber use dat water! We gits all our water from de spring."

"Ol' woman that water has made me sick."

The old cook said, "I'se sho glad uv it. I hopes to God it kills yer, and all the res of dem Yankees!"

29

A YOUNG GIRL SHOOTS A YANKEE

Mrs. R. V. Brayhill, interviewed by John W. Garrett
in an unknown location, an unknown county, no date given

My grandfather, Henry Pennel, was a wealthy farmer and he owned five horses and carriages. When the Civil War came up he had to leave his wife and ten children and join the southern army. My grandfather had a lot of wheat and corn and meat and the Yankees had been coming through the country and carrying away the food supplies, corn and wheat and things like that. My grandmother had hid her meat under the house so that they couldn't find it, and one day a captain came by with some soldiers and grandpa had a big fine carriage with nice red plush seats, and the soldiers took an axe and cut that carriage all to pieces and then they took all the horses except one old mare and was taking them off.

Aunt Clarcy, a young girl of twenty, went upstairs and got Grandpa's gun and came to the window, and the captain saw her standing there with the gun and he asked her, "What are you going to do with that gun?" And she was so mad she said, "I am going to shoot if you don't leave my father's horses alone!" He yelled back, "Shoot the d—— rascal!" Sure enough she pulled off and shot one of the men and ran down and hid in a secret cellar under the house. She couldn't be found and they took the horses and went off. But after that Grandmother had to keep Aunt Clarcy hid until after the Civil War was over.

CONJURE
AND
WITCHCRAFT

The Bible reference "Thou shalt not suffer a witch to live" (Exodus 22:18) was enough to make the New England Puritans believe in, tell stories about, and vigorously punish the supposed witches in their midst. Scholars like George Kittredge and Richard Dorson have documented the witch beliefs, persecutions, and tales in that region.[1] Although there was also widespread belief in witches in colonial Virginia, and much talk about them, no one was ever executed in Virginia for witchcraft.[2] In 1659 a woman named Katherine Grady was hanged for witchcraft on an immigrant ship bound for Virginia; but when the ship arrived, the colonial authorities brought suit against the captain for her death.[3] The most famous witch trial in the Virginia colony was that of Grace Sherwood in Princess Anne County in 1705, and its result demonstrates the difference in the two colonies' attitudes toward witches and witchcraft. She was given the ducking test—if she sank she was innocent; if she survived she was a witch—in the Chesapeake Bay at Lynnhaven, at a point which has henceforth been called "Witch's Duck." She failed the test, but at that point the Virginia magistrates lost their taste for the whole business and, rather than burning, drowning, or hanging her, returned her to prison where she remained for a while before being released. She lived to the age of eighty, surviving her husband, and left 145 acres of land to her eldest son in her will.[4] In several folk versions of the episode, she escaped punishment by disappearing into the air or onto the Chesapeake Bay in an eggshell.[5] The deep sense of malevolence and complicity with Satan that permeates the witch legends of New England, where a few years before Sherwood's trial nineteen women were hanged and one man was pressed to death, is absent from both the official and the folk versions of this story.

The legend "A Witch Gets Caught in a Store" (legend 43), which is also from the Chesapeake Bay area, exemplifies the Cavalier (in both senses) attitude of the Tidewater Virginians toward witchery. In this story, although the witches' binge is taken seriously and capital punishment is mentioned, the atmosphere of demonic evil that typifies Puritan witchcraft tales is simply not present. In fact, the WPA collection witch legends give little reference to either Satan or religion in general as the source of

CONJURE AND WITCHCRAFT

witches' powers. Only in Devil Bill Boggs's name and in the initiation ceremony mentioned in "Witch Mountain" (legend 38) is any demonic basis of witchcraft noted.

In the African American tales the system called voodoo, or hoodoo, is the source of the conjuror's power. As Zora Neale Hurston and others have noted, the rejection (or inversion) of religion associated with European witchcraft is not usually part of the voodoo cosmology.[6] It is not unusual for conjure formulas to invoke God or for a root doctor to be a practicing Christian. Two of the black informants who told conjure stories were ministers, and neither indicated any basic antipathy toward hoodoo belief or practice. Several of the Anglo-American witch legends in the collection show influence from conjure. One example is the small bag found in the chimney in "A Conjured Girl Tries to Jump into the Fire" (legend 42), which is clearly a "mojo hand," or hoodoo power bag. A "mojo hand," often abbreviated as "mojo" or "hand," is "a small cloth sack that is carried in a wallet or purse and may contain parts of dead insects, animals (especially lizards), birds, and items that have had intimate contact with the person being hexed (underclothing, feces, fingernails, and hair). Through sympathetic magic, objects closely associated with the person to be hoodooed are doctored to produce the desired effects, which range from influencing their love to death."[7]

Of course, the influence went both ways, and, as Newbell Niles Puckett and others have argued, many African American conjure practices and beliefs were substantially influenced in form and content by European folklore.[8] Lawrence Levine has suggested that "the African practices and beliefs which had the best chance of survival in the New World were those that had European analogues, as so many of the folk beliefs did."[9] Being ridden by witches is one belief the two cultures shared. This belief is the basis of Della Barksdale's "A Witch Rode a Girl to Riceville, Virginia" (legend 33), a first-person version of a migratory legend which has been widely collected among African and European Americans. The migratory legend "A Slave with a Magic Hoe" (legend 31), on the other hand, has been collected exclusively from blacks. The magic hoe was often a motif of antebellum escape stories: the hoe was left still hoeing the field after the

slaves had made their getaway. Such magic power as the slave/
conjuror in this legend displays is, according to Virginia Hamilton, "often attributed to Gullah (Angolan) African slaves. Angolan slaves were thought by other slaves to have exceptional powers."[10] Another migratory tale, "The Conjuror's Beck" (legend
32), also depicts the special personal powers of the voodoo doctors.
And as "The Conjuror's Revenge" (legend 30) demonstrates, conjurors often were involved in power plays among themselves when
one was called on to undo the work of another.

Power is the major theme of both the black and white tales of
witchcraft and conjure. Tales such as "A Slave with a Magic Hoe"
(legend 31) and "The Boat That Would Not Move" (legend 118,
in the Supernatural Events section) show that conjure was a way
for slaves to assert some control in what was otherwise a totally
powerless situation. Lawrence Levine concluded his survey of
conjure and other aspects of "the sacred world of black slaves" (his
chapter title) by saying what the WPA collection conjure legends
substantiate, that hoodoo and other folk beliefs provided "numerous contexts and ways for slaves to find their own sources of power
and protection."[11] The white witch legends are also tales of power
and also often pit two occult practitioners against each other.
They reveal the same basic pattern that Leonora Herron and Alice
Bacon described for black conjurors: "The conjure doctor has five
distinct services to render to his patient. (1) He must tell him
whether he is conjured or not. (2) He must find out who conjured
him. (3) He must search for and find the 'trick' and destroy it. (4)
He must cure the patient. (5) He will if the patient wishes turn
back the trick upon the one who made it."[12] The only major difference in the pattern for white "witch doctors" is that they are
usually depicted as telling their patients what to do rather than
doing it for them. Also, Herron and Bacon's assumption that all
conjurors are male is contradicted by both the black and white
WPA stories.

Contrary to Brunvand's suggestion that cultural chauvinism
tends to cast male witches as benevolent "wizards" or "healers"
while branding female witches as malicious,[13] the WPA tales are
usually sexually equal in occult matters. Malicious witches come
in both genders, as do benevolent ones who help victims break

their spells. Kate Upp in "Witch Mountain" (legend 38), Jim Baker in "A Witch's Gun Charms the Woods" (legend 39), and the unnamed couple in "Aunt Lucy's Bewitched Cow" (legend 40) are all given malicious roles. And Jim Largin in "Witch Mountain" and the unnamed "old woman" in "Cooking a Witch's Shoulder" (legend 41) are cast as advisers and spell fixers. Montague and Duck Moore run a classic good-cop/bad-cop routine—Duck bewitches her neighbors and her husband Montague offers to cure them, for a price. Perhaps Brunvand's thesis is supported by this division of labor in their extortion scheme, but the narrative makes it clear that both Montague and Duck were equally feared and hated in the community.

Montague and Duck's story also refutes Yvonne J. Milspaw's idea that Appalachian witch practices constituted protective measures on the part of the mountain poor, especially women. She stated that women who were deemed witches benefited "both in terms of the gaining of the material goods necessary for survival (in some cases as basic as food and shelter), and in terms of the creation of an atmosphere of healthy respect around them. People in the community would take care not to anger a person known as a witch, for fear of retaliation."[14] This analysis, based on an examination of thirteen Appalachian witch narratives, fails to note that the people from whom the witches gained materially were also poor. My look at the approximately seventy white witch narratives in the WPA collection suggests that the term *protection* is applicable only in the sense of extortion. Montague and Duck lived well for years as parasites on the labors of those they terrorized. Further, it is hard to see how "respect" for the witches in these narratives was "healthy," given that all but Devil Bill Boggs and the Moores were finally killed, severely burned, or banished from the community.

Perhaps this decidedly negative slant was influenced by the collecting process of the VWP workers. The "Index to Folklore Subjects" in the *Manual for Folklore Workers* gave witchcraft its own subject listing, in which the third subheading was "Evil deeds of witches," a somewhat leading terminology.[15] But neither of the legends in which witches successfully assert control in their communities centers on, as Milspaw put it, "women living alone in male-dominated American society."[16] The numerous and pointed references to the failure of alleged witches to live up to community moral standards indicate that there was tension between the social groups and the individuals whom those groups designated witches, but (unlike the case of conjure doctors in black culture) there is little to back a reading of the witches' behavior as any sort of strategy for surviving or gaining group respect.

A note James Taylor Adams added to "Cooking a Witch's Shoulder" (legend 41) gives some of the historical and social context of Appalachian witch tales in the 1930s:

> My grandfather, Spencer Adams, believed in witches; one of my uncles, William Green Adams, still living at the age of 87, believes in witchcraft, and I have heard it said that he once declared he could overcome a witch's charm, in other words, that he *was* a witch doctor. I am not sure, but I am of the opinion that my father Joseph Adams (he died when I was eight years old) believed that people and things could be bewitched by persons who had gotten some unusual power by selling their souls to the Devil. I can remember hearing my father and mother discuss such things as they sat around the fire on winter evenings, and, somehow I got the impression that they believed there were witches, bewitched things, and witch doctors. And of course I believed in witches just the same as I did in a personal God, until I got old enough to know better. Belief in witchcraft, once general in the Cumberlands, is now found only in the most isolated sections and among the older people. I believe it would be a safe estimate to say that fifty percent of the people above seventy years old believe in witches. They have the Bible to back them up in their belief, so why not.

A sampler of Virginia witch beliefs and narratives has been published in the Virginia Folklore Society's journal *Folklore and Folklife in Virginia*.[17] The texts were collected by Alfreda Peel of Salem, Virginia, and deposited in society's archives. Except that some date from as early as 1924 and some from as late as 1950, these sixty-odd texts are very similar to the WPA witchcraft materials. In fact one text, "The Witches in the Cellar," is a short version of "A Witch Gets Caught in a Store" (legend 43).

NOTES

1. George Lyman Kittredge, *Witchcraft in Old and New England* (rpt. New York: Russell and Russell, 1956); Richard Dorson, *America in Legend: Folklore from the Colonial Period to the Present* (New York: Pantheon, 1973).

2. David Hackett Fischer, *Albion's Seed: Four British Folkways in America* (New York: Oxford Univ. Press, 1989), p. 340.

3. Philip Alexander Bruce, *Institutional History of Virginia in the Seventeenth Century* (rpt. Gloucester, Mass.: Peter Smith, 1964), 1:280–81.

4. Several literary versions of the Grace Sherwood story and extensive background research on her are in box 3, folder 1, items 2, 3, 55, 56, WPA collection.

5. See ibid., items 2 and 3, for texts of these incidents.

6. Hurston, *Mules and Men*, pp. 193–95, 216, 223–25, 245; see also Newbell Niles Puckett, *Folk Beliefs of the Southern Negro* (Chapel Hill: Univ. of North Carolina Press, 1926), and Robert Tallant, *Voodoo in New Orleans* (rpt. New York: Collier Books, 1969).

7. *Encyclopedia of Southern Culture* (Chapel Hill: Univ. of North Carolina Press, 1989), p. 492.

8. Puckett, *Folk Beliefs of the Southern Negro*, pp. vii, 20–21, 583–84.

9. Levine, *Black Culture and Black Consciousness*, p. 60.

10. Virginia Hamilton, *The People Could Fly: American Black Folktales as Told by Virginia Hamilton* (New York: Knopf, 1985), p. 172.

11. Levine, *Black Culture and Black Consciousness*, p. 80.

12. Leonora Herron and Alice M. Bacon, "Conjuring and Conjure Doctors," *Southern Workman* 24 (1895):20–31, rpt. in *Mother Wit from the Laughing Barrel: Readings in the Interpretation of Afro-American Folklore*, ed. Alan Dundes (New York: Garland, 1981), p. 366.

13. Jan Harold Brunvand, *The Study of American Folklore: An Introduction*, 3d ed. (New York: Norton, 1986), p. 44.

14. Yvonne J. Milspaw, "Witchcraft in Appalachia: Protection of the Poor," *Indiana Folklore* 11 (1978): 72.

15. Box 14, folder 4, WPA collection.

16. Milspaw, "Witchcraft in Appalachia," p. 72.

17. "Witch Tales and Beliefs from the Society Archives," *Folklore and Folklife in Virginia: Journal of the Virginia Folklore Society* 2 (1980): 67–86.

30

A CONJUROR'S REVENGE

Rev. P. L. Harvey, interviewed by Roscoe Lewis
in an unknown location in Appomattox County on May 15, 1939

Right down in Appomattox County where I was born I experienced another case of conjuration. Next to my father's farm there was a big plantation owned by a white man who kept folks on his place as tenants and share-croppers who worked so much of the land and received a certain portion of the crop after expenses were deducted. The wife of one of these tenants became sick one day and she continued to grow worse as the weeks passed in spite of the fact that the best doctor in that section attended her. This doctor was noted for miles around as being good at his profession. And when he gave you up it was time for somebody to start digging a grave. He gave this sick woman up and said there was nothing more that he could do other than keep on coming and run up a big bill. So he stopped coming to see her.

One day somebody mentioned the idea of taking the woman to old Lady Calloway over at Grace's Church to see if a spell had been put on the woman. Her husband agreed and took her. In reading her cards, old lady Calloway told the woman that she could cure her without giving her any medicine, for she was not naturally sick, but "fixed."

She told her that she had recently moved on a white man's plantation and had been given one of the best houses, which meant that another family had to move. She said that the family which was ordered to move to another house disliked this woman and her family and planned to get even. Her present condition was the result of that effort. After the old lady had told the story of the woman's sickness, the husband of the sick woman began to check up on the family who lived in the house prior to their coming. He and his wife agreed that the family had been acting rather strange toward them but they had not thought anything about it in a serious way. They had faith in what old lady Calloway told them because she gave an accurate description of the persons involved and also of the conditions upon which they had to move.

Finally old lady Calloway told the woman that she would do anything to the woman who cast the "spell" on her but one thing—that was, she would not kill her. So she was told that all [that was] necessary to do was to see that she left the community to stay. Then the Calloway woman told her exactly what had caused her so much trouble. She told her that at their home, in the spring, the angry woman had placed a little sack of something in the very bottom of the spring under an almost square rock, and the stuff in that little sack was poisoned and was responsible for her sick spell. She also told her that the woman could, by renewing the filling of the bag at intervals, have kept her in the bed helpless just as long as she wanted to unless somebody removed the spell. So she told the man and his wife to go home and remove this sack and rock from the spring and burn the sack and throw the rock far away. She also told them to stop using water from the spring and if necessary go a mile for well water. They returned home and sure enough found the spring just as had been described. They removed the sack and stop[ped] using the water.

A few weeks after that the family who had cast the spell moved away. Most of them went North to work and the woman who actually did her "fixing" had been back to Appomattox County once since that time. On that occasion she came to the funeral of her sister, but she caught the next train out. The woman upon whom the spell was cast was up about her work and doing well within a week or so.

31
A SLAVE WITH A MAGIC HOE

No source information given

er was an ol' nigger who was a false teller, an' was lazy an' didn't lack [like] no work. While all de otter niggers worked hard, he woul res' under a shady tree. One day while he was resting an' all de otters working, the overseer seen 'im and tole 'im he'd bin watchin' 'im fo' a long time. De overseer say, "Git up an' hoe dat groun' or yo'll git nine an' thirty lashes."

De nigger said, "Oh, I git through time de otters do."

"Git up an' go to work, I say," de overseer said.

"Oh I don't have to work. My hoe works for me."

De nigger spoke to his hoe an' de hoe hoed de groun' and made de rows. De Overseer could hardly believe his own eyes. De boss drive de overseer way, dressed de nigger an' give 'im de job.

He said, "Nigger, you too smart to work." De nigger didn't git de nine an' thirty lashes eider.

32
THE CONJUROR'S BECK

Rev. Richard Buster, interviewed by Isaiah Volley
in Lynchburg, on January 29, 1942

believe so[me]pin in conjure, dea people usta do much of it when I was a boy. Dea people was afraid to get mad with [each] other. Dea tell me it [was] a old man in dea community who call himself bettern than any els[e] in doing dis ting. One day a man who was a drunk medle with him and he said to dea drinking man to go way before he make him come to him, w[h]ether he want

[to] come or not. Dea drinking man didn't believe he could do so. So dis old conjure put his hand in his bosom, and took it out, and beck to dea man, and dea man begin to go to him. Dea man try to stay back. He lay back with his mouth wide open, but he had to come to him.

Every body were fraid of dat ol' man. One time he put so[me]pin in dea water for a man, and dea man drink drink dea water, an' got sick. Dea doctor come see him, and said dea man had a snake was in his leg. My mother and father believe in deas tings, and I believe in dem.

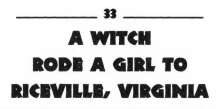

——— 33 ———

A WITCH
RODE A GIRL TO
RICEVILLE, VIRGINIA

Della Barksdale, interviewed by Pearl Morrisett
in Danville, on April 14, 1941

Della Barksdale told the following witch story to the visitor— told it with sincerity and belief in it as a real happening: "I sho do remember hearin' my mammy tell more'n once how a witch rode her one time to de store one night at Riceville. She was a young girl den. Dat witch rode her same as she was a horse and when dey got to Riceville de witch tied her to a tree close to de store. Whilst she was standin' dere tied she said she noticed sumpin shinin' in de dirt—'twas a bright night—and found out 'twas a big brass pin, a shawl pin like de old folks used to pin de shawls wid. Den de witch rode her back home.

De next day she was so tired and stiff she couldn't hardly make it and she told her mistis 'bout it. De mistis jest laughed and she say t'wont nothin' to dat. My mammy she say, "If you don't believe me I ken prove it dis way. Whilst I was standin' tied to de tree at

Riceville a big brass pin kotch my tention layin' down on de ground. I ken take you to de very spot where dat pin lay."

De mistis she say she want to find out for herself, so she take my mammy and they went over to Riceville and to de tree where my mammy say she was tied. So 'nough—dere lay de pin—a big brass one and de mistis saw dat for herself. "Well," she said, "we must do sumpin to get rid of de witch." And here what dey done. Dey killed a yearlin' and cut a square plug of de meat out'n de hind leg. Tied dis raw meat to a string and hung it up in de chimney. When dis meat rotted and dropped off de string, dat was a sign de witch won't goin' to ride nobody else for she goin' to be dead. Dat witch never comed round dere any more and mammy she won't bothered anymore. Folks used to hang horse-shoes over de doors to help keep de witch way from dem. Don't make no difference if a body ain't never done no harm, a witch will come botherin' round if dey think dey ken git anything out'n you.

——— **34** ———

DEVIL BILL BOGGS

Preston Cornett, interviewed by Emory L. Hamilton
in Esserville, Wise County, on November 18, 1940

I guess you've heard of old "Devil Bill" Boggs that used to live on the Roaring Fork. Well, he was always counted a witch. Him and old Andy Sturgill used to hunt together all the time. One time they's out deer hunting and old man Andy got so he couldn't kill a deer. He'd shoot at one at close range and right broadsided and couldn't hit it. He finally told old Devil Bill he was going home because he couldn't hit anything he shot at. Old Devil Bill begged him not to go in. He said, "You'll kill something directly." Andy said, no, he was going in. Devil Bill told him if he would stay he'd guarantee he'd kill something before the hunt was over, if he would let him load his gun.

Well, old Andy agreed to stay and handed Devil Bill his rifle for him to load. I don't know what he loaded it with—some kind of a load he took from his pocket. Well, they hunted along for a spell on the hillside. He told Andy to shoot at a big buck they spied way over on the top of another ridge. Old man Andy fired and sure enough the buck toppled over. Of course the gun was "spelled" and when Devil Bill loaded it he took the spell off it.

They say Devil Bill told Andy that some day he was going to run a deer plum over him. Old Andy thought he was just talking. One day, though, they was out and Andy went up one ridge and Devil Bill up another ridge as they always did when hunting. After a piece up the hill old man Andy sit down on a log to rest. He thought Devil Bill was on the other ridge. Directly something come crashing through the brush and a deer leaped right slap over him. When he saw it coming he didn't have time to get up, but he raised his rifle up and shot the deer in the belly just as it leaped over him.

"Haw, haw, you're a better soldier than I thought you were." Andy looked up and not ten feet above him sit old Devil Bill on a log.

———— 35 ————

THE WITCH TREE

W. Patton Beverly, interviewed by James Taylor Adams
in Norton, Wise County, on November 4, 1941

You know them old people nearly all believed in witches. I know right where there was a tree that was said to be a witch, or to be bewitched. Hit was up on what we called Wagon Track Ridge between the two forks of Clear Creek back of Ramsey. I could take ye to the very spot today.

Old Bill Boggs was said to be a witch. My great-grandda[dd]y Billy Huff lived down there on Clear Creek. There was a big chestnut tree stood on Wagon Track Ridge about a mile up the ridge from his house. That was nothin' uncommon, for the woods was full of big chestnut then. All gone now. Wonder 'f they was bewitched was what killed 'em?

I'll tell you what. Hit was talked aroun' that ol' Bill Boggs would turn hisse'f into all sorts of animals, an' that he had to come to this certain big chestnut before he could do that an' bewitch anything. Guess the tree was believed to be a sort of master witch or whatever ye'd call hit. I know I had heard so much about hit that I was afraid to go near it. Hit stood right on top of the ridge, an' strange as you may think hit, all the timber for an acre or so [around it] had died. I don't know what killed it.

Well sir, this big tree, standin' right thar by itse'f would bear loads of chestnuts, but they would stick in the burrs until they come freezin' weather an' ruin 'em. One fall, hit's been sixty-nine years ago this fall, for I was twelve years old on the twenty-third day of December followin', an' I'll be eighty-one on the twenty-third day of this comin' December, if I live to see it. Yes, that fall the big chestnut had an unusually heavy load of chestnuts on it. So great great-granddaddy Billy Huff was up there one day lookin' fer his hogs an' seed it. The limbs was jis bendin'. He come back to the house an' told Sally, his wife, that he'uz goin' up there an' chop the tree down an' git them chestnuts an' Bill Boggs could find him another tree to practice his witchery under. She tried to keep him from goin' but he went on anyway. He was, I'd say, about eighty years old, but in good health, an' was a great big man, weighed over two hundred.

He'uz gone longer than they thought he ort [ought] to be, an' some of 'em went to see about him. An' they found him layin' there by the tree stone dead. He'd cut the tree about half down an' looked like he'd jis fell away from his axe handle. The axe was stickin' in the notch. There was a little hole in one of his britches legs an' a little blue spot on his leg. Some thought he'd been shot there with a witch ball, but my opinion is that, as he fell, that his britches leg ketched against a little bush he'd cut off an' tore the hole in his britches leg. Anyway, he was stone dead. I he'ped carry him to the grave, an' me jist eleven years old. The ol' tree stood there for a few years and then lightnin' struck hit an' tore it all to pieces. After great-granddaddy was found dead there, not many people would go a-near it.

———— 36 ————

MONTAGUE AND DUCK MOORE

An unknown informant, interviewed by Raymond Sloan
in Rocky Mount, Franklin County, no date given

A family moved into Franklin County about thirty years ago, or, rather "appeared" in Franklin County, settling in a little cabin on a farm near the foothills of the Blue Ridge in the western section of the county. No one seemed know where they might have come from. Evidently just wanderers, Montague Moore and his wife, known only as "Duck," were a peculiar acting couple. And they both dressed oddly and shabbily. No more than paupers really, and without any education or skill, they must have struck a likely place to remain—for they did remain, and fared well.

Living near the Moores were several families that were very superstitious, and it wasn't long before reports began to be circulated that the Moores were witches. Soon proofs of the accusations were forthcoming in the death of livestock from strange causes. Any strange happening was soon attributed to Montague and Duck Moore.

On being approached concerning their ability to hex, to make it stranger still, both freely admitted the fact. Yes, they were witches, but Montague stated that although he had the ability to bewitch, his greatest accomplishment was the ability to "take off the spell." It was his wife Duck, he affirmed, who did all the hexing. It was not very difficult for Montague to follow this up and make it profitable, for, in her visits about the neighborhood, Duck often threatened those who displeased her with a "spell." Dismayed, the superstitious neighbors were relieved, next day, when Montague appeared and announced that he would gladly remove the "spell" for a bushel of potatoes or other household necessities. In this manner, Montague and Duck continued their "racket." Duck was occult in manner and professed to know many secrets

in gaining good fortune and preventing bad luck. This information she dispensed for articles of clothing, food, and even money.

The "spells" were of many types. Duck would suggest causing
everything from a headache to rheumatism in the line of common
ailments, and often would vent her powers on livestock. Children
were especially afraid of her and Montague, and would not pass
near the little shack in which they lived. Even now, years after
their death, many are superstitious about the little shack in which
they lived, and especially wary of the two mounds on the hill, the
graves of Montague and Duck Moore.

Possibly the greatest accomplishment attributed to Duck was
the spell she put upon a young man in the neighborhood. He began to act very strangely and his family thought he was under her
spell. What Montague could do for him didn't help and he went
off in the woods and killed himself. When they had just died
neighbors that had never dared to cross their doorsill came in
crowds to ransack the place. Only a few crude pieces of furniture
were in the little hovel, but a large cave in the hillside nearby was
filled with stuff—tribute they'd got from their neighbors to ward
off their witchery.

———— 37 ————

A SILVER BULLET
FOR A WITCH

P. T. Sloan, interviewed by Raymond Sloan
in Rocky Mount, Franklin County, on March 27, 1939

It seems that Lula Sloan, later Drewry, taught school in a very
remote and mountainous section of Franklin County, near the
Patrick County line, known as Shooting Creek, about the year
1888. While teaching school in this section, she lived in the home
of a resident, still living, whose name will not be mentioned for
obvious reasons.

While living in the house for a number of months, Miss Sloan became intrigued by the old muzzle-loading rifle which hung on the wall in the conventional rifle rack of the day. Just how her curiosity was aroused to the point of questioning, or whether the information below was volunteered, is not clear. But it is safe to assume from my informant's remarks that her host's gun was discussed. The gun was never used, never removed from its rack, although much hunting was done by the family and members of other nearby families, small game being plentiful in the winter months.

Regardless of how the discussion may have occurred, one day Miss Sloan's host, taking the young lady into his confidence, volunteered this information: She was told that a relative by the name of "Joe" had killed his brother. Since this murder, for which "Joe" was not convicted, there had been indications that Joe was a witch. Having always vowed revenge, her host continued, he had decided to "bide his time," but that in order to be sure that his bullet would end the life of his enemy, he had melted a silver coin into the regular lead bullet moulds, fashioning a silver bullet, with which the rifle was now loaded in readiness for his enemy.

The superstition regarding the shooting of a witch was that no bullet, other than one made of silver, would harm a person if he were a witch. Further, the superstition, still remembered and believed by a few, was to the effect that an effigy, or crudely drawn sketch of the person, could be shot with a silver bullet with the resultant effect that a sore "that'll never heal" would appear on the body of the witch.

The rifle remained on its rack during Lula Sloan's stay in the mountains, and there is no data to the effect that the silver bullet was ever used.

———— 38 ————

WITCH MOUNTAIN

An unknown informant, age 70, interviewed by I. M. Warren
in Hillsville, Carroll County, on January 11, 1939

There is a mountain located seven miles northeast of Hillsville, county seat of Carroll County, Virginia, about one mile off to the north of U.S. Route 221. Big Reed Island Creek flows along its western base. It is known as Witch Mountain, a name given to it more than a hundred years ago because it was inhabited by a sect who believed in witches and practiced witchcraft. There are people living now who have associated with these mountain people and have heard their witchery tales.

A gentleman, age seventy, now living in Roanoke, who lived, when a boy, within a mile of Witch Mountain related some of his experiences as follows: "I often asked my mother to let me go across the field to Aunt Nancy Bobbitt's house where she would smoke her pipe and regale me with tales of the witches of Witch Mountain."

"She told me how you become a witch. You climb to the topmost peak of Witch Mountain and place one hand on top of your head and the other on the sole of your foot, saying while standing thus—'I consign all that lies between my two hands to the Devil. I swear to perform all his tasks assigned to me.' Immediately full power will be granted to bewitch others."

"Along with the witches, Carroll County possessed its share of witch doctors. When domestic animals were taken sick and failed to respond to the usual treatments, a hurried trip was made for a witch doctor and his advice was followed to the minutest detail— always, of course, with the expected result."

"I remember one of Aunt Nancy's stories. She said one year Lacy, her husband, had a ewe die when folding [foaling], leaving two lambs. One of these he gave to another ewe with only one lamb, but she refused to take the other one. Aunt Nancy said, 'So he brought [it] in to me, and I raised it by hand. I thought a sight of the little thing, having no baby of my own, right at that time. One morning it was off its food and I was right upset. I put it outside thinking there was something maybe it could find for itself that would cure it better than any physic of mine. But it just ran around and around, butting into things, the same as if it was blind. So I brought it back into the house and dredged it good, pouring herb tea down its throat. But the poor little fellow seemed determined to die in spite of all the simples [remedies] I could brew.'"

"'That night I had him wrapped up and lying on the hearth by the fire, when old Jim Largin, the best witch doctor in the county stopped by to borrow an axe. I got him to look at the lamb. He said it was bewitched and told me to have Lacy bring in a plow share and put it in the fire and before it was red hot someone would come in, but to leave it in the fire until the person began to get sick. And when they did, my lamb would be all right. But I must pull the plow share out and pour cold spring water on it to cool it off in a hurry, or the person would die.'"

"'I was willing to do anything to save my lamb. So I got Lacy up out of bed and made him get the plow share for me and I built a hot fire around it, lit my pipe, and set down to wait. Pretty soon I heard a rapping on the lean-to door. I opened [it] and let in a woman named Kate Upp, who lived about halfway up on the side of Witch Mountain. She said she wanted to borrow my wool cards. But I knew better than to lend anything to a witch, for if you do you put yourself in their power. So I said Mrs. Martin my neighbor had the wool cards, combin' wool for her quilts.'"

"'She sat down and pretty soon leaned over saying she was feeling faint like and asked for a drink, and for me to crack the door. About this time the lamb began to scramble about and got up and nosed me, like he always did when he was hungry. So I pulled the plow share out of the coals and poured on the cold spring water like I was told, and Kate left. I have always worried about that, for late the same month, some neighbors found her dead just off the path leading up the mountain and I always wondered if I had left the plow share in the fire too long.'"

39

A WITCH'S GUN CHARMS THE WOODS

Boyd J. Bolling, interviewed by James Taylor Adams
in Big Laurel, Wise County, on February 4, 1942

I've heard my father (Jesse Bolling) tell a tale about Jim Baker of Baker Flats. This Jim Baker was my great-grandfather. Now I don't know. I don't believe my father or mother would lie, an' I've heard 'em tell some awful tales about people being bewitched. They believed it. This one I'm goin' to tell was about Jim Baker. He left my great-grandmother in North Carolina when my grandmother was a baby an' got him seven women and came here an' lived in the Baker Rocks way back yonder on top of Black Mountain. My folks thought he was a witch. After he'd finally left the flats an' settled on head of Cumberland, he married again an' settled down, but they still thought he was a witch. Father said that he was just a small boy, but Uncle Jerry and Uncle Jim were grown men.

One morning they heard a gun fire way back on Carmel Mountain an' granddaddy said, "that sounded to me like a witch's gun." Now they believed a witch could fire a gun an' as far as it was heard the woods would be "rung." That is the ring within the sound of the gun would be bewitched and nobody could kill a deer [in it] with his gun.

Well, Uncle Jerry went out a huntin'. He saw some deer an' fired at 'em, but he didn't hit any. Hit was jus' that way on and on. Uncle Jim went out an' his gun wouldn't even fire. He had the lock and powder pan worked on. He got new flints, but hit didn't do any good. So at last granddaddy said he'd test it out. So he went out an' run tight up in a herd of deer. He was so close he could almost touch 'em. An' he was a dead shot. So he fired an' never hit a thing. He tried again. Same luck. Some pigeons lit in a tree an' he fired at them an' killed one.

He came back home an' went up on the point an' skinned the

bark off of a tree an' drawed the picture of Jim Baker an' stepped back fifty steps an' shot at it in the three highest names [Father, Son, and Holy Ghost] an' hit it.

He hadn't been back in the house when Jim Baker's wife come over to borrow some meal. They told her they were out. She went home, but hit wasn't long 'till she was back to borrow grandma's windin' blades. They were using them. The next mornin' before they got out of bed they heard her holler at the door an' when they opened the door she was standin' there an' said, "Jerry," that was granddaddy's name, "'f you don't come over an' do somethin' for Jim he won't be alive an hour." So he took a thumb lance an' went over there an' bled him a little an' he got well right then. An' the spell was off their guns.

———— 40 ————

AUNT LUCY'S
BEWITCHED COW

I. M. Warren, from his own recollection
in Roanoke, no date given

A unt Lucy, an old woman who lived in Montgomery County, Virginia, about one hundred years ago, left many tales of her experiences with witches, and these stories are still recounted by her descendants, who are people of integrity in that community. Aunt Lucy was a highly respected and intelligent country woman who lived the simple life of her times on her farm not far from what is now the town of Christiansburg. One day when her best cow began to give bloody milk, the story spread about and her neighbors gathered with the advice that the animal was bewitched. The first thing was to find the witch, and then to undo his evil work. And several fingers of suspicion pointed at once to an ancient couple who lived alone in a hut on a few barren acres of land and whose manner of living did not conform to community precepts. Aunt Lucy sent at once for a man who was reputed to know how to break the spell of witches. She was told to draw a likeness of each of the persons suspected on a piece of paper and to nail these pictures one above the other on the side of her house, then melt a silver coin and mold a bullet from the metal. These preparations made, Aunt Lucy, according to the story, took careful aim and shot the likenesses of the witches. She hit the mark and in doing this not only relieved the afflicted cow, but possibly established a record in killing two witches with one shot.

—————— 41 ——————

COOKING A WITCH'S SHOULDER

James Taylor Adams, from his own recollection
in Big Laurel, Wise County, on March 27, 1939

My mother told me this one when I was a child. I have heard it since then in slightly different versions.

It was a long time ago, when people first came from Eastern Virginia and Western North Carolina and settled here in the Cumberlands. A settler, whose name has been forgotten, had a large flock of sheep. Suddenly his sheep began to die, one a day, seemingly from no particular cause. He watched his flock and would see a ram or ewe suddenly fall dead while it was feeding along in [the] best of health. He believed his sheep were bewitched so [he] hied himself to an old woman who was reputed to be a witch doctor. She told him to go home and skin out the ham or shoulder of a sheep that had just died and put it in an oven and bake it, and by no means allow anyone to come in the house and borrow, steal, or in any way get anything out of the house, above all a drink of water. So he skinned a sheep that had died that same day and put a shoulder on in the oven to bake. The witch doctor had said to let it warm up slowly and start baking gradually for best results. He followed the directions and it was two hours before the shoulder was warmed up to the baking stage.

About that time he looked down the road and saw a neighbor

woman coming, walking as if she was in a hurry. She came on, entered, and asked to borrow some meal. They had no meal. She then asked for a drink of water; and there was no water up [from the well]. She took her departure, but in a short time she was again seen approaching, walking faster than before. This time she seemed unstrung and could not stand still and wanted to borrow some salt. [There was] no salt in the house, and again she asked for water, which was politely but firmly refused her. All the time she was eyeing the oven on the hearth, and this time before she left she asked what they were baking and tried accidentally to overturn the oven.

She had not been gone long until she was seen coming again. This time she was running. The shoulder was getting a nice brown now. She rushed into the house and screamed, "For God's sake, get that off of there. You are killing me. Look here!" And she ripped off her clothes and exposed her own shoulder baked to the same crisp brown as the mutton shoulder. The woman recovered, but if she ever practiced her witchery again it was not found out.

——————— 42 ———————

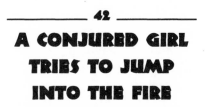

A CONJURED GIRL TRIES TO JUMP INTO THE FIRE

Mr. Wooten, interviewed by John W. Garrett
in Manteo, Buckingham County, no date given

Mr. Harrison Sheaperd, who lived over here at Manteo, well, he had several children and one of his daughters' name was Millie. Now, Millie had always been strong and healthy until she was over twenty and all of a sudden she seemed to go crazy. And when she would have a spell, she'd do her best to jump into the fire. Now the Sheaperd family lived in a big ole fashioned log-house. The big fireplace and the chimney was built of logs filled on the inside with rocks and mud. Now the Sheaperds had to keep their eyes on their daughter Millie all the time to keep her out of the fire. They had the doctor to see her, but he couldn't do her no good. He said he couldn't find what ailed her. Of course, they thought the girl was plum crazy. Some of the people thought she was conjured (or bewitched). So there was an old conjure doctor close [to] there, and Mr. Sheaperd went and got him to come see what he could do fer Millie. Well, he come, and when he saw the girl trying to get into the fire, he says she's conjured sure enough, but it can't be in the fire; whatever it is is in that chimney. And he said, you'll hafta get to work and find it, and I can cure her. But they all was afraid to go try to find it at first, but the old doctor told 'em, go ahead, you got to find it.

So Bill Brown and Tom Wane went out back of the house to the old chimney to look for it. And up in the back of the chimney between two logs they saw a bottle. But Bill and Tom both was afraid to touch the bottle. So they called the conjure doctor and showed him where the bottle was hid and he reached up and got it, and in that bottle was a cross and some liquid and some hair tied up, and something that looked like weeds. The doctor said "That's your trouble. Now I can cure Millie." And sure as we live, the girl never had another one of them spells from then on.

Then he said, "I know who put the trouble on her. And I can send them away if you want me to." And they said "sure, send him away." So they all stayed all night, and the next morning Bill and Tom went with the conjure doctor to Winginer [Wingina] and they had to cross the James River on a ferry, and when he got out in the middle of the river, he held the bottle up and said, "Here goes old Dick Pitman!" and dropped the bottle in the river. And sure enough, in a few days Pitman left the country and he never came back again. And up until that time Pitman had been perfectly satisfied. But the conjure doctor sure sent him away. Now, I must believe this, said Mr. Wooten, as all of these men was truthful men, and I know the girl was well after that.

——— 43 ———

A WITCH GETS
CAUGHT IN A STORE

An unknown informant, interviewed by Lucille B. Jayne
at Hayes Store in Capahosic, Gloucester County, on October 8, 1938

It is said that they [witches] would rub themselves with a brick to make [them]selves small so they could go through small places. And there is a story that has been handed down that four witches rubbed themselves to make themselves small for they had planned to make a raid on a little store in the neighborhood that night; they knew that the store-keeper had just gotten in some whiskey, so they thought they would make a raid, and get all the whiskey they wanted and have a good time in general.

So they started out at about midnight and the first to reach the door said, "Through the key-hole I go," the next "And I after you," and so on until all were through. But when it came to the last one he forgot what to say, so he said "Over the keyhole I go," and "Under the key-hole I go," and he made so much noise bumping around that it aroused the store-keeper, who lived near the store. And he come in and caught the witch. But the other three that got in had a big time; they drank all the whiskey they wanted and tore things up in a great way. The next day, the witch that was caught, they took him out to hang him. [They] had the rope around his neck, when a buzzard flew down and cried, "Up in the air I go!" and the witch replied, "And I after you." And the witch flew right out of the rope, and up in the air.

GHOSTS

The ghosts in the WPA collection are generally peaceful, as the tales included here bear out. The only violence in this section or the haunted house tales are old man Stevenson's ghost shaking a hopvine in "The Haunted House of Saunders" (legend 59), a master's ghost grabbing a servant's arm in "The Old Plantation Master's Ghost" (legend 49), and a ghost causing a horse to throw its rider in "The Slave Trader's Haunted House" (legend 61). Many of these ghosts were involved in grizzly crimes when they were alive, but only as victims; they were beheaded, poisoned, abused, or killed by Indians or Union soldiers. In death they are calm—drifting along the banks of the Clinch River or the sidewalks of Norfolk at midnight, standing silently by a fireplace, or appearing only as a noise or a voice to instruct the living. In fact, one of these ghosts is a Quaker, a member of the Religious Society of Friends, an adamantly nonviolent "peace witness" denomination.

But while they are peaceful, they are not comical. Contrary to Benjamin Botkin's suggestion in A *Treasury of American Folklore*, ghost and haunted house legends do not have to be jokes or narratives with "scare punch lines" to be folklore.[1] In the WPA collection, comic ghost stories are rare. Almost all are taken seriously, and most either have assertions of belief in the events they depict or are told so that belief in them is obvious. "The Ficklin Field Haunted House" (legend 54), a turn on the plot of accepting a dare to stay in a haunted house, is the only comic example included here. The tone of the stories is seldom that of a storyteller's performance either. More often they have the plain style of someone trying to get across the truth.

Over half of the ghost stories in the WPA collection involve a particular house. Because of this, and because the collection files themselves used the classification, I have kept a separate Haunted Houses section. But even those tales which don't feature specific houses describe essentially place-bound ghosts; they haunt one area of town, one stretch of a road, or one strip of railroad track. Not one of the WPA collection ghost stories has a wandering or mobile ghost.

One striking feature of these stories is exemplified in "The Old Woman of the Pies" (legend 51). This image—a sighing ghostly woman offering a pie to passing strangers—is indicative of the giving of gifts, favors, and assistance that occurs so much in these legends. The ghosts typically appear (1) to reveal hidden treasure, (2) to give advice to or change the behavior of the living, (3) to reveal the circumstances of their death, or (4) to straighten out some problem with their burial or remains. In all of these cases the ghosts are either giving help or getting it from the living. Often they must reveal foul play or fix problems with their remains because of the folk belief that they cannot rest until such things are properly settled. And often they point out buried treasure, or help in other ways, as payment for the help they have gotten in these matters. Other folk beliefs are incorporated in the tales too. That ghosts haunt the scene of former violence, crimes, or sins is the one that comes up often. That the use of God's (or the Trinity's) name invokes a spirit or entices it to speak is another, as is the principle that its murderer's touch will cause a corpse to bleed, an element of both "The Ghost's Little Finger Bone" (legend 53) and "A Murder Belief Solves a Crime" (legend 93, in the Murder and Violence section).

Ghosts appear in some of the legends in other sections of the book—see "Indians Kill a Pioneer Family" (legend 65), "How Champion Swamp Got Its Name" (legend 97), and "The Story of Swift and His Compass" (legend 133), for example. I have placed these according to their central concern because their ghost elements are only closing formulas to relate the events of the story to the present day. Some stories in the Supernatural Events section have motifs that are similar to the Ghosts and Haunted Houses tales, too. It is not always simple to determine if a supernatural narrative actually involves a ghost. As William K. McNeil has noted, this is often blurred by the fact that "the returning dead come back in several forms. First, they may come back in the same body they had while alive; second, they may appear in some sort of spectral form; third, they may be invisible and known only by the deeds, noises or mischief they commit."[2] My criterion for a ghost story was a clearly dead human being who had clearly returned to the world of the living. But even this failed to clarify the question sometimes. I suspect, for instance, that "The Woman Dressed in Black" (legend 143), which I placed in the

Unusual Events section, was actually intended by its teller to be a ghost story. But, since it is not stated anywhere in the story that the woman in black is, or even physically appears to be, dead and returning from the dead, it didn't qualify.

Finally, I must clarify one point or risk being haunted until the error is put to rest. In explaining why he includes a chapter on witches in a book titled *Ghost Stories from the American South*, William McNeil said, "In societies such as the South where both witches and ghosts exist, there is no sharp distinction between them."[3] To support this claim he quoted Ernest W. Baughman from the *Type and Motif Index of the Folktales of England and North America* as saying: "It is very difficult to tell whether the haunters under this category are ghosts, witches, or familiar spirits. The actions of these agents are very much alike." But the Baughman quotation is taken out of context. He was discussing a specific motif—E281.0.3, "Ghost haunts house, damaging property or annoying inhabitants"—and a very specific phenomenon, the visitation of a poltergeist (a case of which is described in "The Shower of Stones" [legend 126] in the Supernatural Events section).[4] Baughman was not saying that the general behavior or actions of ghosts and witches are alike. If McNeil had examined even his own texts carefully, he would have seen that there are indeed some very sharp distinctions between witches and ghosts. Besides the obvious fact that witches are live people and ghosts are dead people are the facts that (1) the actions of witches are characteristically motivated by greed, anger, and spite, and that (2) they are very much involved in conflicts and contests of power. Ghosts, on the other hand, are typically (1) motivated by concern, mercy, or a desire to see justice served, and (2) involved in giving gifts, helping humans, and asking for help in return. Further, ghosts are often agents of spiritual powers whose messages from the other side concern religious and moral issues such as changing one's behavior, believing in God, converting to Christianity, and/or living an upright life. Equating ghosts and witches is like equating *Hamlet* and *Macbeth* simply because both plays feature the appearance of supernatural agents. Contrary to McNeil's assertion, stories about ghosts and stories about witches (in the

GHOSTS

South and anywhere else) are in content, themes, and atmosphere poles apart.

NOTES

1. Benjamin A. Botkin, *A Treasury of American Folklore* (rpt. New York: Bantam, 1981), p. 418.

2. William K. McNeil, *Ghost Stories from the American South* (Little Rock, Ark.: August House, 1985), p. 10.

3. Ibid., p. 24.

4. Ernest W. Baughman, *Type and Motif-Index of the Folktales of England and North America*, Indiana Univ. Folklore Series, no. 20 (The Hague: Mouton, 1966), pp. 143–44.

THE QUAKER'S GOLD

Grant Boles, interviewed by Susan R. Morton
in Antioch, Fluvanna County, on April 2, 1942

There was a Quaker settlement in the Bull Run Mountains a long time ago. (This is a recorded fact, it being situated near Hopewell Gap.) There was an old man who came there, built his cabin, and cultivated a little piece of ground. He had a good education and used to write letters and other papers for his neighbors who could not write for themselves. For these services he made no charge, and neither did he raise enough to much more than would pay his annual rent. (The land in that section was nearly all leased and paid [for] in yearly returns of the crops.) However, as he and his wife always seemed to have plenty of everything they needed, it was conceded that he must have some wealth of which no one knew. When they moved there they had several children, but they all died when an epidemic of smallpox came to the neighborhood, and were buried a short distance from the house at a place marked by a large cedar tree. Not very long after that the wife also died, and for some years the Quaker continued to live alone. He was always friendly and ready to do a kindness for his neighbors, but [he] rarely mingled with anyone. And no one knew he was ill until, after a heavy storm that had made the trails impassable for days, a neighbor passing the cabin noticed that there was no smoke coming from the chimney. Entering, he found the old man dead in his bed.

Although it was suspected that he had gold, there was nothing ever found to indicate where it was, and the story grew that he had been robbed, feeling even becoming so high that a young free Negro who lived not far away, and who had been a frequent caller at the Quaker's cabin, was charged with robbery, and even murder. But testimony was brought forth to prove that the old man died of natural causes, and finally the Negro was set free [*words missing*] his protests that he had never seen or even heard of the man having had any wealth whatever.

As the cabin was well built and the land well tended, it was not long before it had a tenant. But the story got about that the old Quaker returned there, usually standing near the bed, and following the sleeper if he rose from his bed.

Several tenants came and went, but at last the schoolmaster who, unlike all his predecessors, was a married man with a family, decided to take the convenient and comfortable cabin. (There was a Quaker school held not far from the site of this story.) To those who warned him of the ghostly visitor, he smilingly replied that he wasn't afraid, and that he was sure if the old man's spirit did return that he meant no harm to anyone.

It was not long after the young schoolmaster was settled in the cabin that his wife awoke him one night to point a terrified finger at the figure of a cloaked and hooded man standing near the hearth. He soon disappeared. But that was only the beginning, and even the patience of the young Quaker became exhausted; and he determined that there must be something sorely troubling the spirit of the former tenant, and he decided to ask him what it was he sought.

It was only a few nights later that the now familiar figure, cloaked and hatted as usual, appeared. It was close to midnight and all the family was asleep except the teacher, who sat reading before the fire. Rising, he approached the apparition with a respectful bow.

"What dost thou want?" he asked. And when no answer [was] forthcoming he repeated it, coming closer to the old man who stood by the chimney end. "What *dost* thou want?"

A faint whisper came from the ghost—"Go to the graveyard and dig one rod east of the cedar tree. Take the gold which thou wilt find there and give half of it to the poor, and the other half thou mayst keep, and God bless thee." With that the ghost disappeared.

The following day the schoolmaster went to the spot indicated and commenced to dig and before long he came upon a small iron pot filled with various coins, mostly gold.

The ghost was never known to make another appearance.

This story was told to Grant Boles by his father and at least three other people, all of whom had heard it with practically the same details and who had no doubt as to its truth.

———— 45 ————

MIDNIGHT ANNIE

Stack Lee, interviewed by Roscoe Lewis
in Hampton, on May 31, 1939

Midnight Annie stayed 'round heah 'bout two years. She was half 'oman an' half ghost, dey say. Sometimes, when folks seed her, she was walkin' on de groun'. Den again sometimes she was floatin' 'bout two an' a half foot off de ground, in de air. Whenever you see her, she be a-hollerin', "Help, Help," an' jes' a-moanin'. Never see her in de day, always see her at night, atter nine o'clock. Mos' de time she had a barrel o' somepin' on her shoulder. Scared dese children 'roun' Hampton to death. Couldn't push 'em out doors at night. Even de old folks went in early. Never did see her myself.

———— 46 ————

A GHOST MAKES
A COUPLE ARGUE

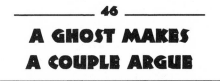

Rachell Gardner, interviewed by James Taylor Adams
in Glamorgan, Wise County, on May 5, 1941

The awfullest haint tale I ever heard was one about old man Smith Fouts who died with typhoid over on Lion Fork of Kentucky River. If Roy [the informant's brother, Roy Mitchell] was here he could tell it [so] that [it] is a sight to hear. Roy told me about it. Roy married old man Fout's girl.

All of the family nearly died one fall with typhoid fever. You know hit used to strike in here an' kill a lot of people. All of his children and his wife had already died, an' he was down with it at brother Roy's. He knowed he was goin' to die. So he told them before he died that he wanted them to burn the bed he was lyin' on.

Well, after he died they didn't burn it. And hit wasn't long till Roy and his wife started fallin' out and fussin'. An' one night they was mad and was a-sleepin' in separate beds. One of 'em was sleepin' on the bed on which ol' man Fouts had died. All at once somebody knocked on the door. Roy said, "Who's thar' an' what do ye want?" Never heard a thing said. Then they knocked ag'in. Roy asked 'em again what they wanted an' who hit was. Then sumpin' says—"Hit's me, Roy, Smith, don't ye know my voice? You promised to burn that bed. You'll never see any peace an' satisfaction 'till ye do."

That was all they heard. So Roy an' his wife got friendly an' talked about it, an' Roy said he'd burn the bed. But she didn't want to burn hit. So it went on a few days an' they had another big racket an got a-past speakin', an' that night they was sleepin' in separate beds when they heard somebody knock again. Roy asked who it was, an' he said "Hit's me, Roy. Burn that bed an' you'll live a happy life, an' if ye don't, you'll never see any more peace."

They put it off an' they just fussed an' fussed. They never had had any trouble 'till then. But then they couldn't give one another a good word. Then they heard it again an' again, five or six times, 'till one mornin' Roy got up an' told his wife she could say what she wanted to, but he's goin' to burn that ol' death bed. An' he rolled it up an' carried hit out in the yard an' burnt hit. They never heard anything again. An' after that they got along as good as any two people ever did.

———— **47** ————

THE HEADLESS GHOST
OF GRIFFITH'S WIFE

Leonard E. Carter, interviewed by James Taylor Adams
in Russell County, on February 17, 1941

Over here in Russell County, about Sword's Creek, a man
named Henry Griffith killed his wife and a feller named Lawson an' his wife one time. I don't know exactly when it happened
but sometime after the railroad was built through that country. I
heard some railroad [men] talkin' 'bout seein' things up thar down
at Norton about fifteen years ago. This feller Griffith was jealous
of his wife, they said, an' she was afraid of him an' had done gone
to stay with a family named Lawson. I believe Lawson had married
her sister, or maybe it was that she was Lawson's sister. Maybe no
kin at all. Anyway, she had left her man an' went to stay at Law-
sons'. An' late one evenin' the three of 'em was down by the
Clinch River, fishin' maybe, I don't know. Griffith foun' out about
them bein' down thar an' he slipped up on them an' killed all three
of 'em an' cut off their heads an' throwed 'em in Clinch River. It
was a month or two before they was found. A railroad man found
'em, I think. They say Griffith's wife's head was not foun'.

Well, Griffith was tried an' sent to prison for a long time. An'
not long after that a train was comin' down Clinch River one
night, an' when it was passing the place where the people was
killed the engineer looked on ahead an' there on the bank of the
river he seed a woman without any head, but carryin' some sort
of light in her han'. An' she acted jes like she was searchin' for
sumpin' along the edge of the water, an' her no head now. What
do you know about that?

Well sir, about the same time the engineer seed her the fireman
seed her too. He looked at the engineer an' the engineer looked
back at him. Neither one spoke until they had got a way past the
place. Then they axed one another 'f the other seed anything. An'

they both said they had seed a woman without any head an' carrying a light as 'f she was lookin' for sumpin'.

They say that ever since then you can go by thar of a night an' you will see her, always with a light, walkin' along the edge of the water. Some folks say it is Griffith's wife lookin' for her head. I don't know what about it. It might be that way.

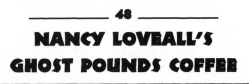

NANCY LOVEALL'S
GHOST POUNDS COFFEE

Dr. J. M. Hill, interviewed by Emory L. Hamilton
in an unknown location in Scott County, on September 26, 1939

In a certain neighborhood in Scott County, Virginia, there lived a family by the name of Loveall, in a small cottage by the side of a lane. The wife of this home on a certain night became a mother, and a certain woman in the neighborhood, who was a mid-wife, was in attendance thereto. The mother passed away the next morning, strange to relate, because she seemed to be getting along so well.

In those days the people had no coffee mills. They bought their coffee green, parched it, tied it in cloth, and then beat it up with a hammer, thus converting it into pulverized coffee. The coffee that was used that night was beaten by the mid-wife who was in attendance.

Soon after the death of this mother the home became vacant, the remainder of the family moving away. In passing to and fro by that house the neighbors could hear a noise—somebody hammering in the deserted house. Thus it became known as a haunted house. Not many people cared to pass that way at night.

Uncle Elias Rhoten, a Justice of the Peace in that neighborhood, a man who was unquestioned for truth and veracity, decided that he would go there one night and investigate the situation.

The time was set at after night[fall] and he went there alone. He stepped inside the gate to a tall apple tree that stood on the lawn and put his arms around the tree. Immediately he heard the the [*sic*] knocking or hammering commence inside of the house. He said, "In the name of High Heaven, what or who is that in there?" A woman stepped to the door and replied, "I am Nancy Loveall." He said, "Well then, what do you want and why are you here?" She said, "Three things I want done, if you'll do the three things and never reveal but one, I'll go away and you'll see me no more." She then told him what the three things were, one of which she said—"I want you to go and fix my grave as I shall here tell you." He agreed and promised to do it. She then stepped down off the little narrow porch, went up the hill, through an old field to the graveyard, and suddenly vanished from his sight.

He said it was a bright moonlight night and that he knew it to be Nancy Loveall, because he knew the dress that she usually wore and which she was wearing that night and that he didn't believe that he could have been mistaken in what he saw there that night. All the neighbors believed that the two [other] things she requested him not to tell, and which he never did, were that she told him the mid-wife, who made the coffee that night, poisoned her, and told him why she poisoned her. But Mr. Rhoten never said that these guesses were correct.

——— **49** ———

THE OLD PLANTATION MASTER'S GHOST

Mrs. Robert Edwards, interviewed by Cornelia Berry
in Fleeton, Northumberland County, no date given

The old pear tree now stands in a field all alone. It is over two hundred years old and once stood in the corner of the yard on an old plantation owned by Robert Edwards of Fleet's Point. This old tree saw many changes and happenings during its life time, but the one most outstanding goes like this.

After Robert Edwards' death there were big times that went on in the "Big House." [There were] parties after parties, feast after feast, much riotous living and squandering of money. The old pear tree stood and watched it all. One night while there was great feast going on, the wine gave out. So a servant was sent to fetch more wine. As he started across the yard to the place where the wine was kept, he saw a man pacing up and down the yard.

The servant waited until the man reached the far end of the yard, and then he ran as fast as he could to the wine cellar. When he started back the man also started back. And when the servant reached the steps of the Big House the man had also reached the steps. He grabbed the servant by the arm, and when the servant looked up, he saw the face of his dead master. For years after the marks of finger prints could be seen on the arm of the Negro. The old pear tree saw it too, and the destruction of the Big House, and the selling of the plantation, but it stands peaceful in its old age alone with its memories.

_____ 50 _____

CONVERTED BY A GHOST

Fletcher Sulfridge, interviewed by James Taylor Adams
in Coeburn, Wise County, on November 18, 1940

It was about twenty-five, maybe thirty, years ago. There was an old man named Greear lived out in the Flatwoods right close to where I was raised. He was called an unbeliever—didn't go to meeting or didn't believe in any church or anything. This old man had a wife and several children. One boy about fifteen years old was an awful good singer. This boy took down sick and died and they buried him in the graveyard up on the point just above the house. About a year, maybe not that long after the boy died, there was a big revival going on near Greear's, and his wife and girls all went. He wouldn't go. Stayed at home by himself. They would try to get him to go to the meetings but he wouldn't do it. They got the preacher to come out one night and talk with him, trying to get him to go. But it done no good. He said, "No! You had just as well hush. I'm not goin'." The revival went on. The girls were all saved; Mrs. Greear had been a Christian a long time.

One night just after the meeting had broke up and they got home and they were setting round talking and Mrs. Greear and the girls was pleading with him to go next night, they heard somebody a-singin'. Went like it was up at the graveyard, and just plimeblank [exactly] like the boy that had died. It come nearer and nearer 'till it seemed to be right over the house. Then it stopped and a little light come right through the wall in the corner of the house and moved right around next [to] the ceiling 'till it was right over the bed where Mr. Greear and his wife slept and come right down the wall and went under the bed. They looked under the bed but couldn't see anything. But after while it came out and went right back up the wall, around the ceiling and out through the wall. Then the singing started again and went off up the hill toward the graveyard. It was exactly ten o'clock when it started.

Next night they got home earlier than usual and had gone to bed by that time. They heard the singing again and again it come on down the point and over the house and hushed. Then the light came through the wall and around the ceiling and down the wall and under the bed. And the bed just lifted up and set over in the floor and began to dance about. They jumped out of it and Mr. Greear grabbed it and tried to hold it, but it just throwed him about and kept on jumpin' about. After a while the bed moved back to where it had been and the light came out from under it, crept back up the wall, around the edge and out through the solid wall. And the singing started off again.

It got rumored around and the whole neighborhood gathered in to see and hear it. The fifth night everybody at meeting nearly come to see it. It done the same thing. Four of the strongest men they could pick out got one at each corner and tried to hold the bed in place, but they couldn't do it. It just throwed them about same as if they had been dolls. It just kept right on. Mr. Greear seemed to be thinking a lot. The sixth night his wife talked him

[in]to going to meeting. That night it came again. The seventh night he went too, and went to the mourner's bench. That night it was just the same thing. The ninth night he confessed religion and the singing was not heard or the light seen any more. I didn't see this or hear it myself, but there are lots of people in the Flatwoods who was there and seen it and heard it. I don't know what it was or what it was for, but it converted old man Greear.

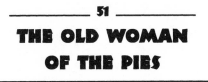

51

THE OLD WOMAN
OF THE PIES

Harry Strickler, interviewed by Susan R. Morton
in White House, Page County, on April 17, 1942

There is a place in the road not far from the White House Bridge in Page County, near the site of the old German settlement where for years travelers who happened to be passing late at night would suddenly find their horse restless. Sometimes it would even refuse to go, and the foot traveler would notice some uncanny presence before reaching a certain spot where a giant chestnut tree spread its branches over the road.

It was all thickly grown about there, but tradition said it was the site of one of the early cabins and that one day when the menfolk were out hunting that the women, the mother [and] one or two daughters, were killed by the Indians.

However, an old woman approaches the traveler, a shawl tightly drawn about her head and offers him—a pie! If the gesture of accepting it is made, she disappears with a peculiar sound that resembles a sigh.

HAUNTED
HOUSES

nderlying many ghost stories is the idea that peoples' spirits are likely to haunt a place where something happened to them, some great tragedy or crime, or even a great love like that of Fiddlin' Mike and his wife for dancing. A headless ghost will haunt the riverbank where she was murdered, and the ghost of an old woman will hand out her pies at the spot where she was killed by Indians. The folktale motif for this is E334.1, "Non-malevolent ghost haunts scene of former crime or sin." Houses are bound to have these connections because people spend so much of their lives in them. Of the 192 ghost stories in the WPA collection, 89 (almost half) are connected to a particular house.

The fascination that old, prominent, or abandoned houses hold for people is attested to throughout the collection. They spawned both ghostly and other legendary tales. In a fragment which Cornelia Berry submitted as an oral history, she reported several non-ghost motifs attached to an old mansion on Fleet's Point in Northumberland County. "All the old heads can tell you about the old house that stood on Fleet's Point and how years ago a hurricane struck it and blew it to pieces. Some say that a straw was blown through the baby's cradle there without harming the baby at all. Others say the baby was blown up into a tree and hung there for several hours by its clothing and didn't get a scratch, while its cradle was blown miles down the river. Which of these stories is true no one seems to know, but all the old folks can tell you about the old house." [1]

A frequent test of courage for an individual in a ghost story is spending the night in a haunted house. The situation usually involves a stranger, a person who is unfamiliar with events that have made the place frightening to those who know what went on there. The atmosphere of this sort of story, however, is usually that of the wonder tale, or märchen. This was not the case with most of the WPA collection's haunted house tales. "The Ficklin Field House" (legend 54) is the only story printed here with that tone; and even though it ends with a punch line which is a migratory folk rhyme/song and involves a traditional speaking animal motif, there are some indications, especially at the opening, that it was believed to have happened. The rest of the WPA collection haunted house stories are clearly believed.

HAUNTED HOUSES

The moral tone of the haunted house tales is as strong as it is in other ghost stories. They often depict clear retribution for sins and crimes. Of the ten given here, six involve such messages, the topics ranging from child abuse and lack of concern for one's employees to heathenism, idol worship, and the evils of slavery and slave trading. "The Dancing Couple" (legend 56) is an exceptional haunted house narrative in this regard. It not only conveys no moral message; it refers to no accident, sin, crime, or wrong in need of correcting. Since their black neighbor is depicted as "kind" and "faithful," even racial relations do not suggest a negative dimension to the tale. Mike and his wife simply loved life; their ghostly return was apparently motivated only by a desire to extend the joyful times they had while living.

NOTES
1. Box 5, folder 4, item 721, WPA collection.

52

THE GHOST THAT
SQUEAKED THE DOOR

Celia Ann Maggard, interviewed by James Taylor Adams
in Norton, Wise County, on October 18, 1940

When I was a little girl, been about forty years ago, Pap bought Little Preacher Wes Collins['s place] out on Collins' Branch and moved out there. Preacher Wes had had a little boy to die there about a year or two before that. They told us they'd heard things there, but we didn't pay any attention to it. The neighbors said the little boy had rid the door, which was an old-fashioned door hung on the outside on pegs, and that Preacher Wes had whupped him for hit. He took down sick and died. And they said they couldn't keep the door shut.

Well sir, the first night after we moved in we was all settin' thar an' the door was fastened with a string on the inside, when all of a sudden that string broke and the door flew open and begin to swing back'ard an' for'ards goin' squeek, squeek. Pap got up and shut hit. Nothing more happened 'till we'd gone to bed and hit waked us all up squeekin' again.

So hit just kept on that way, an' after while Pap said he'd fix hit. So he shut it one night, tied hit with a rope, made a wooden peg and pegged hit shut, an' then leant a big back stick again' hit. He said now he'd like to see anything git hit open. Well sir, we hadn't been in the bed but a little while 'till we heard a kerlatter-ment and the door flew open and started squeaking. Hit went pli-meblank [plumb, exactly] like a child snubbin' an' cryin'. The rope was broke slapdab in two. The peg was out, and the back stick was a-layin' out in the yard.

So Pap said he'd take hit down and hang hit to the stable over across a dreen [drain, ditch] from the house. He did, and all night long we could hear hit goin' squeek, squeek. Never stopped. We couldn't sleep for hit. Then Pap took it down an' put hit up in the stable loft on some fodder. Even that didn't do any good. For from about ten o'clock every night hit would go squeek, squeek, just like hit had when hit was hung. And we'd listen to hit an' we could hear just as plain as could be a child snubbin' an' cryin'. Made a-body feel awful quare, I can tell you. Pap talked of selling the place. But he decided to try one more way to get it to hush. Him and [his] brother Jimmy took hit and carried hit away up in a cove field about a half a mile from the house and laid hit on a big poplar stump. And we never heard anything more.

I b'lieve just as much as I'm settin' here right now that that was that little boy haunting his pap 'cause he'd whupped him for ridin' on the door. I'll never b'lieve nothin' else.

53

THE GHOST'S
LITTLE FINGER BONE

Mrs. Susie Moles, interviewed by Emory L. Hamilton
in Wise, Wise County, no date given

Many years ago in Lee County a man bought a farm and moved into the house standing on this place. He soon found out that the house was so haunted he could not live there. He built a house some distance away and moved out into the new house leaving the old one in [the] possession of the ghost, to rot and fall to decay. One cold rainy night, some travelers came through and asked if he knew where there was a vacant house they could camp in. "Yes," he replied, "up there on the hill is one you can stay in as long as you want to, if you can stay in it." One of the strangers asked what he meant by saying "if you can stay in it." "Because it's haunted," the farmer replied.

"Oh I don't mind the haunts," the strange speaker said. It happened that this speaker was a preacher, and the farmer gave them wood to build a fire and went up to stay with them until about the time for the ghost to arrive. Then he left them with a good-night.

About nine o'clock the ghost came. The preacher had cautioned the other members of his party, that if the ghost came for everybody to be very quiet and let him do the talking. All at once a person was heard to come into the loft overhead and on down the stairs like they were dragging chains. She came on down to the fireplace and turned her back to the fire. None of the crowd spoke except the preacher and he asked, "In the name of the Father, and the Son, and the Holy Ghost, what do you want?" After repeating this three times, the apparition slowly spoke and said, "I was killed here by my sweetheart, who killed me for my money and buried my body in the cellar. I want you to take up my bones and bury all, except the bone of my little finger. Set a dinner and invite all the neighbors in. And after you have asked a blessing, pass this finger bone around on a plate. And the person who killed me, when he touches the bone, it will stick to his hand. My sweetheart didn't get my money, and if you carry out this request, I will return and tell you where my money is hid, which you may have."

As requested, the preacher set a dinner, invited all the neighbors in, and, after saying his blessing, passed the plate around, and the third man who touched the bone was dumfounded when the bone stuck to his fingers. The preacher then had him arrested and he confessed to killing the girl and burying her in the cellar.

Soon after this, one night, the ghost-girl came again and after asking her in the name of the Father, the Son, and the Holy Ghost, three times, what she wanted, she told the preacher that she had come to tell him where the money was hidden. She told him there was a secret drawer in the ceiling of the kitchen and there was where her money was hidden. He found the drawer and to his surprise there was several thousand dollars in gold in it. The old preacher took the money and bought the haunted house and farm. He lived there the balance of his life and the ghost-girl never came again.

THE FICKLIN
FIELD HOUSE

An unknown informant, interviewed by Bessie Scales
in Danville, on September 23, 1940

An old house situated among a thicket of briars, trees, etc. off W[est] Main Street, Danville, Virginia, known as the old Ficklin Field place, was always said to be haunted, and for this reason [was] always avoided by all the Negroes living beyond this field on the outskirts of the city. For many years before this house entirely collapsed from neglect, weird noises were heard during the early hours of the morning. Not for anything would a Negro pass close to this house, although to do so was a much shorter walk to and from town to this settlement, called Po' House Hill. So great was the belief that nolady [*typo*: nobody] could spend the night alone in this old house that a crowd of Negro boys made up a purse of one dollar and offered it to anyone who would spend a night there. The bravest of the lot said he knew there were no sich thing as hants, and he would prove there weren't by spending the night there hisself.

The night was cold and the wind whistled in through the cracks in the walls. So this boy gathered up an armful of sticks, carried them in the old house and made a roaring fire in the big open fireplace. He took a seat in an old rocking chair he found in the room and was soon sleeping soundly.

After several hours when the fire began to die out, he woke, stretched himself, and said, "Well, I jest knowed there were no sich thing as hants. Now I'll git er dollar to spen'. But I sho' is sleepy, gittin' cold too." Then he heard a voice answering "I sho' is sleepy, gittin' cold too." And when the boy looked around there sat a great big black cat, the biggest cat and the greenest eyes he ever saw. And the boy was so scared that he jumped up and ran out of that house as fast as he could and ran about two miles 'till he fell against a tree; and when he caught his breath enough to speak out loud, he said "Well I sho' is tired, but I sho' did run." And the same voice said again "I sho' is tired, and I sho' did run." And the boy looked 'round again and there was that same big black cat, with the big green eyes, and the boy said, "But I sho' is gonna run some mo'. I is gonna keep on runnin'." And the big black cat with the green eyes says "I sho' is gonna run some mo'. I is gonna keep on runnin' too."

And to this day that Nigger boy and that big cat with the green eyes is still running. After a long time when the brave boy didn't come back, the rest of the gang suspicioned what had happen to him. So they made up this song, which all the Nigger children on Po' House Hill sing to this day:

> A big brave boy by de name ob Lous,
> 'Cided spend de night in de Ficklin' Hous.
> A big black cat who eyes were green,
> Was playin' 'round on de sewin' 'chine.
> Sewin' 'chine hit were a-runnin' so fast,
> Hit took a-ninety-nine stitches, in de black cat's britches.
> Now de bo'f [both] is a-runnin' some.

—————— 55 ——————

A CIVIL WAR
HAUNT IN AN
OLD LOG HOUSE

Lemuel Hamilton, interviewed by Emory L. Hamilton
in Wise, Wise County, on September 23, 1940

y mother told this and she said old Mrs. Jones, old Isaiah Jones' wife told her. It happened during the Civil War, and she said it was true stuff. Lizzie Bolton, who was then a young girl, was staying with old Mrs. Jones. They were living in an old log house, two story, in Powell Valley. One night Liz started upstairs, and just as she got to the top of the stairway she saw a woman standing there dressed in white. But she didn't have any head. Liz screamed and fainted and fell down the stairway. Old Mrs. Jones picked her up and asked her what was the matter. She told her about what she saw. Mrs. Jones said, "I didn' allow we'd see that any more. It's been a long time since we had seen it."

Liz asked her what she meant, and she said that during the Civil War the soldiers had killed a young woman on the stairway, cut her head off. She said they hadn't seen her for a long time until this night and she had allowed she wouldn't see her anymore.

My grandmother later lived in this house and mother said it was haunted all the time they lived there. They saw several things. One night grandpa looked out the window and saw a man standing in the yard. It was a pretty light moonshiney night. He thought it was somebody trying to break in the house on them. He got his gun, a double barrel shot gun, and stuck it out the window, and shot both barrels at the man standing there. When he shot they said the man jumped about ten feet into the air. Grandpa thought he'd killed him and went out to see. There was no sign of anybody. He got a light and went out and searched for blood, but not a drop could he find. He said when he shot that the man just disappeared. They never found any sign of a person, tracks or anything, and never found out what it meant.

———— 56 ————

THE DANCING COUPLE

Mrs. Molly Mayhew, interviewed by Susan R. Morton
in Bull Run, Fauquier County, on December 19, 1941

In the midst of the Bull Run mountains in Fauquier County there stood, some fifty years ago, an old log house, the home of an old Irish couple. He was known as "Fiddlin' Mike," for he was one of the best known fiddler players in the community and there was never a dance held for miles around that he and his wife did not attend. She, even in her old days, was a dancer equal to the best of the young ones.

But some years before her death, when in her late sixties, she broke a leg and was always more or less of a cripple after that. So too became Mike when rheumatism overtook him. However, they lived for man[y] years after that, much crushed in spirit by their infirmities. Their children all died before them, and it was to a kind Negro neighbor that they depended for help in the last years of their life. Mike was the fust to go and his wife soon followed. What little property they had they left to the faithful neighbor, Lucy, and the cabin itself soon fell into ruins and was left alone for years.

It was off a traveled road and the woods soon encroached to the very door, nearly hiding it. Night hunters passing by there told of seeing lights at night, and one night Mrs. Mayhew's [the informant's] father coming by there near midnight with his dogs noticed they began to slink close to his heels and howl dismally. It was bright moonlight, and, coming near the cabin, he was sure he saw something pass by the window. So he peered within to see a man and woman dancing, going through the steps of an old-fashioned dance with perfect rhythm. They seemed to be clothed in some luminous apparel and he was certain that it was old Mike and his wife, returning to continue their beloved dance. He left hurriedly, but some venturesome youths went there another night and reported the same scene.

———— 57 ————

GHOST CHAINS
FROM A
LOGGING ACCIDENT

Mrs. Molly Mayhew, interviewed by Susan R. Morton
in Haymarket, Prince William County, on October 10, 1941

When my cousin moved into a house in these mountains she asked me to come and stay with her while she got settled and while her husband had to be away visiting [some] of his kin back home (Fauquier County) that were took suddenly sick. The house was way off from everything, a lonesome sort of place. But they were gettin' it real cheap, and it was clean and tidy for all a man had had the care of it.

Old Mr. Bose Swartz had lived there all alone since his wife died; he was a woodsman (lumberman), and 'tis said he could measure with his eye how much lumber a tree would make and come within a few feet, too. People said he died of remorse for it was his fa[u]lt that young Joe White got killed, or rather, that he died, and him leaving a young wife, too, and a parcel of young ones. Not that old Bose, that's what everyone called him, were to blame or meant any harm to come to anyone. But he forgot the chain one day, and, being in a hurry, he told them to go as best they could and try and get the logs down the mountain while he was gone on some business to the mill.

It's right dangerous to get logs down the side of the mountain without some chains that can be fastened to hold them back until they are eased over the rocks and bad places. But Joe, he never said a thing, and went right ahead. When it was near [dark] and they had got along all day all right, they began to hurry some. And when a big chestnut log slipped it caught Joe on his legs and smashed them good and proper. That night they cut off both his legs, but he died in a few hours.

It was a terrible thing to think that he [Bose] hadn't gone back to fetch that chain as he should. And after that old Bose began to act queer. He wouldn't do no more wo[r]k; jest sat around, and sometimes he would say, as if he were a-thinkin' of that all the time, "With chains we might have saved him." They found him dead in his chair one day. [He] left all he had, and that wasn't much, to the young widow and her children. 'Twas from her that my cousin rented the place.

The first night that we were there we couldn't sleep for the noises, and I said to my cousin that there must be a powerful lot of rats around. We were sleeping in the kitchen that night, as it was right late when we got there, and the critters had to be taken care of. When we started to get settled the next day we couldn't see any sign of a rat. That next night we were sleeping properly upstairs, my cousin and her two boys and myself, when first thing we knew we were all awake and there was the awfullest noise you ever did hear—someone going down the stairs a-draggin' a chain after them. And it went plump, plump, plump on each step. It went on 'till it hit the bottom; then it seemed to disappear like. And all was still. This we heard every night. And my cousin said she'd be hung before she'd stay there.

So [not] long after her man got back—and how he laughed at us, too, 'till he heard the same thing—they moved away. And then some other families took it. But nobody would stay for long. And one Spring when there was a woods' fire, the house burned down. Reckon it was a good thing, for it wasn't much good nohow.

——— 58 ———

A CONFEDERATE SOLDIER IN A HAUNTED ROOM

Cornelia Berry, from her own recollection
in Fleeton, Northumberland County, no date given

When George Edwards was a young man, he was a soldier in the Confederate Army and spent all his "leaves of absence" at his home at Fleets' Point. He came home once for a week and, after spending a pleasant time with his people, he started back late one day on horseback. As his "leave of absence" was growing short he had to ride hard and late at night. He rode until twelve o'clock that night and as he was very tired and his horse almost spent, he decided to stop at a farm house that he came to, which was all aglow with lights. The owner gave him a hearty welcome, seeing that he was a soldier, and gave him supper and invited him to join in the dancing, but as he was very tired he thanked him and said he would much prefer to go to bed, as he had a long ride before him the next day. His host showed him up to his room and bade him good night. Mr. Edwards locked the door, placed his gun near the head of the bed, undressed, blew out the candle, and went to bed. After lying there a short time listening to the music and dancing and thinking of his visit to his home, he slowly sank into a slumber.

He was aroused by the covers being slowly pulled off of him. At first he thought that he was dreaming, so he pulled them up tightly around his neck and dropped off into another doze. He had no more than lost consciousness when he was awakened again by the covers being slowly drawn off of him. This time he sat up in bed, but he could not see anything. So, thinking it must be his nerves and being so very tired, he again pulled up the covers and once more went to sleep. He slept a little longer this time and when he was awakened the covers had been drawn half way off of him. He lay still and waited until the covers had been pulled down to his knees, and then he made a spring for the foot of the bed. But there was nothing there. He jumped out of bed, lighted a candle, and reached for his gun—but it was gone. He searched the room but could not find anything. The door was locked as he left it when he went to bed. He hurriedly dressed and called his host.

They found his gun in the hall outside of his door, and when he told his host about what had happened he said that the room was haunted and the same thing happened to everyone that slept in it. Mr. Edwards did not wait for sunrise, but saddled his horse and left before anything else could happen.

——— **59** ———

THE HAUNTED
HOUSE OF SAUNDERS

Miss Lou Garrett, interviewed by John W. Garrett
in Wingina, Nelson County, on December 2, 1940

Miss Lou, as she is generally known, is an old maid of about seventy years of age. She and her brother Morris have lived in their own home, which they inherited from their parents. They have adopted and reared five boys and girls. Her brother recently died, and Miss Lou has an old colored woman who lives with her and a little girl of eight years, whom Miss Lou is adopting. Miss Lou said "My mother used to tell me that old Mrs. John Radford was the first one to buy the old Saunders' place. He was the grandfather of the Saunders [the place is named for]. Mr. Saunders was Mr. Radford's grandson. My mother said the place was haunted, and one night she and some of the women were sitting up with one of the family [who was sick], and the men folks were sitting out on the front porch, and all at once the men jumped up and ran away, and my mother asked them 'What's the matter?' and they said that old man Stevenson, who had died drunk, was. And he was cripple from being thrown from a horse when he was drunk. Well, they said, there he come hopping around the house, and when he got to the corner of the porch, there was a big hop vine there, and he took hold of it and began to shake it with all his might. And he scared them all so they ran away. I don't know if the sick person died or not. My mother told me so long ago. I don't remember about that."

"But she said that after that she and some more people were sitting up with a corpse, or a sick person one, I forget which one it was, but I think it was a corpse, and along in the night she went into another room and laid down, and all at once the outside door began to shake as if it was being torn down. And it shook until it shook itself open. One of the girls come with a candle and closed the door. But they couldn't keep that door shut. It would begin to shake and shake and open it would come. They said that old man Radford's daughter was coming down the stairs steps and fell and broke her neck, and after that they could hear her come in upstairs and walk around and shut the [bed]room door with a 'bang,' and come tipping on down the stairs, and on she'd come until she reached the bottom step and they couldn't hear her any more, but the front door would come open and they would go to see but nobody would be there."

Miss Lou said "One day my mother was walking with Mrs. Phelps, she was Conrad Radford's grand-daughter, and as they were walking around the Saunders' farm all of a sudden Mrs. Philps [Phelps] said 'There's old man Bob! Don't you see him a-standing there under that apple tree?' Old man Bob was an old colored man who had been dead for years and Mrs. Phelps thought a lot of him. My mother said she looked and looked but she never could see him. But Mrs. Phelps said that old man Bob was standing just like he was before he died, and she saw him just as natural as she ever did in her life. And she said old man Bob reached up and took hold of a limb of the apple tree and vanished from sight. The Saunders' house is on the road going down by the Allie Woods place over here. The old house has been torn down, and a new house has been built there. But everybody knew that old house to be haunted. Nearly everybody has seen and heard things there. I don't believe in ghosts," said Miss Lou, "but my mother told me about these things and my mother wouldn't of told it if it hadn't been true."

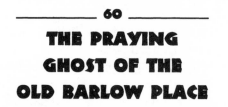

THE PRAYING GHOST OF THE OLD BARLOW PLACE

Moses Johnson, interviewed by Susan R. Morton
in an unknown location in Loudoun County, on March 12, 1942

This old place is located in Loudoun County in a small valley between two of the foothills of the Bull Run Mountains. The house has been gone for many years, a few scraggly lilacs growing in the tangle of underbrush the only sign of a home ever having been there. It had long been deserted and fallen into decay before a fire sweeping down the mountainside finally destroyed it.

Some seventy-five years ago it was occupied by a man named Barlow, and has since been known as the old Barlow Place. This man came into the neighborhood and bought a few acres of land and two log cabins [which were] very old at that time, having been slave cabins on an adjoining plantation of which this place was once a part. He built an addition, joining the two cabins together, and weather-boarded it over, and painted it black with white window frames and trim, making it a sort of curiosity in the neighborhood. He planted the yard with shrubs and fruit trees which he tended carefully.

At the time he came into the community he was well past middle age. He lived alone except for one serving man, who was merely known as "thet furriner," being of very dark complexion yet not being a Negro. They kept to themselves and did not encourage neighborly gestures. Sinister stories grew up about him. It seems that Barlow had followed the sea before his coming to the mountains, and had many curious mementoes of his travels scattered over the house, which the few people who ever went in there said included a "heathen idol" that he worshipped. And [this got] enlarged upon greatly until it came to be believed that he went through some strange rites. That made him an object of awe to the simple folks who were his neighbors.

Finally the "furriner" left and the old man lived alone until finally some relatives came to care for him at his death. Not so long after that they took him away for burial and gathered up the household goods and left the community never to return. Shortly after the relatives came to care for him, a Catholic priest visited him, being brought from the railway station some miles distant by one of the men in the neighborhood. But in spite of his wary questioning, the mission of the priest or anything of the past history of the man he was going to visit was never found out.

The first story of any supernatural manifestation came from a peddlar who, a storm overtaking him, spent the night there. He told of being awakened some time in the middle of the night by the sound of someone wailing as if in great mental anguish. But even by the light of a lantern he placed by his side, he was unable to see anything.

Other stories followed. And a family of squatters who took possession of the tumble-down house some years after its being vacated soon left telling of the praying ghost that lamented throughout the night. And some adventuresome boys, going there one moonlit night, saw an old man kneeling in the house in an attitude of prayer.

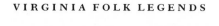

——— **61** ———

THE SLAVE TRADER'S
HAUNTED HOUSE

Mrs. Rebecca Ashby, interviewed by Susan R. Morton
in Waterfall, Prince William County, on January 6, 1942

"Mountain End" still stands just the other side of Hopewell Gap, a large and sturdy stone house built directly against one of the foothills, so that the second floor entrance at the rear opens directly onto the ground level, and the basement, in which are the kitchen and other living quarters, has no windows in the back wall. The house was probably built in the later part of the eighteenth century. It was the home of a man named Bruin, who was a slave trader, the only one in the vicinity and having considerable ill repute among the neighbors on account of his business, and for the same reason was very much dreaded by the Negroes, several of whom he had "sold south," contrary to his promises to the local owners.

Some few years prior to the War Between the States, a man was found dead beside the road one morning, his head crushed, his riderless horse returning home prompting the family to go in search of him. It was claimed that he was thrown from his horse, striking his head, and there was nothing to prove otherwise. But sinister stories were heard of an argument with the slave trader.

Not long after that, people crossing the mountain late at night heard groans coming from the woods at a place where a small branch crosses the road. But [they] never could locate the source. Others saw a Negro woman crying dismally, gliding through the underbrush. And one night, a youth returning late from a visit to his sweetheart who lived [on] the other side of the mountain, had his horse hie and throw him. He died soon after, but be[fore he died he] told that a dark form had suddenly appeared and with a beseeching cry had made a gesture as if to grab the horse's bridle.

INDIANS

The Indian legends of Virginia's Appalachian region are war stories. From the Indians' viewpoint it was a protracted guerrilla effort to prevent the settlers from overrunning their land. To the settlers it was a search and destroy operation to clear the area by killing as many of the Indians as possible and forcing the rest westward. Since no native Americans were interviewed, the WPA collection stories give only the settlers' side. They tell about the grave danger and sudden death that were the stark reality of their lives. A Wise County story from Aunt Sarah Gordon, who was eighty-four years old when she told it to James M. Hylton in 1942, is typical. It also demonstrates the mind-set that viewed the Indians basically as targets in a rifle sight:

> I've heard my grandfather, old Rawleigh Stallard tell many times about when he was huntin' one day an' heard the "gobble"-like call of a wild turkey. . . . But Grandpap was too smart; he'd been raised in th' mountains of Tennessee an' knowed right smart 'bout a lot uh calls an' sech, yes siree. He knowed it wuz a Redskin from thuh very start, an' that 'uz why he stood right still dead in his tracks when he'd heard th' funny turkey call too. Well, he spied that Redskin thar an' with thuh ever trusty aim uh his over thet old rifle stock he pulled away at him an' thuh Redskin drapped into thuh water with a great big splash. They named thuh place Indian Splash. It 'uz on Copper or Raddus Ridge in Scott County where they's plenty Indians runnin' 'round uh lookin' fer some hunter er settler an' allus tryin' tuh decoy them by some uh their fake calls an' whistles, yuh know. . . . He said yuh had to be mighty careful if yuh lived many years then, too, yes siree.[1]

Relations between the Indians and settlers in the other Virginia regions were more peaceful where there were any Indians left. Although the Powhatan Confederacy had been a powerful and warlike union of some thirty Algonquian subtribes in early colonial days, the settlers of Virginia's Tidewater and eastern Piedmont had made peace with them by the late seventeenth century.[2] Also, smallpox and yellow fever had wiped out many of the smaller tribal groups entirely; the Appomattox subtribe, for instance, prosperous when the Jamestown settlers arrived in 1607, was completely extinct by 1722.[3] By the time the settlers began moving into the western Piedmont and Blue Ridge, most of the Indian groups indigenous to the regions had already left. Tribes of northern Indians had gotten muskets from the whites first and with these advanced weapons had cleared their ancient enemies, the Monocans, out of central Virginia.[4]

But in Appalachia there was intense and violent conflict between the settlers and the Indians from the time of their first encounters. Ethnicity was a large factor on both sides. The confrontation in this area pitted the Shawnee against the Scotch-Irish, both of which were cultures with strong warrior ethics. The Shawnee were the dominant aboriginal tribe in the western mountains of Virginia. As the *American Indian Almanac* describes them, "There were no better woodsmen, no better hunters, no better fighters, no more intelligent Indians than the Shawnee. From the earliest time of which there is an authentic record of them, they were feared as warriors by Indians and white men alike. No people struggled with greater ferocity and courage to halt the forces of civilization that were driving the Indians from their ancient homelands."[5]

The Northern British border people who are commonly termed "Scotch-Irish" were by far the largest ethnic group among the settlers of Appalachia. They, too, were warriors seasoned by centuries of raids and set battles along the North British–Scottish border and accustomed to feuds and interclan fighting among themselves.[6] Their fierce independence and swift retribution for insult or injury translated easily from the England-Scotland border to the western highlands. So when the ferocious Shawnee braves attacked these white interlopers, they encountered equal ferocity, blow for blow and scalp for scalp. The Shawnees generally took no combat prisoners; men were tortured to death and women and children were captured and taken to be assimilated into the tribal society.[7] But the Scotch-Irish took no prisoners either and sought quick revenge for any wrong done to family or clan. It must have also come as a surprise to the Shawnee to find the pioneer women as dangerous as the men.[8] "Indians Come Down the Chimney" (legend 71) tells the fate of three Indians who underestimated one pioneer woman.

This dramatic conflict in Appalachia generated most of the Indian legends in the WPA collection. The seven of the collection's seventy Indian narratives that were collected elsewhere portray a much less hostile relationship between the Indians and settlers. One from Augusta County in the Blue Ridge Mountains, for example, tells a romantic tale of an Indian brave who gains strength and gracefulness by bathing in a healing spring.[9] The nonnarrative Indian lore in the WPA collection, which includes notations on such things as herbal cures, indigenous foodways, and weather and crop signs, indicates peaceful domestic and cultural interactions between whites and Indians. Several informants who were not from Appalachia even noted that they were familiar with Indian lore because their ancestors had intermarried with Indians.[10]

The Indian war stories have little moral instruction, either conscious or veiled. The only lesson they impart is the need for constant vigilance against surprise attack. Many have strong warnings to men not to leave their wives and families unprotected. The fear was well-founded, given the Shawnee practice of abducting women and children to assimilate them into their society. In fact, fear of abduction looms larger in the stories and is a more frequent topic than the fear of being killed by Indians. There is sexual anxiety underlying many of the stories that seems related to this fear of abduction. The tale of the woman who is abducted on her wedding day, for example, suggests a struggle between the settlers and the Indians over the white women. A similar one not printed here which also involves a bride's abduction on her wedding day has the groom track her down by following bits of cloth she drops along the way.[11] "The Two Women Who Married Indians" (legend 63) also reveals how possession of the settlers' women was a central issue in the war between the Indians and the whites. The white women actually enter both sides of the wild/civilized conflict and finally decide for themselves which group to accept. Interestingly, there is a male/female resolution as well; the young man whom the women saved from torture by the Indians repays their deed when they return to the white world. One story not printed here tells of a man who had to guard his wife constantly from Indian attacks because they all wanted to scalp her for the prize of her red hair. And another tells how a man realizes an Indian has murdered his wife when he sees him wearing her red shawl.[12] Altogether, the Appalachian Indian tales reveal great stress on the part of the male settlers about the presence and vulnerability of their women in the midst of war.

The stories often characterize the Indians as wild animals. In the narrative "Daniel Boone's Tricks on Indians" (legend 78), Boone deceives a band of Indians in a way the motif index describes as a trick on bears, and European variants for "The Two Women Who Married Indians" indicate the same Indian-for-bear substitution. In "The Friendly Old Hog" (legend 68), an Indian actually takes on the appearance and behavior of an animal to deceive and kill a settler. This "animalized" idea of the Indian was an important part of the settlers' worldview. It was as necessary as stories such as "Indians Kill a Pioneer Family" (legend 65) and "Cry Baby and Your Mammy'll Come" (legend 70), which give the gruesome details of Indian atrocities. Without reinforcement from these stories and from the idea that Indians were simply an unusual species of wild beast, it would have been harder for the pioneers to exterminate the original inhabitants of the Appalachian Plateau.

Virginia once teemed with Indians; now they are almost all gone. These Indian legends make a connection between the present and the past. Each story is a small piece of the large saga of the Indians in Virginia, their once proud domination of the land, and the bloody war they lost trying to defend it. The complex feeling that the stories evoke was aptly described by George Mullins when he recalled how his father told him about "The Indian Boiling Pot" (legend 69). The story involves an Indian whose grave was marked by two hickory saplings tied to grow together over the carved rock—"Well sir, they is two trees crossed right over that rock, an' when I looked up I saw 'em there; but they had growed a mighty lot. They was swayin' in the wind, an' the way Pap was tellin' the tale made me feel quare right then."

NOTES

1. Box 5, folder 5, item 765, WPA collection.

2. J. Norman Heard, *Handbook of the American Frontier: Four Centuries of Indian-White Relationships*, vol. 1, *The Southern Woodlands* (London: Scarecrow Press, 1987), 297.

3. Grace Steele Woodward, *Pocahontas* (Norman: Univ. of Oklahoma Press, 1969), p. 23.

4. Alfred Percy, *Old Place Names* (Madison Hts., Va.: Percy Press, 1950), pp. 10–11.

5. John Upton Terrell, *The American Indian Almanac* (New York: World, 1971), p. 137. Terrell noted that Cherokee Indians had once been as prominent in Appalachia as the Shawnee but that their numbers had greatly diminished in the region by the time the first settlers arrived in Virginia in 1607.

6. Fischer, *Albion's Seed*, pp. 633–39, 765–71.

7. Terrell, *American Indian Almanac*, p. 141.

8. Fischer, *Albion's Seed*, p. 770.

9. Box 5, folder 4, item 741, WPA collection.

10. Box 4, folder 2, item 353 and box 10, folder 1, item 1478, ibid.

11. Box 5, folder 5, item 776, ibid.

12. Items 754, 756, ibid.

THE TEN INDIANS

Spencer Greenfield Adams, interviewed by James Taylor Adams
in Big Laurel, Wise County, on July 21, 1940

One time a man went off from home and just left his wife right by herself. They lived away off from anybody else. So that day she thought she would bake her up some pies and have them for her husband when he come back the next day. So she started baking the pies and it hadn't been long 'till a little Indian dog came in. She knew Indians was about, but she didn't run. And sure enough it wasn't long 'till six Indians come in. One of them was a chief and the others were warriors, all painted up.

She didn't know what to do. But she decided the best thing to do was to be as good to them as she could and maybe they would go on and not kill her.

So she invited them to come in and she went and brought each one of them a big pie and throwed on the pot and cooked them a good supper. They was friendly enough, but they said they wanted to stay all night. She told them she didn't have but one bed. The chief told [her] that was all right. They were not use[d] to sleeping in beds. All they wanted was just to stretch out on the floor and bake their brains before the fire. She told them all right, but she believed he just wanted a chance to kill her during the night.

The little dog, it would run back towards the bed and growl and bark and to keep it quiet the chief put it out of the house and fastened the door.

The woman went to bed and the Indians all stretched out on the floor and the woman lay there awake thinking every minute they would kill her. But after a while she went to sleep in spite of herself; and she was waked up by something sharp sticking up through the bed in her back. She cried out, "I knew you'd kill me, I knew you'd kill me."

The Indian chief he heard her going on and he jumped up and asked her what was the matter. She told him, and he counted his men and they were all there sound asleep. So he told her to go back to sleep, that she'd been dreaming. But it wasn't long 'till he heard her again, "I knew you'd kill me, I knew you'd kill me."

This time he counted his men again and found them all there sound asleep. Then he looked under the bed and there laid a big Negro. He had slipped in the house that morning while the woman had gone to the spring and hid under the bed and was going to kill her. He had a big butcher knife that he was trying to stick in her up through the bed. The Indian chief dragged him out and tied him to a stake and stuck pine splinters in him and set them a-fire and burnt him to death.

——— 63 ———

THE WOMEN WHO MARRIED INDIANS

Mrs. Polly Johnson, interviewed by Emory L. Hamilton
in Wise, Wise County, on August 29, 1940

One time there's two girls and a boy. One of the girls and the boy was brother and sister and the other was a friend to the girl and the brother's sweetheart. They were out walking one day and was captured by Indians. They were taken to the Indian nation. They were took to the place where the old chief was. They tied the boy up and put him under the guard of the old chief and his squaw. They built up a brush heap to burn the boy. The girls were told to lay down and sleep. The Indians went out to hunt some pine knots. They was going to stick the splinters in the boy and set them afire and torture him.

While they was gone the old chief started dozing. His head kept drooping lower and lower, 'till finally he went to sleep. It was getting dark and neither one of the girls had gone to sleep. They was watching the old chief. The boy's sister said to the other girl, "Shhhh, be quiet. I'm going to let my brother loose." The old chief had a knife in his hand that he'd been whittling with before he went to sleep. She got up easy like and slipped the knife from his hand and cut the ropes from her brother and let him loose. She slipped the knife back in his [the chief's] hand and laid down again. When the Indians come and found him gone they waked up the old chief and squaw and asked who turned him [the boy] loose. They said if the girls has done it we'll kill 'em. The old squaw said, "No, they didn't do it. They've been asleep all the time." The Indians said, "Whooeee, white man gone."

Two of the Indians asked the girls which they'd druther do— be burned in the brush heap alive, stabbed and killed, shot, or marry me and be dressed in silk and have good things to eat. One of the girls said, "I'd druther marry you," and the other one said the same. They married the Indians and lived with them three years. They done what they said and dressed them in silk. They wore fine beaded moccasins and beads around their necks. The boy's sister had learned to love the Indian she married.

One day they said to the old squaw, "Mama, we're going to go get some grapes." They had lived with the Indians three years and they trusted them to go anywhere now. They got their silk aprons full of grapes and set down on a log to rest. One of the girls, the one who was the boy's sweetheart said, "I'm gone, I'm going back to my people." The one who loved her Indian husband says, "I'm not going. I'm going to stay." The other'n said, "I'm going. You can stay if you want to." And she started out. The other girl watched her out of sight and then throwed [down] her grapes and hollered, "I'm coming too."

They traveled 'till night, running and walking. When the Indians come in they started out hunting for them. The Indians had a fiest [feist] dog and the two girls heard it coming after them— barking. One of them jumped into a sink hole and covered herself with leaves. The other one crawled in a hollow log. The fiest dog come up and run in the log. She grabbed it and smothered it to death with her clothes. They heard the Indians coming. The husband of the one in the sink hole was hollering "Honey's gone, Oh, Honey's lost." They said when she heard him hollering she come very nigh making herself known. They come up to the log and hacked on it with their tomahawks, and said, "Whooee, Honey's gone. We'll go back and take a soon start in the morning and find them and kill 'em."

As soon as the Indians got gone they crawled out and went on. They traveled 'till they come to a river, and on the other side was houses. They hollered and a man come out. He saw them and said, "There's my sister." He got a boat and come across after them. Just as they got on the other side the Indians come, and the white men killed them.

———— 64 ————

DISTURBING
INDIAN GRAVES

Elbert J. Bond, interviewed by James Taylor Adams
in Big Laurel, Wise County, on May 26, 1941

Yes, I've heard the old people say that the best an' only way to keep a gun from being spelled was to mix Indian bone filings with your powder. They used to say that the old timers would hunt everywhere for an Indian grave an' dig up the bones an' file or scrape 'em to get the dust for their gunpowder. That was a long time ago. Guess they hain't any Indian bones left now, an' if they was, people wouldn't use 'em. Some would, too, for I've heard people say right here lately they believed their gun was spelled.

One time they say that an old man went up on the hill above where Willie Kilgore lives to dig in an Indian grave, an' the first lick he struck the whole earth all 'round him started to tremble an' shake an' he heard a rumblin' down under 'im jes' like thunder. He tried ag'in an' hit done the same way. So he got scared an' run off an' they never could git 'im back thar any more.

INDIANS KILL
A PIONEER FAMILY

Eva Fair Pegram, interviewed by James Taylor Adams
in Big Laurel, Wise County, on November 14, 1940

Long, long time ago there was a man and his wife and three little children living away back in the woods, far off from anybody else. I don't know where it happened, but somewhere in this country, I guess, maybe in North Carolina. One day the man put a turn on his horse and started off to mill. It was a long ways to the mill, and he would be gone all day.

He hadn't been gone but a little while 'till his wife heard somebody a-comin', riding up the rocky road. She looked out and saw two Indians coming riding on their ponies. She told the children to crawl in the closet and no matter what happened to stay there and not cry. The woman didn't have a thing to fight with. They had but one gun and her husband had took it with him. And the axe was sticking in the chop-block out in the yard. So she got down on [her] knees and began to pray.

The Indians come on up and got down and knocked on the door. She wouldn't open it. Then the chief broke it down. They come in and found her kneeling there on the hearth a-praying. They took her up and tied her hands and feet and carried her down to the edge of a high cliff and danced around her and then threw her over the bluff into the river. Then they went back and got everything out of the house they wanted and burnt the house down on the three little children.

That night when the man come back from the mill he found his house in ashes. He soon found the burnt bones of his three little children and their hearts. You know they say a person's heart won't burn. He hunted and hunted for his wife's heart, but of course couldn't find it. So he went crazy, and he run off in the woods and jumped over the cliff and killed himself. A few days later somebody found his wife's body in the river.

And now they say that ever since then the ashes of that cabin stays right there and nothing will grow in them, and that many a person passing there of a night have seen an old man with [a] long gray beard and a stick in his hand hunkered down there stirrin' in the ashes, hunting for his wife's heart.

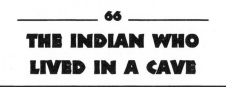

——— 66 ———

THE INDIAN WHO LIVED IN A CAVE

Unknown informants, interviewed by I. M. Warren
in Fredericksburg, Spotsylvania County, no date given

In the ravine to the north of the famous old home, Chatham, there is a square room hewn out of the rock, with a hole upward through the rock and sod for an outlet for smoke. The cave has for years been falling in, from the front. Very old people say that, within the memory of such people, the front was not wide open, but was a door-like entrance, and that at the bottom of the ravine were fragments of a hewn, polished slab of stone that once was used as the door to the cave.

There are many legends about this cave. The one related here appears to be as well founded as any. It is known to many older people. The writer heard it from tenants of Chatham.

When the white men began to drive the Indians back, there was one young chief who fought them, and was captured. An Indian princess was at that time imprisoned in Fredericksburg in the old Warehouse Building, as a hostage. This young chief—he was probably only the chief of a petty tribe of a hundred or two—had known her. He too was given as a hostage, but he was not imprisoned long. He gave his word he would not run away. But he had no way to live, and the Indians would not work for the whites.

So he carved out the cave at Chatham and lived there, on game, fish, and what fruits and berries he could gather. The owner of the place, William Fitzhugh, let him stay, and loaned him a small piece of land to grow corn and yams and so forth. In return, the young Indian kept Mr. Fitzhugh supplied with wild turkeys, ducks, venison, and partridges.

When the Indian princess was released from the old Warehouse in Fredericksburg, her people had gone back toward the mountains. The dweller in Chatham cave saw her and they were married—but what ceremony no one says—and lived in Indian Cave for many years. The cave is still in good condition.

——— 67 ———

TWO INDIANS KILLED
WITH A BOULDER

Hector Lane, interviewed by James M. Hylton
in Hurricane, Wise County, on June 6, 1941

I can tell you a tale my wife's aunt told me many years ago about some Indians that got atter her father when things was just tol'able in that neck of the woods out in the Hurricane country. He was a brave old man an' I don't doubt but what it's the truth too. My wife's aunt was on up in years when she told it to us, but I've heard her tell it to others besides me an' my wife different times since. They's a stiff curve right at Trace Fork and the road turns comin' from Coeburn and circles back up the hillside going on in to Wise. They's a little rise there in the road and that is just where this took place.

Uncle George Lane, his name was, an' he wasn't scared of anything on foot nor wing and he always tended to his business too. But when he got riled he could lay the fist on heavy, or anything in reach of him, like a club or sand stone. He was comin' there one day with his long old rifle gun, but he had it strapped over his shoulder some way and tied with a rawhide thong and another thong with his caps an' powder in a pouch an' he was thinkin' 'bout something he oughtn't to when he heard a scream behind him a[nd] saw a Redskin about so many yards away from him in the rear on the trail.

Well, he done what anybody most likely'd do an' tuck out runnin' fast as he could. But jist as he topped the little rise where the road turns back toward Wise he run right smack into another Redskin, almost face to face. An' they wasn't anything fer him to do but turn ag'in, an' this time he turned quick. But he knowed he'd run into the other one behind him at first an' he angled off up the hill at about a 35 degree angle an' dug his heels in the soft dirt an' made every step count as much as he could.

Well, on up the hill he went, as fast as his legs would carry him until he give plumb out an' jus' had to set down an' rest. He could see below him the two Indians as they tried to get back on his trail. An' then he saw them start out over the tracks he'd made in the soft dirt on the hillside. He knowed he couldn't run another step, as he was out o' breath, an' he looked around him to see what in the world he could do to save hisself. Well, they was a big boulder in back of him there on the hill, and it was round. He pulled a old dead log out from under it an' held it 'till he could see them below him as they tried to come on up the steep hillside.

He waited until they got together an' give the big rock a shove an' down the hill it went, takin' all the small bushes with it as it went. The brush on each side of the path he had tuck was so thick they couldn't git out of the way, an' the rock hit 'em both, right about the knees. They both laid there fer a while an' then tried to get up but saw they couldn't. An' he went up a little deeper on the hill an' got him some smaller rocks an' peppered them both with 'em 'till they's dead, or dyin'. He went down to them an' they told him at the spot that they's goin' to kill him if they lived. But he had pelted 'em so hard he knowed they was talkin' their last an' he just listened to 'em talk.

They both died there, an' he went back home an' got his kin folks an' they all went back there to see 'em. An' they made a path that day lookin' at the Redskins he kilt. They buried them there, an' their graves is in them woods today. Turnin' back at the place where he met them started the path there, an' later the road turned there too. So that's why it['s] so steep.

——————— 68 ———————

THE FRIENDLY OLD HOG

Mrs. Dicy Adams, interviewed by James Taylor Adams
in Big Laurel, Wise County, on August 1, 1940

One time a man had been to see some of his people and as he come back he had to travel through a big wilderness. One night he lay down in the edge of a deep wood to sleep. He had built him up a fire to keep him company. Away long in the night he heard something rattling the leaves up on the side of the hill, and, thinking it might be a wild animal that would jump on him, he set up and listened. At last he seen it was a big hog.

It come on down the hill rooting along in the leaves, and every now and then it would throw up its head and grunt and wind him. It kept coming on down the hill and went all the way around him. And it would root along and jerk its head up and look at him and grunt. He did not care about being bothered with it so he throwed sticks at it and it run off. But it was not gone long 'till here it come again. And it would go round and round his fire, and every now [and] then throw up its head and look at him and grunt. Then it would go back to rooting in the leaves.

At last he decided to let it alone and watch it. Right round and round it went, rooting in the leaves and grunting. And he noticed that every time it went around that its circle got a little closer to him. And he got to noticing it and it didn't seem to act the way a hog would act. So he run it off again. That time it was gone a long time. But after while he heard it coming again grunting and rooting in the leaves. And this time it come right close up to the fire and rooted, and when he throwed at it, it would just run off a little piece and turn and come right back.

At last he said to himself, "I bet I do get rid of you!" And the next time it come back it got right close up to him and he noticed that it seemed to stop every now and then and look at him. He just couldn't stand it any longer and he grabbed his gun and shot it. It fell and he run over to it and turned it over, and there lay an Indian, with a big knife in his hand. He had put the hog skin over him and was trying to slip up on the fellow to stab him.

———— 69 ————

THE INDIAN BOILING POT

George Mullins, interviewed by James M. Hylton
in Wise, Wise County, on April 21, 1941

We was goin' through the hills back on Indian Creek one time when I was pretty young an' spry, an' run on a big rock in the path that I don't think I had ever seen before. Pap was with me an' as we got up to it I saw a big roun' hole in the center of it that was smooth and roun' an' looked like it would hold 'bout two gallons. I asked Pap if he knew what it was an' he said sure, he knew. It was a place where the Indians boiled their water an' cooked their meat in the wintertime, as the clay they made their pots up of in the summer wouldn't stan' a freeze an' would crack an' break up in winter an' they had to find some way to boil an' cook. An' they would wait 'till some brave done some little something wrong in camp an' for his punishment they would make him stan' on a big flat rock near the camp an' drill away with flints on poles 'till they had got down in the rock far 'nuff to hold a good 'mount of water an' the likes.

Pap said that his pap told him that how this particular rock had been drilled was that a young brave was sent 'long behind a party of hunters one day an' told to bend down two saplin's ever' now an' then over the path they took so the Indians could foller them later, an' that the brave got to this place an' he had bent so awful many already that he was tired an' laid down to rest. An' [he] slep' a little longer than his Indians thought he ought to an' [they] went to look for him an' found him layin' there by this big rock. And for his punishment they bent the two saplin's above him an' tied them together; an' then they tied his han's in the fork and fixed him so the pole with the flint on the end would dig into the rock ever' time he moved, as his feet lacked a little [of] touchin' the rock they hung him over an' that the win' blowed him roun' an' round an' back an' forth 'till it had cut this hole in the rock. But he died from hunger an' water, an' later when the Indians come back to see 'bout him, they found him dead an' was awful sorry an' they took stout vines an' leather thongs an' tied the saplings ag'in so they would grow that way as a sign of their misdeed to their brother, as he was one of the best in the tribe.

Well sir, they's two trees crossed right over that rock, an' when I looked up I saw 'em there but they had growed a mighty lot. An' they was swayin' in the win', an' the way Pap was tellin' the tale made me feel quare right then. Anyway, if they's anything to the tale, it's a lastin' memory to the Indian brave for his mistake, and theirs too, as them trees was hickories, an' they last a long, long time.

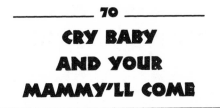

70

CRY BABY
AND YOUR
MAMMY'LL COME

Etta Kilgore Hamilton, interviewed by Emory L. Hamilton
in Wise, Wise County, on October 5, 1940

One time they's a woman making soap and she had a little baby. She had this little baby in a crib out where she's makin' soap. She happened to look up and she seed a little Indian dog and she knew the Indians was coming, and she didn't think about the Indians hurting the baby, and so she run and hid. She took her a kittle of soap with her when she went and she got down in a barrel of feathers. When the Indians got there they couldn't find the mother and they decided to hurt the baby and make it cry and she'd come. So they picked the baby up and stuck one little foot in the hot soap and said, "Cry baby and your mammy'll come." Then they stuck the other little foot in and said, "Cry baby and your mammy'll come." Then they put both hands and arms in the soap and said, "Cry baby and your mammy'll come." Then they stuck its head under and said, "Cry baby and your mammy'll come." Then they just stuck it every bit under and said, "Cry baby and your mammy'll come." [She didn't come] so they laid the baby back in the crib then and went to hunt for the mother. They looked everywhere but the barrel of feathers and they left that for the last. When they looked down in the barrel of feathers she poured the hot soap in their faces and they run away. And when she went downstairs to her baby it was burned up. I used to hear Grandma tell this and I wanted so bad for her to say that the mother doctored the baby up and it got well. I was a child and I guess [I] didn't realize what it was to be stuck in boilin' soap.

—— 71 ——
INDIANS COME DOWN THE CHIMNEY

Mrs. Etta Lawson, interviewed by Emory L. Hamilton
in Wise, Wise County, on October 8, 1940

I guess Aunt Nancy Renfro told me this. She said way back in Indian times a woman's husband was gone away and left her to stay all night by herself. She was living in a little one room house with a mud chimney [*ELH note:* stick and clay]. She had her doors barred up for fear the Indians would come. Well, it was night and she was still afraid of the Indians. She was listening for them. Said she heard something coming and when they give the war whoop she knew it was Indians. They give the war whoop when they found the house.

They tried to prize the door open to break in on her. She had it barred, though. She had the bed and heavy things up against the door—set against the door and clear across the room to the other wall. That was the way she had her door barred. She wouldn't open the door and heard the Indians say, "We will get her, we'll [get] up on top of the house and come down the chimney."

They went up on top of the house. She got her axe and laid it down on the hearth and tore a featherbed open. And when she heard the first Indian start down the chimney, come head fo'emost, she threw the feathers in the fire. The smoke stifled him and when he come down he couldn't see. She took up the axe and split his head. When she split his head and the next one come down, she did the same thing, 'till she had killed three warriors.

She said she was afraid there'd be more. She stayed in the dark house with the three dead Indians 'till her husband come home. Then she told how she had killed the three Indians. And many women [after that] tried the method of stifling the Indians as they come down the big chimneys.

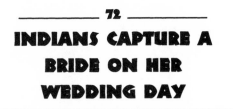

72

INDIANS CAPTURE A BRIDE ON HER WEDDING DAY

Raleigh Kilgore, interviewed by Emory L. Hamilton
at Indian Creek, Wise County, on December 12, 1940

Daddy said one time a woman and man was fixing to get married and the day she was to be married the woman went down to the creek to wash. It wasn't time for the marriage and the man hadn't yet come. While she was there washing some Indians come along and captured her and carried her off with them.

In a little while the man come and asked where she was, and they told him the Indians had stole her. He asked how many of the men there would go with him after the Indians and none of them would go with him. He told them then to get him the fastest horse that was there and two pistols, and he'd go.

He got the horse and pistols and started after them. He soon saw them and he run up shooting both the pistols and the horse flying off the earth. They turned the woman loose and started running off. He chased them about a half mile and then come back and got his woman and married her.

LEGENDARY PEOPLE
(FROM THE
AFRICAN AMERICAN FILES)

Most of the legendary figures in the African American files of the WPA collection were actual local people. Railroad Bill is the only one in the stories given here whom the storytellers did not know personally, and his is the only African American WPA collection legend that has been collected widely outside Virginia.[1] The black storytellers typically cared more for the local scene and their own neighbors than for famous names or exemplary heroes. There are a few black heroes besides Railroad Bill—James Bowser, the free black who spied for the North (in the Civil War and Emancipation section), for example, or the nameless old black man who stopped a train to ask for a ride (in the Unusual Events section), but the John Henrys, John Hardys, High John the Conquerors, and Slave Johns of the black heroic impulse are conspicuously missing from these files.

Surprisingly, tricksters are also scarce. Again, Railroad Bill is the exception. Perhaps the fact that she was talking to a white VWP worker influenced Bettie Stevens's choice to tell about the heroic trickster Bill. Hers is the only story that portrays a figure who operates with freedom and success outside the law and in spite of the white authorities. The others, who were talking to black collectors, told tales of frustration. Henry Armstrong, for example, was locally famous for the failure of his tricks. His attempt to get money and the admiration of his woman bring him to jail and ruin. In the narrative tradition of the outlaw, a woman is blamed for his downfall, but his career was rather circumscribed even before his fall.

"William Wydeman: Peacock and the Soldiers" (legend 77) tells a similar story. A woman figures in his demise, and his heroic deed lands him in jail. But there is no connection in this tale to the tradition of the trickster. The man who told Peacock's story used the nickname "Stack," which, when connected with his last name Lee, produces the name of one of black legendry's most famous figures—Stackolee.[2] Peacock is best seen in this light, as a black badman outlaw, a Stackolee. He was "jus' like dynamite goin' off" and "strong as a bull ox." The story Stack Lee told is actually an etiological story; it gives us the origin of Peacock's career in crime. Of course, he does not exactly fit the pattern of the "bad nigger,"[3] the completely asocial violent bully, because he is nice until provoked, doesn't go looking for trouble, and, initially anyhow, works for a living. In this he is more like the traditional white badman, who is often turned into a criminal by circumstances beyond his control. In this case the circumstances beyond Peacock's control were white people with rifles. "Bill Cabell, a Badman at de Bar" (legend 74), on the other hand, fits the prototypical black badman pattern perfectly. The only problem in his case is that he is a fake. He reaches for the legendary badman ideal but fails when he meets a true badman. These stories are clearly explorations of the danger involved in mistaking a heroic ideal for reality. They point out that no matter how bad you think you are, there is always someone badder.

I have included stories of the Richmond judge John Crutchfield in this section even though he was white. "Justice John" was the subject of many tales and anecdotes among the blacks interviewed in Richmond. He was certainly notable because he was a powerful white man who affected their day-to-day lives, but that was not the source of his fame. Other white judges who came in regular contact with black Richmonders were not remembered. But Judge Crutchfield was a "man of words" in the African American tradition. Like the winners of such street corner verbal contests as the "dozens," the diminutive judge won his arguments and his fame through verbal skill, wit, and humor. His legal power may have come from his robe, but his power as a legendary figure came from the fact that he played the African American game of words, and played it so well.[4]

NOTES

1. Carl Carmer's *The Stars Fell on Alabama* (New York: Literary Guild, 1934), pp. 122–25, gives the background to the Railroad Bill legend, which originated in Alabama and is based on the life of a black turpentine worker named Robert Slater. In 1893 Slater shot a white policeman during an argument and escaped on a train. Lawrence Levine, in *Black Culture and Black Consciousness*, p. 415, said that the noble social bandit, "the Robin Hood figure so familiar in the folklore of other Americans," is entirely missing from black lore, but clearly the WPA collection's version of the Railroad Bill legend portrays him as a black Robin Hood.

2. Levine, in *Black Culture and Black Consciousness*, pp. 413–15, discusses Stackolee's place in the pantheon of black badmen heroes.

3. Levine's chapter titled "Bad Men and Bandits," ibid., pp. 407–20, is an excellent discussion of the lore of the bullying violent badman in black tradition,

as is Roger Abrahams's *Deep Down in the Jungle: Negro Narrative Folklore from the Streets of Philadelphia*, rev. ed. (Chicago: Aldine, 1970).

4. Abrahams's *Deep Down in the Jungle* is the best source of general information about verbal competition in black folk culture; he discusses the dozens specifically in "Playing the Dozens," *Journal of American Folklore* 75 (1962): 209–20.

73

HENRY ARMSTRONG, DE FORGIN' MAN

George Bowden, interviewed by Roscoe Lewis
in Hampton, on May 15, 1939

De forger was, an' is, dat ole coon, Henry Armstrong, what useta live 'roun' heah on Grant Street. Lives in de penitentiary up in Richmond now, but hit ain't 'is fault, an' dat's why I'm gonna tell you all 'bout hit.

Henry Armstrong be a World War veteran. He was a captain in de Eighth Illinois. I 'spec' he took right smart beatin' over dere in abroad, which didn' help 'is state o' mind out any too much anyhow. Atter de war was over, he come to Hampton to live. Some folks didn' like 'im, said he was too high an' mighty. But I always thought he was a purty nice feller. Anyway, Henry he chauffer fer a white 'oman up heah in Lincoln Park somewheres. Atter he got dat job, he met de cause o' 'is downfall—dat be 'is wife what lives over on Grace Street now.

Now I wanna tell you somepin 'bout her. Henry her second husban'. She use to be de leadin' shout songster 'round heah in de Queen Street Church, an' I mus' say she was right smart o' a singer. Ole sweet preacher name o' Reverend —— come heah to run a revival at Queen Street, an' Mabel jes' wen' wild over 'im. Laid dat sister in two weeks, dat brother did. Married her an' carried her on way from heah wid 'im. Got her up dere in [New] Jersey somewhere's an' beat her so bad she didn' know which end she was standin' on. An' believe me, she come on home a-flyin'. Reckon she got a 'vorce from 'im, you cain' always tell, you know.

An' Henry started courtin' her. She was lookin' fer money, an' Henry sure was a sweet man to her. He useta call in dat big car what he drive fer de white folks, an' had her believing hit were his. Tol' her he had a lot o' property and money. She jes' married him real quick.

Den she foun' out he ain' got nuttin' an' she gits turrible mad. Ragged 'im all de time 'bout hit 'till he musta lost what li'l sense he did have, poor man. One day he went down de street an' bought a nice seventy-five cent shad. Scarce season fer shad too. Brung hit home to her to cook for de supper. She threw hit out de winder. Say she used to eatin' mo' 'xpensive food den dat. Cats in de back-yard jes' a-eatin' six-bits shad; poor Henry in de house hungry.

Well, 'pears like dat done 'ffect Henry's mind, like I done tol' you. He feel like he jes' mus' git dat 'oman some money. So he forge 'is first check. Forged hit on de 'oman he wukin' fer in Lin-coln Park. He was ketched an' put in jail fer several months. He come on back an' was doin' purty good for a while. Den dat 'oman got on 'im again an' he messed up again. Went in de D. P. Store down here on de corner o' Marsh Mount Corner an' bought a lot o' groceries, to please dat wife. He ain't got no money so he jes' reach in 'is pocket an' pull out a book an' write a fake check to pay fer 'em. Wrote hit jes' big 'nough so's dere 'ud be a li'l money lef' over fer 'im to carry home. Well, de police comed by an' get 'im again. Dis time de court sends 'im to de pen. He stay in de pen a long while. Atter a while dey lets 'im out.

An' lissen to what de fool did, son! He ketched de 9:27 train from de Main Street Station in Richmond, de C & O dat comes down, you know. Well de first stop de train makes is at Williams-burg. Do you know dat coon gets off de train in Williamsburg an' forges 'nother check! Yessuh, he sure did. Den he come flyin' on home. Everybody see 'im on de streets a-yellin'—"Hello Henry! Did you make yo' grades in de state college?" He call back, "Yeh boy, I made good grades. I'se goin' home now an' eat dinner wid de ole 'oman." Henry walked on up Grant Street to 'is house an' met de cops at 'is door. Foun' 'is pockets full o' forged money fer 'is money-lovin' wife an' taken 'im right on back to jail dat same day. Didn' even git to eat any dinner. Got 'im back to de penitentiary dat same night. Poor fool's bed at de pen didn' even git time to cool off. He's still up dere. I don't know who got 'is bonus.

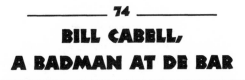

74

BILL CABELL,
A BADMAN AT DE BAR

William Johnson, interviewed by Jesse R. Williams
in Lynchburg, no date given

Yes, I know ole Bill Cabell. He uster be tough as pig iron an' didn't keer 'bout nobody or nothin'. Funny thing 'bout him though is he always played bad but got a lotta bad breaks. He's been shot, cut, and beat every which way. He could work, though. Sho' 'nough tobacco man. He uster work fo' de Zullan Company here [in Lynchburg], and then in bright tobacco season he uster go as far [as] Winston-Salem and down in Georgia.

I recollect one time, one Sadday night down on Twelfth Street, sompun' happened to Bill that he'll git hot [about] now if you mention it to him. In them days Twelfth was one o' the streets where niggers uster crawl lak flies on spiled meat, 'specially on Sadday night. You see, they was a saloon down there 'bout where Grace Street runs in. That place uster stay full of niggers an' po' white men from all over town an' everywhere. Some bad ducks uster hang 'round there too.

Well, Bill was a big six-footer and always wore a big broad brim black hat. And you know he's got a roaring voice—you know 'im, don't you? He had a lotta little niggers, an' white folks too, bluffed, an' mi' near all of 'em was scared o' Bill. Pretty near every night he was up an' down Ninth and Twelfth Street raisin' hell.

This night I'm talking 'bout Bill walks in, walks in de saloon an' a lotta boys was standing at de bar drinking an' talking. I was setting over at a table eatin'. Bill walks in 'bout haf drunk an' says, "Well, I'se here. Who don't lak it?" Most of de boys jes' laffed.

Den Bill walks over to de rail where a fella was jes' oderin' a drink. When de bar man poured it, Bill picks up de glass an' throws his head back lak dis an' drinks de po' boy's likker at one tilt an' hollered, "Who don't lak it?" Ain't nobody said nothin' fo' most of 'em scared o' Bill.

Well, I seed 'im do two or three mo' lak dat. But dere was a strange fella in dere dat had bought a drink an' jes' leave it set dere on de counter in front of 'im all de time an' wouldn't drink his. At las' Bill spied 'im an' said, "Hey dere stranger, looks lak you don't lak dis company. Where you come from, nohow?" The fella ain't said nothing yet. An' 'is glass o' likker was still settin' dere. He was jes' a little fella, didn't weigh an ounce better'n 145 pounds. But he don' say nothin' to Bill. Jes' looks at 'im an' smokes 'is cig'rette. Den everything got quiet lak. Everybody watch Bill an' dis nigger. Jes' knowed Bill gonna mop de flo' wid 'im if he said anything.

So Bill walks ovah to whar de nigger was standin', picks up de glass an' starts to throw it up to 'is mouth an' drink it jes' lak he did de others. But jes' as Bill got his head back 'bout lak dis, dat nigger caught 'im right here, jes' under 'is throat an' chin wid his fist.

Well sir, Bill was fallin' ten minutes an' landed on de flo' flat on his back, gaggin' an' slobberin' at de mouth. I thought de nigger had killed 'im. But dat little fella jes' looked at Bill an ordered another drink.

After de fellas worked wid Bill a while, he come to, rubbed his head an' face a little, and jumped up from dere a[nd] flew outta dat saloon. We couldn't find Bill nowhere an' didn't nobody see Bill on Twelfth Street fo' three or four weeks after dat. After dat when de boys would see Bill dey would say, "Bill, yo' want a drink?" An' Bill would say, "Go to Hell!" Right now if you want to make 'im mad, jes' say, "Bill, yo' want a drink?"

Well I didn't see it but Alec Turner told me 'bout it. Bill an' two of his buddies was went to Winston-Salem to work at the openin' of the [to]bacco season. None of 'em knowed nobody down dere in No'th Carolina. So Alec said after de first day dey worked, Bill, him and de other buddy washed up, eat, an' went down de street to a joint eatin' place whar a lotta niggers hung out. All three of them walked by the place to the next corner to whar dey saw some gals and started talkin' to them. After the gals left, Alec said Bill said to him an' his buddy, "I gotta let dese No'th Ca'lina niggers know who I am. See dat joint up dere? Well you all go in dere an' order some pie. About five or ten minutes from now, I'm comin' in. When I comes in, you all start eatin' yo' pie an' I'll walk over to you, throw de pie on the flo', an' play hard. I'll put the fear o' God in dese niggers' hearts an' we won't have no trouble wid 'em long as we stay here. I been tole dere's some bad niggers down here ev'ry year."

Dey done lak Bill said. So he comes in de place an' takes Alec's pie an' throws it on de flo' and brushes the other boy's off de table, plate an' all. Then Bill hollers, "Who don't lak it?" Alec said he noticed two niggers settin' ovah at a table sorta nudgin' one another an' 'bout dat time de woman running the place come out fussin' an' tellin' Bill ef he didn't leave her place she gonna call de man. So then Bill gits bad sho' 'nuff. He walks ovah to a table in the corner an' reaches fo' a man's plate. But jes' 'bout time he reached good, [a bottle] come voongin' through the air an' landed Bill on the head. Well sir, dat bottle knocked Bill cold. They drug him out in de street and poured water on 'im, an' at las' Bill come to runnin'. Alec said he ain't never seen a man run so fas' in all his bo'n days.

Alec said when him an' his buddy got back to dere boa'ding place Bill had two heads and was packed up ready to leave dat town. Nothin' they said could 'courage him to stay. So Bill left sometime dat night an' come on back to Lynchburg. Alec said the fella dat hit Bill wid dat bottle was called "Road Man Sam" an' dat he had been ev'rywhere working wid gangs on grades an' in de mines an' didn't never say nothin' much to nobody.

———— 75 ————

JUDGE
JOHN CRUTCHFIELD:
"JUSTICE JOHN"

An unknown informant, interviewed by an unknown worker
in Richmond, no date given

Ole Judge John Crutchfield was a magistrate of Richmond for more than forty years. He was alternatively damned and praised by Negroes who appeared before him for justice. Judge Crutchfield was very much more sympathetic to Negroes in trouble than to those who chanced to plead their cases. One morning a Negro wearing a long frock coat and black bow tie was brought in charged with the theft of a watch. "What you got to say, nigger, before I send you away?" asked Judge Crutchfield. The old colored man spread wide the tails of his coat and got on his knees. "Thanking your honor, I'd jus' like to have a few words of prayer." The judge dismissed him.

"Justice John," a very small man, "endured," it is said, a single Negro lawyer in Richmond during the first two decades of the century. The fortunate man was Giles B. Jackson, also of small stature, whose native wit and facile tongue talked many Richmond Negroes out of Judge Crutchfield's court. Giles B. Jackson appeared before Judge Crutchfield one day in defense of a Negro charged with stealing a hound from a white man. "Judge," Giles is said to have declared, in the vernacular he customarily adopted when talking to white men, "you knows dat a yaller dog will follow a nigger anywhere. My client ain't stole him. Dat dog jus' followed him home." [*An edited copy adds:* "Case dismissed," growled the Judge.]

Another of Jackson's clients, a woman, was charged with smacking a Negro woman. Before Jackson could plead her case she won it herself. Standing before Judge Crutchfield, she declared—"Dat woman tole me dat if I smack her she was gwine take me 'fo' dat ole gray-haired, no toothed devil down at police cote. An' judge, I jus' couldn't hear nobody call you no such names as dat, so I smacked her, good an' hard." "Get out of here," bawled Judge Crutchfield.

"Justice John" was commonly thought to have a secret understanding with the Negro preachers of Richmond, and he frequently turned over erring church members to their pastors' care instead of jailing them. Favored of his Negro associates was the Reverend John Jasper, of "the Sun Do Move" fame [a sermon Jasper preached throughout the state to great acclaim at the turn of the century]. One case appearing before "Justice John" hinged on the exact date of Jasper's death. Before Judge Crutchfield could speak, a police sergeant called out—"the twenty-ninth day of March, 1901." "How do you know?" asked the judge. "Because three bad things happened that day; Rev. Jasper died, the Jefferson Hotel burned down, and I was sworn in on the police force." "Yes," retorted Crutchfield tartly, "three of the worst things that could happen to the city."

A favorite stop of tourists in Richmond was "Justice John's" court. He could spot a Yankee at a glance, legend says, and woe be it to Negroes coming before him when curious northerners sat in his court. But he always gave them a show for their interest. One day when the courtroom was packed with visitors Jesse Green appeared before Crutchfield. Knowing how well the judge liked music, Green's lawyer asked him to sing "Sweet Adeline" for the court. Green started in beautifully, and soon Crutchfield joined in. But when Green finished "Justice John" sang one more bar to words of his own making: "Ten dol-lars fine!"

On another occasion Mack Forster, an eighty year old Negro, came before a crowded court charged with being drunk. "Mack, you're an old-time Virginia nigger, ain't you," asked the judge. "Yessir, dat I is," "Mack, wouldn't you like to go up north an' live with some of these good Yankees who are visiting us here today?" "No sir, Judge, befo' God, no sir." "Git out of here then, else that's jus' where I'll send you," roared "Justice John."

Sometimes Judge Crutchfield took the losing end of a duel of wits in good spirits. A methodist-baptist church quarrel came into court one day. Lawyer Pollard for the methodists was rather hard on the baptists. The judge interrupted his embittered plea, declaring that he wasn't going to have anything mean said about good old baptist niggers. "You see," he told the man, "I'm the daddy of that church." "Why your honor," spoke up the lawyer, "It's quite possible that you are the father of some of the members, but I hardly believe you are the father of the whole church." Judge Crutchfield slapped his sides with laughter and called to his court clerk—"He sure got me that time, didn't he, Edgar? Case dismissed."

And finally there is the story that is told about almost every court in the south. But Richmonders are all willing to swear on a stack of Bibles that it really happened in Judge Crutchfield's court. The accused was named Joshua. "Are you the same Joshua who made the sun move?" asked Judge Crutchfield. "No sir, I'se de Joshua who made de moonshine," came the reply.

———— 76 ————

HOW RAILROAD BILL
CHASED HIMSELF
TO HIS GIRL'S HOUSE

Bettie Stevens, interviewed by Bessie A. Scales
in Danville, on February 17, 1941

Railroad Bill has been a popular fellow among the Negroes living in the little cabins among the dark North Carolina pines for a long time. Everywhere, if you listen hard enough you can hear a whispering about him. White folks say his real name was not Railroad Bill, but black boys and girls who tell stories and sing songs about him have never known him by any other name.

He still lives, they say, in the North Carolina woods near the railroad. Sometimes when a poor old black woman opens her cabin door in the morning she finds a little pile of canned foods on her door-step. "God bless Railroad Bill," she says, as she hides away the cans, because she knows Railroad Bill has taken the cans of food, sacks of flour and sugar, and all kinds of things out of the freight cars to divide them with all the poor black folks he knows.

Nobody could ever catch up with him, but all the black folks know why. One time, as the sheriff and a large crowd of white men who were looking for him raced through a clearing in the woods, they saw a little black sheep standing there watching them run. Some of them don't believe to this day that the little black sheep was Railroad Bill. But it was.

Another time the sheriff and his men rode a train to a lonesome place where they thought he was hiding, but Bill was in the car behind them all the time. And when they got off the train and went looking for him, he just stayed on the train and collected up all the canned goods, which he gave away to all the poor folks all over the countryside that night.

Another time the sheriff and his men were looking for Bill in an dense wood. They spied a red fox run out of an old hollow tree, and fired twice. But neither of the shots hit the red fox. And when he ran away off to the top of a hill he looked back and laughed out loud at all this crowd of men trying to catch one poor little red fox who turned into a man right before their eyes, but he was too far off for them to do anything about it.

When that story got out it made the sheriff mighty mad and he swore he would catch him yet. That sheriff sent way off to Mississippi and rented some bloodhounds, saying he knew he would catch the varmint now. He found one of Railroad Bill's old shoes in the road, and when he gave the dogs the scent, they started right off following a track straight to a cabin where his girl lived on the other side of the mountain. When they got to the cabin of Bill's best girl the sheriff saw her on the porch. But she told him she hadn't seen Bill in a month. After searching all around he couldn't find Railroad Bill. All at once he asked, "Did I start with three dogs or four?" Nobody seemed to be able to remember, but now there were four dogs on the trail. And one of them was a black bloodhound.

The dogs seemed to want to go on and so the sheriff and his men followed them. But now the sheriff noticed there were only three bloodhounds on the trail. The black one was gone. The sheriff never really did know that the black dog was Railroad Bill, who had chased himself all the way out to his girlfriend's house and had just stayed when the sheriff and his men left. White folks say that the sheriff finally caught Railroad Bill, but the blacks folks who live in the cabins in the woods just laugh when they hear that. And they tune up their banjos and sing a song called Railroad Bill.

RAILROAD BILL

From Bettie Stevens, collected by Bessie A. Scales, February 14, 1941
box 29, song 1171C, WPA collection

Railroad Bill, mighty bad man,
Shot all the lights out de brakeman's hand,
Was lookin' for Railroad Bill.

Dat old sheriff had a special train,
When he got dere dere was a shower of rain,
Was lookin' for Railroad Bill.

The policemen all was dressed in blue,
Comin' down the street two by two,
Lookin' for Railroad Bill.

Everybody tol' 'em they better go back,
Policemen comin' down the railroad track,
A-lookin' for Railroad Bill.

Railroad Bill a mighty big spo't,
Shot all de buttons off de sheriff's coat,
Was lookin' for Railroad Bill.

RAILROAD BILL

From John Hooker, collected by Bessie A. Scales, January 1, 1941
box 29, song 1171A, WPA collection

Railroad Bill was a mighty bad man,
He shot all the lights out o' the brakeman's hand,
Now we all's lookin' fer Railroad Bill.

Railroad Bill was a mighty big sport,
He shot all the buttons off o' the sheriff's coat,
Now we all's lookin' fer Railroad Bill.

Railroad Bill was the worse old coon,
He killed McCarty by the light o' the moon,
Now we all's lookin' fer Railroad Bill.

───── 77 ─────

WILLIAM WYDEMAN:
PEACOCK AND
THE SOLDIERS

Stack Lee, interviewed by Claude W. Anderson
in Hampton, on May 23, 1939

Whar he git dat name "Peacock" I don' know. 'Is real name be William Wydeman. Come outen a large fambly. Got lots o' brothers an' sisters 'roun' heah. He wen' up to de Union Street School fer a while an' den he quit. Ain' try to go to college like de other boys. Jes' quit. Peacock warn' de type to like dat Normal School stuff dey teach 'cross de crick. Ret smart boy too, an' real nice lookin'. Allus min' 'is own business. Ole Peacock never bother anybody. He won' bother you lessen you rile 'im an' effen you rile 'im, den somepin's gonna happen quick, 'cause he jes' like dynamite goin' off. Yessuh!

W'en Peacock quit school, he start a-wukin' down dere at Ol' P'int in one o' dem crab factories. *Long's*, I think hit was. Dat were not so long 'go; musta bin 'roun' nineteen thirty one er two. He jes' a youn' feller den, 'cause w'en he die heah las' winter, he warn' but twenty-fo'. But lemme tell you one thing, son. Was he strong? My lawd! He one o' de strongest younguns I seen fer to be 'is size. He warn' much larger den you is w'en he died. But he were strong as a bull ox.

Anyway, as I was sayin', Peacock be a-wukin' fer de *Long's Crab Factory* when a one o' dem bad early sto'ms come rushin' up heah one night. Sto'med all night. De nex' mornin' de waves done wash thousan's and thousan's o' daid crabs up ret on de shore o' Buckroe Beach. De crab comp'ny heahs 'bout hit an' dey sen's Peacock down to gadder dese crabs. So Peacock wen' on down to de white folks' beach fer to gadder dese crabs. Wen' down in a oyster boat 'roun' Ol' P'int. He warn' botherin' nobody, an' he warn' sayin' nuttin' to nobody. But, son, you know hit seem like dese white folks in dis day jes' won' leave nigguhs 'lone. Peacock was busy pickin' up crabs w'en three white men come a-steppin' up. Dey was sojers f'om de Fort Monroe, an' felt ret 'sponsible fer everythin', I guess. One o' 'em say, "Hey you, darky. What in de hell is you doin' down heah pickin' up crabs? Whatcha gonna do wid daid crabs anyhow?" Peacock ain' sayed nuttin' yit. Den dey gits to badgerin' 'im an' he got riled.

Now, I dunno how he done hit. De papers ain' say how an' ain' none o' de nigguhs seed it. But Peacock jumped dem officers an' taken a gun 'way f'om one o' 'em an' had 'em all drillin' up an' down de beach. Dey say he was jes' yellin' "Yes, by Gawd, now you'll do as I say! March! One, two, three, fo'! Turn ret! One, two, three, fo'!" Nigguh jes' a yellin' an' dem white sojers a-drillin' fer all dey's wu'th. One o' dem sojers ax some o' de onlookers— Lawd yes! Dey's plenty o' white folks lookin', but dey's all 'fraid to mess wid dat bad nigger. Ain' he already taken de soldier's guns! As I was sayin', one o' de sojers 'quested dat somebody call de law. And dey did. Called de law in Hampun [Hampton] an' tol' 'em fer to hurry down to Buckroe Beach, 'cause dey's a nigguh done run crazy down dere an' was drillin' white sojers wid de sojers' own guns turned on 'em. De law jumped in de fastes' car dey had an' rushed on down quick as dey could, but 'fore dat car git dere, one o' dem sojers ain' turned as quick as Peacock want 'im to turn an' Peacock done shot 'im ret in de laig.

Well, w'en de law 'rived, dey done broke up de party, 'cause, while Peacock ain' 'fraid o' all de sojers an' guns in de whole fort, he kinda 'fraid o' de Hampun polices. Atter Peacock done give de white mens dere guns back, de law 'rest 'im an' carry 'im on up to de cou'thouse jail. Den dey had a big trial about hit. De crab company stood ret up fer Peacock, 'cause dey done sent 'im down dere to git dem crabs. If he jes' ain' shot dat sojer, he git off clean. But he already shot 'im, so dey give 'im one year in de pen. He ain' hardly serve six months, dough, 'fore de company got 'im out an' put 'im back at wuk ag'in.

Well, dat kinda spile [spoil] Peacock, an' atter a while he lose 'is job. Den he git real hongry. He ain' got no money an' he ain' got no place to sleep. So he start bootleggin' an' runnin' wid bad mens and wimmens. Dere was an ole no 'count woman 'roun' heah by de name o' Gladys what runned wid six mens 'sides her common law husban'. Peacock taken up wid her. Den he start goin' down. De law raid a house an' fin' liquor what 'sposen to be his. Mos' nigh ketched 'im, too. Law breakin' de front do' and Peacock jes' breakin' out de side winder. Close shave! Dey look an' look fer Peacock, an' him jes' a-hidin'.

Den one day dey fin' 'im. But dey ain' foun' 'im like dey want 'im. Heah de way de 'terpretations run terday. Gladys return to her home one night an' w'en she wen' upstairs she foun' de room done bin on fire, but de fire was out. Everything in de room done bin burned up, but de fire ain' burned de house down. Peacock, he was layin' in de mid o' de flo' like he done roll offen de bed. Peacock was daid. He were half burned an' layin' in a pool o' blood an' holdin' a open knife a-stickin' out o' one o' 'is hands. All de clo'es an' everything burnable in de room was burned. Gladys call de law. Dat w'en de law nex' saw Peacock.

'Cose dey had de 'quest. Dey ain' make much over hit, dough, 'cause de law was already lookin' fer Peacock w'en dey foun' 'im. De co'ner say Peacock was drunk. But he ain' 'hale [inhaled] 'nough o' dem flames to kill 'imse'f, an' dat hit look mighty funny. Gladys tell de law she ain' even know Peacock was anywhar 'roun' 'till she come an' seed 'im layin' in de flo'. Everybody knowed she was lyin'. All de other mens an' wimmens what stayed in de house ain't knowed nuttin' 'bout hit either. 'Twere a rhythm house [a private house being used as a juke joint], you know. So de law kinda wink dere eyes an' write down dat Peacock done died o' accident'ly suffocatin' in a fire.

Everybody knows, dough, dat Gladys done had some o' her men kill Peacock fer somepin'. An' everybody still axes' why Peacock was a-layin' in a pool o' blood an' whar de knife come f'om, an' why, effen everything in de room burn up, jes' why ain' de house burn down. House ain' no more dan a two story frame house, an' nobody ain' 'spose to hab put de fire out. Fires jes' don' go out dat easy wid out somebody doin' somepin' to 'em. Whoever kill 'im got off 'cause dey done it slick, Nossuh!

Den, atter de funeral w'en dey's easin' Peacock in de groun', dat hussy Gladys seed 'nother 'oman standin' by her 'longside de grave a-cryin' an' she snap out, "What in de hell is you cryin' fer?" De 'oman snap ret back, "By Gawd, he was jes' as much my nigguh as he ever was yo's!"

I 'spec' you done seen Peacock an' ain' knowed 'im. He was 'roun' heah las' year. Jes' was buried in thurty-six.

LEGENDARY PEOPLE
(FROM THE
ANGLO-AMERICAN
FILES)

The stories in this section depict people of admirable character and high deeds. The undercurrent of frustration, rebellion, and failure common in the black material is rare in these Anglo-American legends of exemplary individuals. Only Doc Taylor, the "Red Fox of the Cumberlands," shows a dark side, and as a kind of Daniel Boone gone wrong, even he provides a model of approved behavior by negative example. He was fearless, strong, cunning, a great man of the woods, and seemingly even possessed of supernatural powers; but when he chose a path outside the law, these heroic attributes could not save him from hanging. Like the two given here (legends 86 and 87), many of the Doc Taylor stories also involve Riley Mullins, the man he killed. Taylor comes across as the better of the two in courage, integrity, and wilderness skills; but, the stories conclude, not even such as man as Doc Taylor is above justice. The Doc Taylor legends, which always bring up his execution no matter what good things they tell about him, are not unlike the "criminal's farewell" songs of the broadside ballad tradition; they describe a man whose life went wrong, show how he lived to regret it and confess his crimes, and offer him as a clear moral example at the close. The WPA collection has two other such repenting criminals, Talt (Talton) Hall and Clifton Branham, although Doc Taylor seems to have been the best known and most widely discussed of the three.[1]

Such criminals, however, are in the minority in these legends; the stories more often take a positive approach. They also usually take an anecdotal one. Rather than giving the entire life story of their noteworthy individual, they center on specific incidents and events to demonstrate the behaviors and character traits they applaud. The story of "Daniel Boone's Tricks on Indians" (legend 78), for example, never mentions his frontier explorations or his major role in the settlement of the West. The listener would have to know who Boone was to understand that the tale is about a famous man. It offers an appreciation of wilderness skills, ingenuity, and grace under pressure, but it does not put the man himself on a pedestal. By placing Boone in the role of tobacco farmer, father, and neighbor, the story narrows the gap between the legendary man and ordinary people. Thus, besides giving practical advice on how to act in critical pioneer emergencies, it implies that anyone could, and should, be able to manage in such dire circumstances.

The legend about Thomas Jefferson also focuses on a particular incident to make a specific point, in this case an ethical one. One of the towering figures of history, Thomas Jefferson's name alone invokes the idea of greatness, which is basically all the story needs from him. The same incident has been attributed to other Virginians, such as Washington and Robert E. Lee, so any great man will suffice. The moral is straightforward: in a society with rigid racial and class stratification, one must be mindful of the dignity and humanity of those at the bottom. The story's teller believed this was its point and also believed that it worked and had a definite social effect on ordinary people. Willard Freeman told project worker James M. Hylton that the legend was "the reason so many old people in the Kentucky mountains would always try to be polite to the colored man instead of slighting him as lots of people do."[2]

Johnny Appleseed's admirable traits are that he was kind, thoughtful, religious, and dedicated to his mission of covering the country with beautiful blossoming fruit trees. If his whole life story is told, it is compressed, essentially to his one great significant deed. The message of his legend is not that his particular task should be taken up but that his general disposition and dedication are a model for a well-lived life. But Johnny Appleseed is not only a moral example. Although those hearing Nancy Wooding tell the story would probably not have recognized it, he is also symbolic. He is a civilizing hero of the cultural/religious variety, an American saint. The version of the tale given here resembles stories of medieval saints. Johnny's spirituality and the peaceful reaction he received from animals and Indians alike suggest Saint Francis of Assisi's ability to commune with nature, and his arrival by boat to civilize a wild country harks back to Saint Patrick's conversion of Ireland. As Saint Patrick Christianized that country and drove out its snakes (symbolic of wildness and evil), so Johnny Appleseed spread "the news fresh from heaven" and replaced the American wilderness flora with domesticated food-bearing trees (symbolic of civilization and good). Beneath Johnny's mild manners and love of animals is the pattern of the saintly missionary bringing religion and civilization to the wilderness.

Daniel Boone, Thomas Jefferson, and Johnny Appleseed are famous names. Stories about them have been collected around the state, region, and country. They represent one of the two types of legendary figures in the WPA collection stories. Ira Roberts, Gowl James, Molly Mulhollun, Booker Mullins, and Major Mike Wallace represent the other. These are names of local people whose fame was based only on specific personality traits or on some specialty, such as catching rats or fighting bears. These stories also celebrate character traits and behavior valued by their tellers, such as physical strength, gumption, courage, initiative, and fair play. As a comparison of the three strongman legends reveals, these virtues were valued across socioeconomic levels. Booker Mullins, or at least his brother, insists on the same decency and fair play as any gentleman of Major Mike's station would, and with a bear no less! The story of Molly Mulhollun, the only female legendary figure in the collection, upholds these same "manly" values and also makes the point that men do not have the corner on them. In effect, the story takes the teller's society to task for allowing only the men to display them. I should point out that this legend was submitted by a VWP worker from her own recollection, so we cannot assume that the story had wide circulation in oral tradition.

The curious story of Gowl James adds skill at one's work and the worth of honest labor to the list of approved traits and values. The fact that his work is so bizarre and distasteful only highlights the moral of the story, that whatever one does is worth doing well. That it pits a wealthy politician against Gowl, the workingman, also gives the story a somewhat democratic slant.

NOTES

1. Box 5, folder 4, items 722, 723, WPA collection. Talt Hall had the distinction of being the first criminal to be hanged in Wise County.
2. Circumstances of interview sheet, box 5, folder 1, item 545, ibid.

DANIEL BOONE'S
TRICKS ON INDIANS

Joe Hubbard, interviewed by James M. Hylton
in Esserville, Wise County, on October 12, 1940

Daniel Boone and a Stuart fellow that lived by him each had two girls a piece. Boone had taught his girls to keep a ball of red yarn handy so that if the Indians carried them off they could leave bits of yarn for him to track them by. One day the Indians carried off Boone's girls and the two Stuart girls too. They went to hunt for them and Boone tracked them by the bits of red yarn and found all four of them, and seven Indians that stole them. They killed the seven Indians and took the girls back home.

One time Daniel Boone was re-hanging some tobacco in his barnloft and was busy with the tobacco and wasn't watching out for the Indians. Four Indians come up on him and took him unawares. They had their guns on him and said, "We've got you now!" He stood looking at them, and all the time he was crumblin up tobacco leaves in his hands. All at once he throwed the crumbled tobacco in their eyes. And while they's getting it out he run off.

One time Boone's out splittin' rails and five Indians come up on him and throwed their guns on him. He told them he'd go with them, but first he had some deer meat on cooking and wanted them to eat some first. He had a log partly split open—gluts [wedges] drove in it. He told them to take hold and help him pull the log open and they'd eat and then he'd go with them. The Indians put their fingers down in the split place to pull the log open, and then Boone knocked the gluts out and the log closed back on their fingers and held them so tight they couldn't get them out. He took his axe and cut all five's brains out.

————— 79 —————

IRA ROBERTS,
THE STRONGMAN

George Hill, interviewed by James Taylor Adams
in Norton, Wise County, on August 19, 1940

I've seen a lot of stout people in my time, but I b'lieve that Ira Roberts was the stoutest man I ever seed in my life. I know he was when he was in his prime. One time they had a big fencing at the Beaver Dam farm and they was a lot of people there. Some cutting logs, some splitting rails, and others a-puttin' up the fence. I forget just now who it was a-carrying the rails up the hill besides me and Ral Roberts, little Ral, your wife's brother Ral. We was a-packin' them right straight up a steep hill about a hundred yards and Ira, he was your wife's own uncle, you know, and went west after that, well, he was a-splittin' the rails at the foot of the hill. Me an' Ral got to grumbling about how heavy the rails was to pack all the way up that steep hill.

Uncle Ira said, "Humph! I can carry a quarter of airy [any] cut here!" We laughed at him, for the rail cuts he was splitting was making an average of a hundred rails to the cut. "Don't you believe it?" he asked us. We told him no, and we didn't believe there was a man alive who could carry a quarter of one of them cuts up that hill. We even didn't believe him nor anybody else could shoulder a quarter of a cut, let alone carry it.

He just reached down and picked up one end of the biggest quarter there was there and shouldered [it] as easy as I would a rail. He sort of shook himself and told somebody who was standing there to set Ral up on one end and me on the other. Now we weighed about one hundred and sixty apiece then. They done that and I'll swear that he walked right up the hill with all that load and got someone to help us off and laid down the load and never took a long breath.

Another time they was a-puttin' a bridge up at the Starns' Place where the iron bridge is now. They had two big stringers to put across; they'd got the end of one down in the creek and the team, with all the help the men could give it, couldn't pull it out. Uncle Ira had been to Gladeville and was a-coming back. He rode up and set there on his horse a few minutes and watched them. "Why don't some of you get down there and lift that log out of there?" he asked the crowd. Everybody laughed. They told him that every man there and the team couldn't pull that log out. He slid off his horse, pulled off his shirt and breeches and shoes and socks, and waded down in the creek. He got his shoulder under the log and the veins begin to bulge out on his neck and the muscles to stand out on his shoulders as big as my fist. Then the log begin to move sort of slow and he just crawled right on up the bank with it. Then he just sort of laughed, put his clothes on, and got on his horse and clicked to him and rode on up the river.

I never seed such a man in all my life. I hear Uncle Ira died not long ago out in Taney County, Missouri. He sure was a man in his day.

_____ 80 _____

MOLLY MULHOLLUN, THE CABIN BUILDER

Mary E. W. Smith, from her own recollection
in an unknown location in Alleghany County, no date given

When Virginia was being settled land from the King of England was granted through the governor to those who transported future citizens to the colony. It sometimes happened that there would be among the passengers one or more who would serve in the household of the person who brought them from foreign shores. There was, in what is now Allegheny County, one such personage by the name of Molly Mulhollun. She was brought to Staunton and became a servant in the home of a Mr. Bell.

Benjamin Borden was the possessor of a large tract of land. He was very ambitious in regard to the encouragement of settlements along the James River, the Cowpasture, and the Jackson River. As an incentive, he made known far and near that for every cabin built he would give the builder a plot of ground. This happened during the closing year of Molly Mulhollun's indenture [and], Molly being possessed of the adventurous spirit, [she] was very impressed with the Borden proposition. The desire of owning a home with surrounding land made her determined to enter the arena of cabin building.

Upon the end of her servitude in the Bell home she trekked out from Staunton to the site of the city of Covington. Undaunted, she donned the wearing apparel of men over her own clothing, and, equipped with tools, she began viewing the surroundings. Molly lost no time in starting work on her future abode. In due time the first cabin was built. The builder was known as John Mulhollun in her new role. Time passed, [and] with it there came into existence thirty cabins on the site of what has developed into an outstanding manufacturing town in Allegheny County.

When Borden arrived on the place where he supposed one cabin had been built, he was astounded to see houses for a small sized settlement, all built by one "man." These he was viewing [were] something unthought of. He admitted he had not made any bargain with anyone by the name of John Mulhollun.

People became suspicious as to the reality of the person who had built the thirty cabins. It happened that Molly Mulhollun visited Staunton wearing her adopted attire of leather shirt, pants, and moccasins. She was recognized by people who had known her when she served in the home of Mr. Bell. She, finally, was prevailed upon to acknowledge her identity. She afterward discarded the masculine garb and appeared among her old acquaintances as Molly Mulhollun who [had] paid her transportation [to America] by working in the capacity of a servant.

————— 81 —————

MAJOR MIKE WALLACE

G. B. Wallace, interviewed by John T. Goolrick
in Ellerslie, Stafford County, on February 8, 1939

Major Michael Wallace, of the American Revolutionary Army, was an enormous man, more than six feet six inches tall, broad and powerful. He was a brother of General Gustavus B. Wallace, and after he had fought through the war with distinction, he and the general, bachelors, returned to live at "Ellerslie," the family home, where their father and mother were still living.

"Major Mike" became a tradition, a legendary figure in the current annals of Stafford—a gigantic, immensely strong, good-natured but fearsome figure. No man, after a short time, dared to engage him in an altercation. His vast deep voice was so potent that, it is said, standing on the porch of Ellerslie, he could call a servant two miles away. When angered he roared like a wild bull and, when going through the woods, he sang to himself, the song echoed over the countryside.

In those days men met in physical contact on court days, or at assemblages, in a mere spirit of bravado; and Major Mike had not been long from the war when he was the admitted conqueror of all the Staffordians. One day there came to the Port of Falmouth a ship from England, commanded by a brawny, old-faced, flaming Irishman whose very heart's joy was a fight. Having about the taverns found one or two brawls in the taverns that ended, for him, in easy victories, he found no more of the hardy rough and terrible fighters of the day willing to fight him, and abandoned hope of further fray. Then someone thought of Major Michael Wallace, and, while the Irish fighter waited eagerly, a horseman rode to Ellerslie. Major Mike had no grudge against the sea captain, but, ever ready for any encounter, he readily ordered his horse saddled and rode to Falmouth. In the center of the street that is now U. S. Highway 1, a ring was formed. The Irish sea captain and Major Mike agreed to fight to the finish, no rules. [They] divested themselves of their coats, and the fray began.

The first blow from the fist of Major Mike killed the Irishman.

Somewhat sobered, Major Mike now refrained from battles—there was no one to fight him anyway—and continued his pursuits at Ellerslie. It was his custom, save in very cold weather, to sleep upon the bare floor. And there he always lay down when he wanted to rest. He was lying thus one day when a parson from somewhere "up the country" rode by and stopped. He was going, he said, to the home some ten miles away on the King's Highway, of the Widow Wishart, widow of the well-known Parson Wishart. He had been chosen, he said, as one of those to settle the late Parson's Wishart's estate, which was quite valuable. He recited that the widow was possessed of about 6000 acres of land, a very fine brick house with many out buildings and stables, fine carriages and riding horses, many cattle and sheep and oxen, and some sixty slaves. The giant Major Mike had arisen from his couch on the floor by now and asked the traveling stranger "And when are you going?" "I shall accept your hospitality tonight and remain here," answered the guest, "I ride at sunup tomorrow." "And I ride with you," declared Major Mike, "and I'll marry the widow!" which is exactly what he did. From that union came a large branch of the Wallace family in Virginia, all of them big, powerful men.

——— 82 ———

BOOKER MULLINS, THE BEAR FIGHTER

Boyd J. Bolling, interviewed by James Taylor Adams
in Flat Gap, Wise County, on March 11, 1942

Guess you've heard about old Booker Mullins. He was said to be the greatest bear hunter and fist and skull fighter that was ever in this part of the country. I've heard my father talk about him. Said that one time him and his brother were out bear hunting and they run up on a big bear. Booker told his brother to hold the dogs and let him fight the bear with his bare hands. Agreed. He lit into the bear, which seemed willing for the match. They had around and around and at last the bear got Booker in hits hug and was about to squeeze him to death. He hollered to his brother, "Turn the dogs loose!" "Not do sich a thing!" his brother said, "I'm not goin' to show foul play in a fight." And he didn't; but Booker finally killed the bear. Booker called him[self] the champion fighter, and I guess he was.

One time he was traveling through Kentucky and passed where they were raising a house. He boasted around some, and after he went on one of the fellows said "Jis' wait 'till he comes back by and I'll beat the devil out of him." Well that evenin' Booker come back by, and this fellow picked a fuss with him. They went into it. And Booker whipped him and three others who run in and took hit up for him.

83

THOMAS JEFFERSON'S MANNERS

Willard Freeman, interviewed by James M. Hylton
in Wise, Wise County, on January 9, 1942

I don't know where it started, but over in Kentucky there's a tale that is as old as the hills that Thomas Jefferson with one of his friends was in a town one day near Washington while he was President and met an old colored an' weather-beaten slave, who bowed nearly to his knees to the President and made a nice gesture to him. The President in turn bowed to him and spoke most kindly to him and drew him into conversation and on turning to leave him he wished him well. But at the same time he saw that the officer who was with him was not liking the idea of his talking to the old negro so kindly. "Shame on you, my man, I would not want to admit to the fact that an old and aged slave who is colored have more manners than I." With this the other turned away in much shame as President Jefferson added, "By all means the negro was more polite to me than you could be at any time."

———— 84 ————

JOHNNY APPLESEED

Mrs. Nancy C. Wooding, interviewed by Bessie A. Scales
in Danville, on March 4, 1941

Many many years ago a little sail-boat came sailing in from the ocean and landed on a shore that was afterwards named Virginia. In this boat came a queer, blue-eyed man with long hair hanging to his shoulders, barefooted and wearing ragged clothes. The first people he saw were the Indians, who treated him kindly, dressed him in clothes made of skins, and helped him on his way. His friends were the animals he met and one day he was seen playing with three bear cubs, while their mother looked on greatly pleased.

On his back he carried a big sack of apple-seed, brought from nobody knew where, and everywhere he went he planted apple-seed. For ten long years he journeyed far into the mountains planting his appleseed everywhere 'till they all gave out. Then he started back in the way he had come. Apple trees had sprung up everywhere, hundred of acres were a-bloom, and the people were all rejoicing at the sight of the beautiful apple blossoms, soon to turn to fruit, and they were all talking about the strange man who had brought them such beauty and such luscious fruit—they called him Johnny Appleseed.

Everywhere Johnny Appleseed was welcomed by the grateful people. When he sat down at table with them he would not eat until he was sure that there was plenty of food for the children. After he had eaten he would stretch himself out on the floor, take out the Bible he always carried in his sack, and read aloud what he called "news fresh from heaven." His voice was loud as the roar of the wind and waves, then soft and soothing as the balmy air.

One day he walked along for twenty miles to reach the home of a friend. He sat down on the doorstep to eat his evening meal of bread and milk. Then he read aloud from his Bible for a while. Then he went to sleep stretched out on the floor, and he did not wake up.

And all the folks bless Johnny Appleseed, for they know that when spring comes to the land there will be many acres of pink and white apple blossoms.

85

GOWL JAMES, THE HUMAN RATTER

Mrs. William Tolliver, interviewed by James M. Hylton
in Norton, Wise County, on May 5, 1942

Over in Edmonson County, Kentucky there lives a man by the name of Gowl James, a middle-aged man who makes his living killing rats. So the story goes and I'm sure its true. The funny thing about it is that he uses no gun or no poison, nothing but his bare hands, that's all. He mashes them to death with them big hands of his, yes sir. When anybody has a barn or a hog pen or a corn crib to be cleared out for rats they usually send for Gowl too. They all know his reputation as a rat killer, an' know he's good too. He charges as a price on them, a nickel each, or five cents. That sounds small but when he has got started you soon learn that they's more rats around your place than you ever would a dreamt of, though. Something sure about it he gets 'em all when he gets started too. Sometimes he fools the farmer who hires him, an' they see where they wasn't so smart in hirin' him after all. It runs into money when he gets started on a big barn or farmhouse of some kind.

A congressman who is from Brownsville hired him not long ago and told him to go ahead and clear up the rats on his place, which was a big barn on the Honorable B. M. Vincent's place up the way a piece. And the first thing you know he had killed three hundred rats in no time at all. The honorable congressman thought he was makin' too much money and thought that anybody else could do as well cheaper, and told him to stop. He thought he could kill them hisself by just grabbin' them an' squeezin' them to death. He run his hand in a hole an' tried to pull out one like Gowl James did an' the big rat in the hole bit the end of his finger almost off. Then he decided to let James finish the job, an' he did. In the end he had killed 432 big rats, 132 more'n he'd killed when Vincent had stopped him. So he showed by that that he knowed his business, I guess.

The way he says he does it is he locates the holes in a barn or place an' the next thing is to get all the rats into these holes. An' he moves everything around and makes a lot of noise doin' it. An' sometimes when they scamper out from hidin' he grabs two or three at a time an' gets them before they get to the holes. He is quick as a cat in a way, with his big hands. But the big kill comes when they get into their own holes in the ground. If they's a water hose he uses it; if not he carries big buckets of water an' pours into the holes where the rats have gone in and waits at the outlets or the other end of the holes. He knows which is which an' never gets bawled up any. He grabs them as they come out an' squeezes out their breath. When he reaches into a hole they never bite him for he says he knows how to get hold of them before they have a chance to bite his fingers. As a rule, when the hole has no long outlet or way out, he just reaches in an' the dead rats are there an' he just pulls out dead rats.

No matter where he goes he likes to clear the rats out. Even if he isn't hired to do it, he'll get all of them before he leaves the place. He is just eager to see to it that they all get caught an' killed. Gowl had a neighbor that didn't like him but had a lot of rats he wanted to get rid of, but wouldn't ask him; an' James knowed it an' slipped in an' got them all with him not knowin' it. An' he never did know he'd slipped in when he was gone an' killed off all his rats. People call him James the Ratter there.

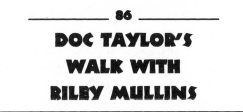

86

DOC TAYLOR'S WALK WITH RILEY MULLINS

White Coon Hubbard, interviewed by James M. Hylton
in Wise, Wise County, on April 17, 1941

Shore, I knew Riley Mullins, an' I know he was a mean'un too. I saw him get his hand called time after time, though. But he was mean as the devil hisself though anyway. He tole me a tale one time 'bout runnin' 'cross Doc Taylor, the Red Fox of the Mountains, you know, that you've heard an' read so much 'bout when ever'thing was wild as hell in this neck of the woods. Well he said he was walkin' 'long one day in the road that run through the Pound Gap where he later kilt Ira Mullins an' some of his family an' that they wasn't anybody [with]in a mile of him that he knowed uv, an' ever'thing was quiet-like, when all uv a sudden who should be walkin' by his side but old Doc Taylor, the Red Fox of the Cumberlands, an' who made history in this country when he did at last go wrong.

Well Doc had heerd 'bout some big talk that Riley had had 'bout not bein' feared uv any man [other] than the devil hisself, an' Riley knowed what was comin', I guess. Well, anyway old Doc jest went right on in the road 'side of him an' never said one word to him, but by that time Riley said he was gettin' scared as the devil an' if he was goin' to be kilt he wished it was soon over with an' done. "Well, sir," said Uncle Riley, "he never did speak to me, but jest kind of looked kind uv mean at me, an' I thought my en' had come shore. But the next thing I knowed he was all gone, jest like he appeared, an' nowhere to be seen. But as I went on in the road an' decided to take a chew uv 'backer an' rech [reached] in my pocket to get my 'star navy' I found a little piece of a candy poke, an' on it was the words, in all kinds of fancy writin'—'Watch out

Uncle Riley or the Devil will get you when you mess with the Fox.'"

An' so he was so all-fired scared he said that "I jest took out runnin' down the road 'till I got to where Jenkins is now to a man's house by the name of Poindexter who lived at the foot of the mountain an' stayed there 'till I was shore Doc Taylor was good an' far from that neck of the woods."

But Riley got over his scare an' was braggin' 'bout what he had said to Doc on this walk as he was talkin' with a friend later. An' what do you think, old Doc stepped out of the woods right in front of him; an' he like to a-tore the [w]hole woods down gettin' 'way from there. But old Doc had raised his big .390, about the only one in this country, an' cut loose at his [Riley's] feet an' cut down the bushes all 'roun' him as he run. But he got 'way.

But after that Uncle Riley never talked too much 'bout him, an' on the day he was hung in Gladeville, here now Wise, Uncle Riley was there to see it was well done an' helped guard the jail where he was, an' was the best pleased man in the whole crowd of hundreds when it was all over. After that he changed his tale an' swore by the Almighty that he had made Doc Taylor run and cut brush, but it was really the other way, I know.

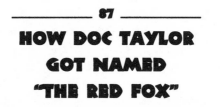

87

HOW DOC TAYLOR
GOT NAMED
"THE RED FOX"

Jefferson ("Jeff") Mullins, interviewed by James M. Hylton
in Payne Gap, Wise County, on April 17, 1941

This wuz 'bout thuh time Arch Hopkins kilt bad Ed Hall from a upstairs winder over at Donkey where Pound is, you know. Henderson Mullins wuz a brother to Ira Mullins thet thuh "Fox" later kilt in his wagon thar in thuh gap an' hung fer in Wise here.

Him [Henderson] run 'round lots with Campbell Carter an' thuh Fox, you know an' they's a bad three I'm here tuh tell you too.

They'uz many a man wanted tuh kill ole Doc Taylor, or thuh Fox, an' thuh ole feller wuz slick as glass, an' when they'd foller him in thuh hills they'd be goin' one way lookin' fer him on his trail an' he'd be goin' in t'uther d'rection all the time though. He'd wear moccasins made outten groun' hog hide an' he'd lace 'em up so's he could wear them uther way, an' hit'd look like he'uz goin' in thuh opposite d'rection than he'uz sure 'nuff goin', you see.

They'uz alluz tryin' tuh git a pot-shot at 'im, but they'd foller 'im fer days some times an' then find out he'd been in thuh tuther end uh thuh county all thuh time. He'd fooled 'em by his tracks bein' made back[w]ards. He'uz so slick an' so sly an' smart thet way thet one time Ira Mullins an' Campbell Carter wuz tryin' tuh pot-shot 'im an' failed an' ole Ira said, "He's slick as a red fox." An' from thet day 'till his hangin' he went by thet name too.

He shore wuz slick an' I'se with 'im 'nuff to know an' laid out in thuh hills with 'im many a bad night an' listened to 'im talk an' tell how he'd fooled many a man. It'uz awful funny how hit all came about too, fer he later kilt ole Ira, thuh man thet named him thet, his wife, a feller Chapell from North Carolina, an' a Wilson too, an' some more. An' they hung 'im later fer it in Wise here, an' I wuz thar too. (He pointed towards town and the spot where Taylor was hanged.) He got his name from thuh man thet he hung fer killin'. But they'd all knew not to try an' foller in his ol' moccasin tracks later on, as hit'uz too dangerous tuh try. A feller wasn't apt tuh git back from sech a trip as thet an' they all knowed hit too.

It'uz funny I guess, but one side uh thuh Fox's face wuz sorta [w]rinkled an' he had some kind uh scar tuh thuh right, but thuh other side wuz clean as uh pin, an' when shaved hit looked purty good. But iffen you knowed 'im you'd notice thuh wrinkled side fust off hand.

MURDER
AND
VIOLENCE

When one sarcastic southerner was asked why the murder rate was so high in his region, he said he reckoned that there were "just more folks in the South that need killing."[1] Whether this wisecrack is true or not, data support the stereotype behind it. The South is statistically the most violent region of the country. In 1988 the murder rate per 100,000 people in New England was 3.24, in the Pacific Northwest it was 3.21, but in the South it was 12.47.[2] This regional difference in the level of violence is not new. Between 1930 and 1950 Louisiana, which had the lowest crime rate of the eleven former Confederate states, still had 74 percent more violent crime than the national average.[3]

Historically, the South has been a particularly violent region ever since colonial times. With settlement motivated by economic rather than religious incentives, the southern colonies started out wilder than their Puritan, Baptist, and Quaker counterparts to the north. Laws against mayhem, the willful maiming or crippling of a person, had to be enacted as early as 1748 in the Virginia colony, although these did little to diminish the common fighting practices of eye extracting, ear ripping, and nose biting in the southern colonies and on the frontier.[4] As Mark Twain so graphically depicted in *The Adventures of Huckleberry Finn*, violence continued as a basic element of southern culture into the nineteenth century. Huck encountered greater cruelty and violence in direct proportion to his descent into the South. At the Grangerford plantation he saw the finery, culture, and romance of the southern plantation system. But finally the brutal violence of its dark underside overwhelmed him, and by the time his young friend Buck was killed in a skirmish of the Grangerford-Shepherdson feud, he was too sickened to continue describing it. Farther down the river he saw a man shot down in the street over an insult, and later the same day he witnessed the ultimate symbol of southern violence, a lynch mob.

The most often cited reasons for southern violence are its colonial and frontier survivals, slavery and its need to keep blacks subdued and fearful, the inherited British traditions of dueling and the cult of honor, the bloody legacy of the Civil War, Reconstruction, and the South's subsequent position of shame as an economic dependent of the industrial North. Some historians have argued that there is a sense of defeat, grievance, and guilt at the heart of the southern identity which the rest of America does not share.[5] Defeated and overrun so often—by Indians, Yankees, carpetbaggers, abolitionists, and later union organizers and civil rights workers—southerners feel guilt from the fact that the invading outsiders have been morally right and superior to the defenders, which exacerbates the violent streak in their regional character.

That there is some basis for this kind of cultural psychologizing can be seen in what Willard Thorpe has called "the psychopathology of lynching." Sociologists have shown distinct correlations between economic slumps in the South and increased numbers of lynchings, which also increased significantly immediately following both world wars, "when the white population was made angry and apprehensive by the self-reliance and self-assertiveness of the returning Negro veterans."[6]

But even though it is real and statistically verifiable, the violence of southern culture should not be equated with the traditional stories about violence and murder that circulate within that culture. Just as we recognize that contemporary American movies and television reflect a deeply violent society, we also recognize that these media exaggerate and emphasize it. No matter what neighborhood we live in, it is extremely unlikely that we will hear as many actual gunshots on any given evening as we hear nightly on TV. So the question underlying both our modern popular culture and the Virginia folk legends in this section is this: Why are we drawn to depictions and stories of murder and violence that we would abhor in reality?

The answer is both psychological and moral. To understand the psychological dimension, we need only look at the last line of "Killing an Unwanted Infant" (legend 90). We are shocked by this graphic rendering of the thing we fear most—uncontained, gratuitous, cruel violence. It is all the more horrible because its victim is a helpless baby. In hearing this story and contemplating this deed, we face the unpleasant reality of human depravity head-on. Like the film *The Texas Chainsaw Massacre*, which, according to folklorist Harold Schechter, is modeled after a German folktale,[7] legends of violence and murder dredge up and consciously project our most deeply suppressed psychological fears, emotions, and violent impulses. But if our unconscious urges draw us to these narratives, our moral imaginations generally take over to give them acceptable social messages. Most of the legends in this section do come around to some moral point, and most eventually mete out justice, repaying their villains eye for eye and tooth for tooth. In "A Murder Belief Solves a Crime" (legend 93), for instance, the cruel murderer is himself slowly and cruelly executed; and the narrator of "A Strange Light at a Murder Site" (legend 88) says, "I believe the murderers died on account of the crime they done." When there is no moral point, as in "The Murderous Tavern Keepers," "Killing an Unwanted Infant," or "A Strange Funeral" (legends 89, 90, 94), the story may be less satisfying, but its visceral impact is actually increased. In these cases we are left to grapple with the stark reality of evil that the legends with straight moral messages conveniently resolve for us.

NOTES

1. Sheldon Hackney, "Southern Violence," *American Historical Review* 74 (1969): 908.

2. *Statistical Abstract of the United States, 1990* (Washington, D.C.: U.S. Department of Commerce), p. 171.

3. Lyle Shannon, "The Spacial Distribution of Criminal Offenses by States," *Journal of Criminal Law and Criminology* 45 (1954): 264–73.

4. Elliott J. Gorn, "Gouge and Bite, Pull Hair and Scratch: The Social Significance of Fighting in the Southern Back Country," *American Historical Review* 90 (1985): 18–32.

5. Three historians who have explored this issue are Wilbur J. Cash, *The Mind of the South* (rpt. New York: Vintage, 1969), C. Vann Woodward, *The Burden of Southern History*, rev. ed. (Baton Rouge: Louisiana State Univ. Press, 1968), and Sheldon Hackney in "Southern Violence," pp. 906–19.

6. Willard Thorpe, *A Southern Reader* (New York: Knopf, 1955), pp. 404–5.

7. Harold Schechter, *The Bosom Serpent: Folklore and Popular Art* (Iowa City: Univ. of Iowa Press, 1988), pp. 36–48.

88

A STRANGE
LIGHT AT A
MURDER SITE

Mr. Bryant, interviewed by John W. Garrett
in an unknown location in Buckingham County, no date given

Bill and Tom Stuart had returned home from Texas where they
had worked as cowboys, and it was the general belief of the
people that the Stuart boys had plenty of money. They lived in a
little log cabin near Buckingham courthouse and one night
Dal[l]as Wright and three Negroes, Richard Perkins, Ed Jones,
and Eliot Johnson went to the Stuart home and Bill was shot with
a shot gun as the gun was put through a crack between the logs,
while he was in bed.

His brother Tom was sleeping in the room upstairs and when
he heard the sound of the gun, he came downstairs. And the four
men grabbed him and forced him to tell where their money was
hid. And under a loose brick in the hearth was fifty dollars, and
then they cut Tom's head off with an axe. His brother Bill drew
himself up in the bed groaning, and the men found some kerosene
oil and poured it on the floor and set the house on fire, and they
thought the crime was well-concealed.

When the neighbors saw the house on fire, Dallas Wright said,
"I've said many a time that chimney would burn that house sometime." But it wasn't long before the murderers were arrested and
brought to trial by the deputy sheriff, Eddy Carter. The murderers were convicted, but an appeal was granted, as Dallas Wright's

people had a little money to fight the case. And when the trial was on again, the [deputy] sheriff was on his way home from court—he lived near Sper's Mountain—and he was murdered and left laying in the road near his home.

And at the place where his body was found there come a light which appears every night. I've seen it many a time; the deputy sheriff was killed fifty years ago, but that [light] appears every night over a place about the size of a grave, an' it will shine until one gets close to the spot, and then go out. Then after one passes on the light will appear ag'in.

The murderers were cleared and set free, but two of the Negroes soon died with the T.B., and the other one went to West Virginia to work in a mine, and the mine caught fire someway, and he was burned alive. Dallas Wright may be still living somewhere. I believe the murderers died on account of the crime they done. But that light on the place where Eddie Carter was killed is a great mystery, and I've seen it many a time. It's been a few years since I've been there, but they tell me it still appears every night.

———— 89 ————

THE MURDEROUS
TAVERN KEEPERS

Mrs. Minnie Collins, interviewed by James Taylor Adams
in Glamorgan, Wise County, on September 30, 1941

This is a true tale. I've heard Ples an' Berry Collins both tell it. Hit happened to them. Said they'uz goin' to Tennessee or Kaintucky one time to visit their people. I've forgot where hit'uz, Tennessee or Kaintucky, but [I] b'lieve hit was Tennessee. They put up one night to stay all night, an' they put 'em both in one bed to sleep. The place they stopped was a sort of country tavern. Place where people had [a] habit of puttin' up to stay all night when they'uz travelin' through that country.

Ples said that they didn't like the actions of the man an' woman, that they got off an' whispered an' cauckused an' cauckused. An' then the man, he went off, an' the woman set up before the far-place.

They said they laid there an' wouldn't go to sleep, an' from where they laid they could see the woman settin' thar. An' ever' time anything moved outside she'd git up an' go to the door an' listen.

At last Berry said to Ples "Reach over an' git your gun out o' yo' britches pocket an' hol' hit in your han' ready to shoot, fer we're goin' to have trouble here." Then they agreed to let on like they'uz asleep an' begin snorin'.

Wudn't long tell they heard somebody walkin' an' the woman got up an' went to the door. An' they heard her an' a man whis-perin'. Heard him say "Are you shore they are soun' asleep?" She said, "Yes, they are snorin' like hogs." Then he come in, an' he had two pole axes in his han'. He give one to her an' they heard him say, "Now be shore you don't make a mislick, an' when I say 'now,' hit, an' hit to kill."

She nodded her head an' they started easin' across the floor torge the bed. They let 'em git right up close to the bed, but not in strikin' distance, when Ples Collins raired up in the bed with his pistol in his han' an' said "Drop 'em axes or I'll shoot you both in two!" They throwed down the axes an' run out of the house. The Collins's got up an' put on their clothes an' hit out away from thar. They never seed either one of 'em ag'in.

—————— 90 ——————

KILLING AN
UNWANTED INFANT

Mrs. Martha Shupe, interviewed by Emory L. Hamilton
in Esserville, Wise County, on November 23, 1940

I've heard another tale about a family trying to kill a little child. I heard Tom Evans tell it and I believe I heard mother talk about it too. There was a certain family that had a child they didn't want. I don't remember if it was their child or a grandchild, but anyway they wanted to get rid of it. One night they took it to the stable and put it in with the horses. They thought sure they'd tramp it to death that night. But they didn't. They said the horses would step over it. Well, they saw that wasn't going to work and they put it in the hog pen for the hogs to eat. Next morning they got up and the hogs hadn't touched it. They got it and went to the house and the old man heated a red hot poker and stuck [it] up its rectum and killed it.

—————— 91 ——————

SCARING THE WIDOW

Rev. John A. Robbins, interviewed by James Taylor Adams
in Big Laurel, Wise County, on August 30, 1941

One time two men went into a new county and took up lan' right side by side. Great big boundaries. Went on an' one of the men died. His widow an' children decided to jes stay on an' make the best of it.

The other feller got to thinkin' that he'd like to have both places. He tried to buy the widow out by offering some little sum for her place. She wouldn't sell. So he planned out how he'd make her sell.

He'd killed an owl an' that gave him an idea. He took the owl's claws an' went up close [to] her house one night an' squealed like a panther. The woman heard it an' told her children she'd heard a panther. The screamin' come right on up closer an' closer. She barred up the doors. There was a big tree stood by the house. After while they heard something climbing the tree, then "ker-thump" hit struck the roof an' began clawin' an' scratchin' with them owl claws, jes like it was goin' to tear the boards off. The woman grabbed her husband's old rifle gun an' stuck it up through the loft an' fired. She heard somethin' goin' rollin' an' tumblin' an' strike the ground in the yard. She'uz afraid to open the door. But next mornin' she opened the door an' there laid her neighbor, dead an' stiff.

——— 92 ———

THE ROBINETT
DEATH HOLE

John Elkins, Jr., interviewed by James M. Hylton
in Jonesville, Wise County, on September 3, 1941

The Robinetts and the Elys all had a grudge since I can recollect, an' I know they had lots of trouble back in the days when things wuz just so-so in this country. Well, they's a big water hole up next to the Ely farm not but several hundred yards from Main Street here, an' all the folks tuck their cattle an' horses there to git water. They fell out 'bout it some way or 'nother an' one said the water was his an' the other said it wuz his an' I reckon as that's the way the feud started. Anyway, anybody you talk to can tell you all 'bout it, as it lasted until a few years ago. Anyway, back in the early part of the century Bill Ely and Job Robinett, the two leaders of the two families, met there one day and fit it out, fist and skull. They found them both beat up so bad that neither one got over it, an' both died later.

Later, two of their boys met there an' a Robinett killed a Ely an' it started all over ag'in. It had the boys an' girls fightin' in school an' on the ways home. Everywhere a Robinett met a Ely hell wuz sure to pop. But in later years for a while everybody had sort of forgotten about it all, until a Robinett woman, Aunt Liza, by name, dreamed one night 'bout her boy Hugh Robinett an' told him the next mornin' not to be 'bout the [watering] place no more as she dreamed he would be found dead there.

Well, Hugh wuz strong-headed like all other young fellers an' just laughed it off for the time bein'. Anyway, the boys got to drinkin' 'round the ole water hole, an' on Sunday they'd go there too. One mornin' a feller called by Aunt Lou's an' asked fer Hugh, as he wanted some work done. But when they went to his room, he wasn't there. They figured he'd just up an' stayed with a friend. Anyway, 'bout noon a woman found him layin' with his head in the water at the hole. An' after a 'xamination they couldn't find a single mark or anything on him. They tried to pin it on a Ely, but couldn't git proof.

That wuz twenty years ago, an' soon it went forgotten. Then one mornin' a woman got a note to go to the hole an' she'd find something. An' as she got to it she found Rob Ely layin' just as they had found the Robinett boy, Hugh, layin', with his head just in the water. No marks wuz to be found, an' try as they might, they couldn't pin it on anyone attal. No more has ever been found there as to yet, but they expect it any time. I don't know what it wuz all about myself.

MURDER AND VIOLENCE

————— 93 —————

A MURDER BELIEF
SOLVES A CRIME

Mrs. Polly Johnson, interviewed by James M. Hylton
in Wise, Wise County, on November 21, 1941

About a hundred years ago two men slipped up behind a wider
women an' kilt her while she was nursing a young baby child.
The way it all happened, my dad, or Pa, as we called him, tole me
years ago over in Johnson County, Kaintucky. He said a feller by
the name of De Lapp, a big feller, an' a feller named McCullin, a
little runt uv a man, got together in uh bad way tuh start with.
That they met one time when thuh big feller was hidin' uh bidy
[body] under uh bridge. An' thuh little man started tuh run an'
thuh big feller knowed he'd tell, but he got hold uh him an' made
him tell him he'd never tell it to a soul. Well thuh big feller bullied
thuh runt around all thuh time an' made him do as he tole him
tuh do.

One time at a place not far from Pa's house these same two
robbed uh feller later an' kilt him an' wuz hidin' his bidy unner
uh little wood bridge when uh woman comin' down thuh road
seed 'em. They caught her an' started tuh do her in too, but she
begged an' prayed tuh them thet her children wuz home with nuthin' tuh eat an' she'd been tuh beg some meal for tuh make some
hoe-cakes for them, which wuz thuh truth. She'd been left uh
wider an' uh little child'd been born since then. She had several
other little ones besides at home too. Thuh little runt [McCullin]
sided with her an' so long thuh big feller give in an' let her go.
Thuh fact wuz thuh woman had had uh awful hard time rearin'
her little ones since her husband had died, an' all the folks wuz
glad tuh do what they could tuh help her. An' when she ran outta
food they'd give her somethin' ever' time she'd go ask fer it. An'
she'd been to borry meal as she'd said this day she saw the two
hide uh dead bidy unner thuh little wooden bridge she had tuh
cross.

Well, she went on home an' wuz thankful an' glad she'd got away from the two. She made them the hoe-cakes an' they all eat, an' fer thuh time wuz fairly contented. That night early she put them tuh bed an' went tuh bed herself as usual with thuh little baby thet wuz nursin' from her breast. She went to sleep this way an' all thuh house wuz still. But thuh two men never forgot her, an' they laid plans an' wuz ready thet night to do her harm as if she'd tell on them an' they'd git caught in their killin'. They went tuh thuh house an' slipped up outside in thuh cold deep snow an' thuh big one made thuh little feller put the barrel uh his gun through uh chimney pit an' shoot. He never wanted tuh do it, but thuh big De Lapp feller put uh pistol tuh his head an' swore an' bedamned he'd blow his head off iffen he didn't do it. So thuh little feller closed his eyes an' shot an' they slipped off in thuh dark.

Well, uh neighbor, three days later, noticed no smoke comin' from thuh chimney an' thought they might need wood or coal an' went tuh see if they needed help when they found thuh dead woman shot through thuh back so's thuh bullet went through her heart an' had kilt her dead. Then officers wuz called an' a inves- tigation started an' thuh tracks in the snow found. They found thet thuh little children had got up in thuh two mornin's as ever an' played about thuh house an' then went back tuh bed at night thinkin' their mother was sick or asleep. Thuh little baby had stayed in thuh bed an' when thuh woman found them thuh little baby wuz still nursing thuh breasts uh thuh dead mother. Some- how they got it tuh uh hospital, as such wuz in them days, an' iffen it hadn't been real cold weather, it'd died from pisen [poison] shore. Well thuh kids had played about thuh room an' all thuh time blood run down from thuh bed an' they'd tramped through it an' their little tracks wuz all over thuh house.

The sheriff wuz a awful good man an' knowed he wuz stumped. So he called in uh hired detective tuh help him an' it wasn't long 'till they'd simmered thuh suspects down tuh about eight feller[s], an' De Lapp and McCullin wuz two uh them, too. Thuh bidy hadn't been moved yit, an' they got all these men in thuh house an' then thuh sheriff said, "They's uh sayin' thet iffen a man mur- ders, an' iffen he touches thuh person he murders, thuh blood will flow from thuh wounds. So I want yuh men tuh go one at a time an' put yore finger on thet bullet hole on her breast an' see what happens."

Well, six uh thuh men gladly went forward an' nuthin' happened. So thet left only thuh other two, McCullin and De Lapp. So they stood there but thuh sheriff uz not easy tuh fool, so he said tuh thuh little feller, "Go ahead McCullin." But thuh little runt drawed back from thuh bed an' put his hands over his eyes. He said he couldn't do it, an' then admitted tuh what him an' De Lapp had done. De Lapp started tuh run out, but they caught him 'fore he got through thuh door. They tuck them tuh thuh jail in town an' thuh detective went tuh work on 'em with questions.

Then McCullin tole how De Lapp had forced him intuh uh life uh bad crimes an' tole thuh whole story. De Lapp, though, wouldn't budge uh inch an' jest set thar an' cussed 'em all. Anyway they sentenced them both tuh be hung, an' in a short time they wuz all ready fer 'em too. Ever'bidy had been worked up over thuh killin' uh thuh good woman an' wuz ready tuh see thet jestice wuz done. In them days they stood 'em up in uh wagon an' placed uh rope 'round their necks an' then pulled thuh wagon away from 'em, an' I guess jest choked 'em tuh death.

Anyway, McCullin wuz hung first, as they thought De Lapp would break too, but he didn't. An' McCullin hung an' twisted uh few minutes an' then his people got him an' galloped off down thuh road with him. They say tuh this day he come to an' lived uh better life. But they done different with De Lapp. They let him hang uh few minutes an' then drove thuh wagon back in unner him an' let him rest uh while. An' so in uh few minutes they'd pull it out from unner him an' let him choke uh little more. For one hour they done this 'till finally he died by sufferin'. And ever'bidy thought he'd deserved it. Thet wuz one time ever'bidy said thet uh folk belief, or superstition, solved uh crime, with thuh help uf uh good, honest sheriff uh thuh mountains, an' uh honest detective too.

———— **94** ————

Jeff Mullins, interviewed by James M. Hylton
in Payne Gap, Wise County, August 2, 1941

I heard my Pap Geo[rge] Washington Mullins tell this years ago. An' in speakin' of funerals it beat all I've seed. He said a nigger assaulted a white woman at Making, Kentucky, not so far from here an' they's huntin' fer him soon atterds [afterwards]. It's been a long time ago, I don't recollect jist how long. A long time, anyway. He's a mean nigger an' ever'body knowed hit too an' was skeered of him too. When he done this to the Whittaker woman there they lost no time huntin' him down an' findin' him too. They found him holed up next day under a store porch an' snaked him outten there right fast lick [like].

They'se a bridge from the railroad to the other side of the old river there, or wus then. [There was] a swingin' bridge of some kind I think then. They tuck him there an' strung him up from the bridge, or the side of the bridge, I mean. They let him down 'till his feet an' legs hung jist into the water, an' it wuz swift an' sort o' swung him back an' forth, you know. When he's dead a feller got up on the bridge an' preached his funeral, in a funny sort of way, I guess, but hits the way they done fellers like him back in them days, I guess.

He held a big 45 colt in his hand an' as he talked he would swing the 45 'roun' an' 'roun' in his hands. "Gentlemen," he said, "we 'un are all here fer a solem[n] occashun an' hits my duty to see that jestice is done. Fred Rankin (that was the nigger's name) is dead here an' by his own acts on this here earth. He is below us here today an' I pint to him now." He pointed down to him swingin' from the rope with his feet in the water.

"As I now preach this here funell [funeral], 'cause nobidy else'd do hit. An' as I say 'Ashes to ashes, an' dust to dust,' I mean it!" An' with that he shot a volley of shots in the top of the nigger's head as he hung below him, atter he rech [reached] over the side of the bridge. An' he added as he pulled a barlow knife from out-ten his pockets, "I now commit yore body to the grave," an' with that he cut the rope an' th' nigger slid away on down the river.

Some time later they drug him outten the river at Whitesburg, the county seat of Letcher County, an' knowed who hit wuz. They poured ile [oil] on him an' set fire to him an' then dug a big hole an' pitched him in. They's most fifty people present when he wuz hung but you never could git anybidy to say anythin' then, you know. Nothin' wuz ever done, though, 'bout hit attal. Niggers, though, wuz sca[r]ce atter thet in Whitesburg an' most of Letcher County. (Letcher County jines Wise County, you know.) I've heerd others tell 'bout hit too. Pap wuz a stock dealer an' wuz buyin' stock sech as cows an' horses there then when hit hap-pened, you know. I have heerd it mentioned several times since then in this part of the country too.

PLACE-NAMES

The subject matter of the place-name stories in the WPA collection is essentially the same as the section headings of this book—animals, Indians, violent crimes, treasure, legendary people, and unusual and supernatural events. In fact, the frequency with which these subjects come up in explanations of place-names and features of the landscape reinforces the proposition that they are the core topics of Virginia folk legends in general. Place-name stories also generally serve the same purposes as other kinds of legends. They support the attitudes and morals of their group, express its anxieties, give advice, and recognize and sometimes resolve social and personal ambiguities. "How Dragon Run Got Its Name" (legend 95), for example, is a clear moral lesson about keeping the Sabbath day holy. And "How Bloody Branch Got Its Name" (legend 96) is a reminder that crime doesn't pay, even though "nobody could ever pin anything" on the murderers in question. The tale insists that "murder will out" and shows how nature itself may step in when human justice fails.

The opening of the Bloody Branch story also shows how learning the place-name stories of a locality is essential to getting to know the place. Mrs. Ortha Moore set her story during the time she was just getting acquainted with her new neighborhood. When she asked an old-timer about the red color of the creek running by her house, she was told a story which explained its color and its name. But it also explained the wild old days of Big Stone Gap, when drinking, lawlessness, and sudden violence were common. And more than that, it demonstrated that those days were gone, that the neighborhood was not that way anymore, that the group disapproved of such behavior, and that they taught the story to schoolchildren to ensure that its values were passed on. The color of the creek is reminiscent of the biblical "rainbow sign," a promise that the bad old days and ways will never return.

In this story an alternative reason for the redness of Bloody Branch is mentioned. But it is refuted, which in effect strengthens the argument for Mrs. Moore's more exotic and mysterious explanation. As one place-name scholar has noted, "To a person using a name it makes no difference what the name really means."¹ In other words, a name's connection to a story which is meaningful to the group that lives with it is its reality, no matter what the historical records say. Two historical sources indicate, for instance, that Dragon Run was so named because the stream, a small tributary of the Piankatank River, looks like a dragon on maps, although one notes that you need a vivid imagination to see the resemblance.² But the people who lived around Dragon Creek saw more than that. Their imagination saw a chance to turn a suggestive place-name into a strong warning against ignoring religious obligations and taboos.

Place-name legends often grow around the sites of great tragedies or crimes. "How Haddix's Branch Got Its Name" (legend 98) and "How the Bull Run Mountains Got Named" (legend 99) are two examples. Place-name legends share this tendency with ghost stories; in fact, the two often merge. In the Champion Swamp tale (legend 97), for instance, the place is named for an event which also explains the ghostly presence that haunts the site.

Thus Champion Swamp, little more than a highway culvert across a stretch of marsh, gains a name and a story. Notice how the opening juxtaposes travelers speeding by in their cars with the local folks who know the "real story" that makes this small and insignificant place a little larger and more significant. A particular purpose of place-name stories is revealed here; they are locality ego-builders. The legend scholar Américo Paredes has put it this way: "Legends are ego-supporting devices. They may appeal to the group or to individuals by affording them pride, dignity, and self-esteem: local or national heroes to identify with, for example, or place name legends giving an aura of importance to some familiar and undistinguished feature of the local landscape."³ This aura of importance is doubled when the place-name refers to a feature of the landscape and to a national hero as well. Hence, "How Mother Leather Coat Mountain Was Named" (legend 100) reminded its audience in Haymarket, Prince William County, that the peak they saw every day was named by no less a figure than George Washington and that this great individual had a definite connection to their little town. The name "Mother Leather Coat" even carries Freudian overtones connecting the "father" of the country with this local "mother," in the tradition of the "Washington slept here" signs displayed by so many proud localities.

There are forty-eight entries for place-names in the WPA collection, but this number does not reflect the actual count of individual items; one entry alone contains fifty-six place-names collected from five different informants.[4] Most of the multiple-item entries are just lists of names followed by short descriptions, such as "The Pound, a corn pounding mill. People would say 'I'm going to *the* pound to grind up my corn,'" or "Snow Creek, snow stays on the banks here longer than [at] other spots. It was an ice house source," or "Crow's Mill, mill owned by John Crow. He kept and would ride around on a pet bear." But some include fully developed stories. Curiously, more of both the short-entry descriptions and the developed stories refer to natural features on the landscape than to man-made ones. There are numerous descriptions and stories about the names of creeks, caves, mountains, rock outcroppings, swamps, and springs, but only a few about towns, estates, and roads. The origins of the names Hickory Gap and Sontag (which was named for a burlesque dancer) are the only town name explanations that amount to fully developed narratives. I don't know if Johnny Gilliam's Hickory Gap "Church" is still around, by the way, but as of 1974 the town of Hickory Gap was still in the state municipality listings.[5]

The fact that only one place-name entry in the WPA collection comes from the African American material demonstrates that those in power do the naming of things. As its title indicates, "Why Chestnut Street Was So Called" focuses on a smaller unit than a town.[6] A street is more of a folk social unit than an official political one; it is small enough to be controlled, and therefore named, by the people who actually live on it. An entry from the white material notes that Liberty Street in Falmouth, Virginia, was named because it was "a street where slaves could go unmolested."[7]

The collection of place-name stories seems to have been stimulated by Benjamin Botkin's *Manual for Folklore Studies*, which specifically mentioned them along with local legends under the category of "Tales." The VWP workers got the manual in August

1938, and place-name legends started coming in to the Richmond office regularly after that date; only two had been submitted before. The workers may also have been stimulated by a notice that there were plans for a Virginia place-names book. The letter which announced the plan pointed out that "folklore can make a real contribution" and urged workers to "get all the versions of name origins, and any unusual stories connected with the names."[8]

NOTES

1. Ronald Baker, "The Role of Folk Legends in Place Name Research," *Journal of American Folklore* 85 (1972): 368.

2. Raus McDill Hanson, *Virginia Place Names, Derivations, Historical Uses* (Verona, Va.: McClure, 1969), p. 6, and James Hagemann, *The Heritage of Virginia: The Story of Place Names in the Old Dominion* (Norfolk: Donning, 1986), p. 72. Hagemann said that a vivid imagination is needed to see the dragon; he also noted that "many of the records of Middlesex County were hidden 'in the Dragon' during the Civil War to save them from Union soldiers who loved to burn valuable papers in county courthouses."

3. Américo Paredes, "Mexican Legendry and the Rise of the Mestizo: A Survey," in *American Folk Legend: A Symposium*, ed. Wayland D. Hand (Los Angeles: Univ. of California Press, 1971), p. 98.

4. Box 6, folder 2, item 846, WPA collection.

5. Thomas H. Biggs, *Geographic and Cultural Names in Virginia* (Charlottesville: Virginia Department of Mineral Resources, 1974), p. 47.

6. Box 1, folder 7, item 55, WPA collection.

7. Box 6, folder 1, item 830, ibid.

8. Box 14, the "instructions to workers" folder, ibid.

95

HOW DRAGON RUN
GOT ITS NAME

From an unknown informant, interviewed by Lucille B. Jayne
in Capahosic, Gloucester County, on December 10, 1938

The story of "Dragon Run" was told me this way, that one Sunday a man went out to fish in a stream in the upper part of Gloucester that was then called "Pinankatank Stream" that connected Gloucester and Middlesex at Glenns in Gloucester and Saluda in Middlesex, the center of the bridge being the dividing line.

Well, while the man was there very intent on his fishing, suddenly he heard a terrible roar. Looking up quickly he saw a short distance from him, coming at a rapid pace, the most horrible and gruesome looking creature imaginable, driving a chariot that roared like thunder and sent out flashes of light like lightning. He was so terrified that he sat spell-bound for a few seconds, for he knew that it was the "Dragon," or the devil, and he had come for him. He took up his oar and began paddling frantically and at last reach[ed] the shore and started running as fast as he could to his cabin. Finally he reached home and he told his wife that he was very sick and was going right to bed, which he did.

The story goes that in the morning they found him dead in his bed. And they said that they knew that the "Dragon" had gotten him. From that time to the present day, the stream has been known as the "Dragon Run." The old gentleman that told me this story said his mother, Mrs. Sarah Fary, told him that it had been handed down from one generation to another for over two hundred years.

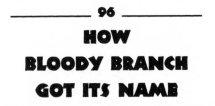

96

HOW
BLOODY BRANCH
GOT ITS NAME

Mrs. Ortha Samantha Moore, interviewed by James M. Hylton
in Big Stone Gap, Wise County, on September 24, 1941

I recollect Aunt Sue Phillips tellin' me this when I'd first moved into this house with my Pap an' we wuz gettin' 'quainted with thuh folks around 'bout. They's uh branch run down past thuh house, an' I recollect[ed] its red color when she wuz settin' there with us on thuh porch an' I ask her if she knowed what made it thet way. "I shore do," she said, as she smoked her old clay pipe, settin' there in thuh straight chere. "Dan Wampler used tuh be uh reg'lar roustabout 'round here, an' he'd alluz go into a patch uh laurel thar 'bove this place yuh see." An' she pointed from here on the porch an' showed us a patch 'way up on the hill. "He drunk a lot and [wasn't] no good fer any thing attal," said Aunt Sue. An' he done nuthin' but go git thuh cow fer 'iz dad, an' that'us all." I listened as she unwound thuh tale an' she never once quavered or stopped a time.

"He'd been drinkin' with some boys thet lived in this very house here, an' they'd fell out 'bout sumpin', an' they'uz settin' on this very porch hyer when they seed him go atter thuh cow, one day late in thuh evenin' lak. An' they went up thuh branch too. They come on back soon, though, later an' went to bed. Dan never showed up at home that night, though, an' next mornin' thuh ole man, er his pap yuh know, went lookin' fer thuh cow, thinkin' Dan'd got drunk with some uh thuh boys an' let thuh cow go hang. Well, when he rech [reached] thuh place whar thuh cow alluz hung 'round, he foun' Dan with'iz throat slit an' dead. He'd fell sorta down torrds [towards] thuh little branch an' his head wuz jest uh little above it, an' blood'd run in thuh branch. When they carried him down they could see blood in thuh little branch all along it too.

Well, nobody could ever pin anything on thuh boys, but they thought a lot, though. Nearly ever' time thuh boys wuz settin' out on this here porch, they c'd look out thar an' see red in thuh creek. An' they finally moved on thet 'count. They got scared, they did. Well, soon after we moved here my dad went up an' looked at the place, an' he says they's a place there in the laurel where poke berries grow, but they ain't close to thuh branch. Some folks, you know, said they'd fell in the branch an' caused it tuh turn red. But dad said no, said they's too far away to get in thuh water. Anyway, they call it the bloody branch, and all thuh people 'round here say it wuz to make thuh boys thet kilt him repent, er make them remember poor ole Dan Wampler they'd kilt. Thet tale's old as itself, an' every school child can tell you thuh whole story too, as they's alluz told it by their folks. An' I know most uh them believe it is Dan's blood comin' down to scare them fer their crime.

—————— 97 ——————

HOW
CHAMPION SWAMP
GOT ITS NAME

Mrs. John Cofer, John Underwood,
and William Wilson, interviewed by Grace Williams
in Smithfield, Isle of Wight County, on December 25, 1938

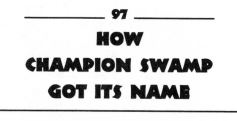n route 158 three miles from Smithfield there is a concrete culvert over what is known as "Champion Swamp." And many a traveler goes flashing by knowing nothing of the old legend from

whence it got its name. The story goes that early in the Eighteenth Century, two duelist[s], each claiming the title of champion, arranged to meet by this stream to prove, by actual test, their supremacy. At the appointed time, they arrived, each on horseback. They dismounted, took their stands, and drew their swords, beginning the conflict. Long and hard they fought until one fell, mortally wounded. The victor walked over to his fallen [sic] adversary, cut off his head, mounted his horse and rode away.

After this tragedy, the shadow of mystery hung about this place and finally strange rumors went the rounds. It was told that a lone night traveler, passing that way, saw two ghostly figures on horseback coming slowly through the shadows, one from one side of the branch, one from the other. They met at the swamp-run and sat silently side by side. One of the riders was headless. Others declared that they too had witnessed this weird meeting, and the old swamp became "Champion Swamp." Through the years this old story has passed on from one generation to another. Time has wrought many changes, but the air of mystery continues to surround this spot, and the story of the ghostly riders continues to be told.

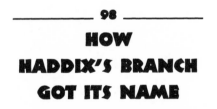

98

HOW HADDIX'S BRANCH GOT ITS NAME

Elbert J. Bond, interviewed by James Taylor Adams in Big Laurel, Wise County, on September 3, 1940

My father always said that how Haddix's Branch got its name was that way back yonder before anybody had ever settled in this country that a company of hunters come into this country to camp and hunt. They were camping somewhere about the beaver dams on Beaver Dam Fork of the Guesses River and hunting in the Black Mountain and the small streams of the Guesses River.

One of the hunters was a man named Haddix. One day him and the others had left camp and come up the little creek that's called Haddix's Branch. They had got up in the forks of the branch just above where Irvin Mullins lives now at the old Harrison Chizenhall place, and there they say they bounced a big bear. If I remember right my father said they had bounced the bear the day before and lost it and was back there to roust him out again. It seems Haddix had went on stand, that is, he had took a stand at the fork of the branch just below the Lewis Roberts graveyard above Mullins' house, and the others were out thrashing the brush to roust the bear.

All at once they heard Haddix's gun fire, and the next minute they heard him screaming for help. Then he hushed. They run to him as fast as they could and when they got there the bear had killed him. They said he had shot it and slightly wounded it, and you know a wounded bear is said to be the dangerousest animal on earth. It had rushed him, and him being in a laurel bed, he couldn't get away, and it had caught him. They said it had tore his guts out, and almost had his head eat off when they got there.

They killed the bear. And I have heard it said they dug a grave and buried Haddix right there. You see, it was probably a hundred miles to the nearest settlement then, fifty anyway. And ever since then, I rec[k]on, this branch has been called Haddix's Branch.

─────── 99 ───────

HOW THE
BULL RUN MOUNTAINS
GOT NAMED

Miss M. A. Ewell, interviewed by Susan R. Morton
in Haymarket, Prince William County, no date given

When the first settlers made their way along the Carolina Road which led from the Susquehannah to the Carolinas, the mountains to the west were of sinister repute. Wolves abounded, catamounts yowled in the night, and always there was the danger of brigands who hid there to waylay the travelers along the trail, to say nothing of the fierce Indians. So cattle that escaped from the droves along the road were often left behind rather than risk the dangers of a prolonged hunt for them on the mountainside. Thus it was a young bull breaking away from some settlers bringing their stock with them was left to roam at will. It grew to unusual proportions, and together with its great size, became so fierce that it was before long felt to be as great a menace to the peace of the community within a few miles of the mountain as the wild animals that roamed there at will. Hunters came home with tales of being chased by this ferocious beast, who seemed to have a great dislike for men. His body was massive and the footprints showed a cloven hoof that might have belonged to some animal that roamed the hills before the advent of man. His roar could be heard over a half a mile, yet, in spite of his size, which would have been supposed to make him ungainly, he was so swift that none had ever been able to [get] within shot of him. With the approach of winter he came near the dwellings of the settlers at the foot of the mountain, frightening women and children, several of whom had had a narrow escape; so it was finally decided to form a group of well-armed men and run the bull until captured, the one to fire the fatal shot to have the meat.

The news of the proposed chase was spread throughout the countryside, and it was a challenge to the men to show their courage and skill, as well as a promise of a good supply of meat. The day designated found a large sports-loving group assembled at the foot of the mountain where the trail could be easily followed. So[me] of the men went from a sense of duty to rid the section of a menace; others in the hope of adding to their frugal fare in the winter to come; and the younger men for the joy of such heroic sport. They started at sunrise, and it was not until after several hours of hard and futile riding that they came in sight of their quarry, who took them in mad pursuit over the rough trails, through heavy underbrush, showing remarkable speed for an animal of his size. Some of the horses became exhausted, some riders too, until finally as the autumn dusk became near there were but a very few left. However, the bull had slowed his pace, and

222

VIRGINIA FOLK LEGENDS

finally he turned in a small ravine and was about to charge when two almost simultaneous shots felled him.

This led to an argument as to who had fired the shot that reached his heart first. But it was finally settled to the apparent satisfaction [of both hunters], and the victor proceeded to claim the spoils. Finding the carcass more than he could handle, he promised a hundred weight to anybody who would stay and help him skin it and cut it up. This was accomplished, but darkness was upon them by then, so the helper left with a forequarter for himself, and a hindquarter strapped to the back of the victor's horse, which he was to lead back and get the man's son to come with a fresh horse as well as his to carry down the remainder of the meat. He built a fire to warm himself as well as keep prowling beasts away. He cooked himself bits of the meat while he waited with growing impatience for the returning rider. He was very exhausted from the day's work and excitement, and it was cold as the night drew on, so he wrapped himself in the hide of the bull and before long was in a sound sleep.

So sound in fact that he did not hear a rider approach. The rider, instead of his expected son, was the one that had helped with the skinning of the bull. He had merely taken it to his home, kept the other horse there, and returned with a fresh horse to get the rest of the meat, expecting that by a delay he would find the owner asleep. He proceeded to cut up the meat so that it could be tied to the horse. He worked hastily in the darkness so he could get away before the return of the owner, whom he thought had merely gone a short distance in search of help. To complete the job, he tied the tail of the bull to the horse and started off at a gallop to get out of sight as soon as possible. All at once he heard terrified screams and curses coming out of the hide, the sleeper being so rudely awakened and realizing that he, as well as the meat, was being stolen. [He] soon caught the culprit, a desperate fight ensuing. Searchers later found them both, too battered to make their way home, and an easy prey for wolves.

—————— 100 ——————
HOW
MOTHER LEATHER COAT
MOUNTAIN WAS NAMED

Susan R. Morton, from her own recollection
in Haymarket, Prince William County, on February 22, 1941

One of the peaks in the Bull Run Mountains to the west of Thoroughfare Gap is called "Mother Leather Coat." (This is proved by old records, indentures, etc.) Tradition says that it was given this name by George Washington who as a very young man surveyed there for his friend, Fairfax.

There was an old woman who lived on the southerly side of the mountain and who, both winter and summer, wore [a] leather apron and jacket. She offered food and lodging for any traveler who happened by, and it was at her cabin that youthful Washington sought hospitality during his sojourn in that section. She had a reputation for being a very fine cook, and in appreciation of her kindly ministrations to him and his party, he named that peak in her honor. Until a few years ago there were a few rotting logs of her cabin that could be seen among the thick undergrowth.

—— 101 ——

HICKORY GAP
AND THE
HICKORY GAP "CHURCH"

Lee Gilliam, interviewed by James M. Hylton
in Hickory Gap, Wise County, on February 3, 1941

About sixty-five years ago, Johnny Gilliam moved here from North Carolina and settled at what is now known as Hickory Gap. He homesteaded a good tract of land and cleared the place for a home site near the gap of the ridge that runs to the north. Hickory nuts were gathered and stored away in the loft along with other fruits for winter use. When he went to visit any of the older folks in the Hurricane section or at Wise, he would always refer to being from the Hickory Gap. Now there is a school house near the old place that accommodates all the children living in that part of the country. Good homes and farms dot the countryside and a good road leads from Hickory Gap to the nearby town of Wise. The farms and home[s] are owned and operated by widely known citizens and apples and berries are raised on a considerable scale. Wise furnishes a good market for the berries and one such farmer makes a good living selling berries and yellow root. The name Hickory Gap has held on and everyone in this section of the country knows it by that name. There is a comic legend told my [by] a gentleman of Wise about the Hickory Gap Church.

Charles Freeman, interviewed by James M. Hylton
in Wise, Wise County, February 4, 1941

A legend well known about Hickory Gap Church is well known by the residents of Wise who enjoy hearing Mr. Freeman tell it in his own way. It relates to membership in the Church and a hickory nut is given to all members and carried at all times. Membership was given to all newly weds who come in to obtain [a] marriage license while Mr. Freeman was working in the capacity of deputy clerk. A new hickory nut was given to the groom and he was told to carry it at all times and when he changes clothes the nut should be also moved and placed in the [new] pants pocket. He was told to pull a cord that operated the switch of the electric light over the counter [in the county clerk's office] and from which dangled a shiny new hickory nut. Thereupon he became a full-fledged member of the "Hickory Gap Church." When a member meets another member he at once presents his hickory nut. Much conversation usually follows and great enjoyment is experienced my [by] the two members before they depart. Some members have carried the nuts so long that they obtain a bright cherry-like hue after being constantly carried and handled.

SIMON KENTON

Susan R. Morton, the VWP worker who collected the Simon Kenton legends, knew she had uncovered something interesting when she found tales of this famous pioneer figure still in circulation in the 1930s. But she worried about their deviation from the written records of his life. Apparently disappointed that the local legends failed to echo the official facts, she wrote in her notes that they were inaccurate, imaginative stories "told for the sole purpose of entertainment." But fortunately she recorded them anyhow, noting that the people who told them believed they were telling the truth.

The "official facts" may be gleaned from such books as Charles McKnight's *Our Western Border* and Theodore Roosevelt's *The Winning of the West.*[1] Simon Kenton was born in 1755 in Fauquier County's Bull Run Mountains, the seventh son of an Irish couple from County Down who had come to Virginia in 1737 and built a cabin near Dumfries at a place called Devil's Bed. His brothers were industrious and successful; one helped George Washington survey Fauquier and Prince William counties, and another became wealthy in banking and land speculation. But Simon earned the reputation of being lazy and wild, excelling only in hunting and tracking. At sixteen he provoked a fight with a man named William Leachman who married the woman he wanted to wed. Thinking he had killed Leachman, Kenton left the area, assumed the name of Simon Butler, and joined a hunting expedition to the Ohio River near Fort Pitt. He met an Indian trader on that trip named David Duncan, who had been stolen as a child and raised by Indians; Duncan taught him the Shawnee language and told him about the rich hunting region the Indians called Kentucky.

While exploring the Kentucky territory, Kenton met and befriended both Daniel Boone and George Rogers Clark. In 1774 he served as a scout and dispatch runner in a military operation against the Shawnees, and after their defeat he claimed a tract of land near the present site of Maysville, Kentucky. In 1775 he joined the Boonesborough settlement, scouted the Indian country, and helped defeat two Shawnee attacks against that settlement. It was here that he saved Daniel Boone's life by shooting an Indian who was about to kill him with a tomahawk. He accompanied George Rogers Clark on an expedition to the Illinois territory and then returned to work as a scout for Boone's raids against Shawnee villages. During this time he was captured by the Shawnee and underwent his most famous ordeals. He was made to run the gauntlet eight times, almost having his arm severed; he was lashed to a wild horse which was then turned loose; he was tied to a stake to be burned three times, being rescued each time; and finally, he escaped and made his way to Detroit before returning to Louisville in 1779.

Between 1780 and 1782 he scouted for Clark and others in Kentucky and Ohio. When the American Revolutionary army disbanded, he recruited several Kentucky families to settle on the Maysville land he had claimed. When he learned that the man he thought he had killed was alive, he dropped his false name, returned to Virginia, and recruited his relatives and neighbors to his settlement in Kentucky. In 1794 he served in Mad Anthony Wayne's campaigns that closed the Indian wars in the Old Northwest. In 1798 he moved to Ohio and became a brigadier general in the militia there. He fought in the War of 1812 and later settled near Zanesville, Ohio, where he died in 1836.

Susan Morton's informants told her almost none of this. They focused on his early years in Virginia and viewed him almost exclusively from a local perspective. Their interest in Simon Kenton was directly proportional to his proximity to the Bull Run Mountains and Fauquier or Prince William counties. Their main topics were the circumstances of his birth, his leaving home, his disguised return, and his half-Indian descendants in the area. They also typically gave this extraordinary man an ordinary context. In the first two stories given here, for example, older female informants told how the hero's future fame was influenced by the folk beliefs and sympathetic magic of two elderly local women. The first, which is itself the talk of an old woman, self-reflexively attributes Kenton's greatness to "the talk of an old woman." While most of Kenton's feats of strength and endurance are typical of a heroic woodsman demigod, "Simon Kenton's Exploits" (legend 104) mentions his domestic abilities, too. In connecting his deeds among the Indians, bears, and wolves with his skill at breaking hominy, this narrative collapses the distance between the hero's world and that of normal local people, as does "Simon Kenton's

Growing Tree" (legend 103), which ties his western exploits to a local tree.

Ambivalence about Kenton is apparent in the stories. Several informants noted his low regard for work, although most of them hastened to show how his woodlore skills eventually compensated for his "lazy, ornery" traits. His identification with the Indians was a source of ambivalence, too. As early as the Boston Tea Party, American colonists had been pretending to be Indians, and as they attempted to deal with the frontier environment, they settled the Indian clearings and followed the Indian trails until the most successful adapters actually became like Indians themselves. Kenton was such a man, and the emphasis on his Indian ways, disguises, and family life shows how large this loomed in the narrators' minds. Winter Owen's tale describes how Kenton's courage and endurance won the Indians over, even though they remained savage and cruel to whites in general. The tale of his Indian wife grapples with his apparent defection to Indian culture, too, but it carefully shows that he was eventually enticed to return to the white world.

His unusual "growing tree" invokes another ambivalence his narrators felt about him. A strange and atypical tree was chosen, suggesting a strange and atypical life. The problem was that Simon's values and behavior were not those of his group, but this difference was his essence, the thing that made him a legendary figure about whom stories are told. The stories attribute magical circumstances to his birth and growth, note his early deviation from group norms, and confirm it when he becomes an outlaw. His outsider status is capped by his passing as an Indian when he returns to his own home community. The idea of predestination in the legends resolves the ambiguity their tellers felt. The behavior as well as the destiny of a man like Simon Kenton, they suggest, was a matter of fate. He had to act the way he did. And from the unique perspective of his birthplace, this could be seen from the beginning.

NOTES

1. Charles McKnight, *Our Western Border, One Hundred Years Ago* (Philadelphia: J. C. McCurdy, 1875), pp. 302–61; Theodore Roosevelt, *The Winning of the West*, 4 vols. (New York: G. P. Putnam's Sons, 1889–96).

HOW SIMON KENTON
LEFT HOME

Mrs. Rebecca Ashby, interviewed by Susan R. Morton
at Waterfall, Prince William County, on August 15, 1941

'Twas most likely th' talk of an old woman what made Simon Kenton th' great man he turned out t' be. When he was borned there was a big dark mole on his neck an' [the old woman said] that was a sure sign that he would be hung. His mammy tried all th' things she ever heard of t' get shet of it—she made poultices of herbs an' soaked a coin in vinegar, an' made him wear it over th' mole. But nothin' ever did any good. So when Simon got into a fight with th' Leachman man that had married th' gal he wanted, he fit right courageous, but though he were big an' strong, he weren't but a boy an' this man were heavy an' more powerful. He were gittin' th' best o' him an' they were near some young trees, so Simon he stept on on[e]. Now if'n he meant t' do it nobody won't ever know. An' it caught in th' other fellow's hair an' pulled him off'n his feet so quick that it took his breath. An' then Simon heaved a powerful knock on his chin an' he 'peared t' be dead fer sure.

An' then Simon were sure he had done a deed that would make that mark come true an' he were sure he would be hung; so he started off an' kep' a-goin', being so scairt that he took no mind of his thin cloth[e]s, which th' branches tore 'most off'n him. But otherwise he might never have started his travels what made him such a great man, what shows [how a] little thing can work out t' do th' Lord's will as He had a planned things.

———— **103** ————

SIMON KENTON'S
GROWING TREE

Aunt Fannie Beale, interviewed by Susan R. Morton
in Waterfall, Prince William County, on August 15, 1941

Tis said as how there were an old woman lived by hersel' on the mountains, it don't 'pear t' be certain who she were, or whar she comed from, but she had a gif' o' doctorin' wi' herbs and roots she got hersel' and th' proper time t' use 'em. She said she got her knowledge frum th' Indians, but it ain't likely. She were jes' a natur'l born doctor and she were th' midwife fer the countryside an' there were those as said she had a lot t' do wi' the start a baby hed.

One o' her tricks were t' tek a bit o' the baby's hair, 'fore ever it were washed, an' as soon as she could git it a young tree, she'd cut a slit in th' tree an put in th' hair an' chink it up ag'in. An' as th' tree grew, so'd the child. Most always [she] took a poplar, fer they grow quick an' straight, but though it were th' favored tree, a poplar tree were likely t' be cut young, fer they grew tall quicker'n mos'. An' if th' tree were cut 'fore hit got hits growth, it were bad fer the hair owner; an' then too 't'is bad fer the one what cuts down th' tree 'cause it'd make a secret en'my o' th' one whose life'd been cut short.

But fer some reason, th' ole woman choosen a gum tree [for Simon Kenton], what ev'ry one knows grows slow an' sometimes gits crooked. But this here tree stood fer years, an' lightning tore off a part o' it, an' somebody took off'n a limb t' make gun stocks out'n. An' t' cut mos' trees like that woulda stunted 'em, but not this a one. Storm an' man both tortured hit, but it stood right on, which were jes' what Simon did. He were near kilt a heap o' times, but he stood up straight, which were likely what thet ole woman meant he would do when she picked out the gum tree fer a growin' tree.

——————— 104 ———————

SIMON KENTON'S EXPLOITS

Mr. Winter Owen, interviewed by Susan R. Morton
in Waterfall, Prince William County, on August 15, 1941

This Simon Kenton, I reckon he was about th' strongest man that ever growed up in these hills. I heerd tell many th' time as how when he was fittin' th' Indians they'd captur'd him and got ready t' burn him at th' stake, an' got th' fire all laid, an' had him tied up tight with strips o' leather all 'round his arms. He, bein' as he'd lived with th' Indians, knew how to make their kind o' talk, an' he told [them] he'd break th' ties if'n they'd let him go free. An' they talked together an' the Chief Man he said he could go free, fer that were somethin' no man could do unless he had some kind o' spirit in him. So Simon he strained at th' leather an' it cut him so thet th' blood kept a-runnin' down, but he never let on as how it hurt him. An' that made th' Indians think he were somethin' strange, fer they didn't see how he could stand the pain an' not show any o' it. An' after he'd strained an' tugged, one o' th' strips o' leather broke. An' then he easy got free.

'T'is said he'd kill a b'ar an' take it home on his back. An' one time he fit a wolf with his bare hands. T'were in th' winter an' he had gone into th' woods t' cut some hickory fer makin' into handles, fer he were powerful clever in usin' a knife when he'd a mind t' settle down to doin' hit. He saw this critter right at him 'fore he could grab a holt o' his knife what he had just laid down. He made a jump at the beast's throat an' they fit and rolled over th' ground. But Simon held on t' it an' strangled it right an' proper. An' then he cut th' head off'n it an' got paid a bounty fer it, fer they was a-payin' fer the heads o' varmints in them days.

He could break enough hominy to last th' whole family all day, 'fore breakfast 'tis said, an' that were hard work just usin' a mortar 'bout th' same as what th' Indians used. I reckon you won't ever see th' likes o' Simon 'round these parts ag'in. He were a great man.

―――――― 105 ――――――
SIMON KENTON'S INDIAN WIFE AND FAMILY

Maggie Hensley, interviewed by Susan R. Morton
in Waterfall, Prince William County, on September 13, 1941

Simon Kenton, after he'd gone to the wild land of Kentucky, married an Indian girl who had pleaded with her father to save his life one time when they already had him tied to the stake to burn him. She was a right pretty girl too, an' they lived peaceable together, he a-huntin' and a-trappin'. But after a while he hankered t' see his old home, and so he up and left his squaw wife an' their three children an' come on back home, which made her so mad she up an' followed him a-carryin' the papoose on her back an' leavin' the other two behind with her Indian kin. An' bein' an Indian she could get [along] about as well as Simon, an' all th' time she knew he was not far ahead. Once, when he was about t' be caught by some o' his enemies, she turned 'em off his trail, 'cause, while she was mad at him herself, she wanted her own pleasure of revenge, an' she was a-plannin' t' creep up on him when he was with his kinfolk an' make him own up he'd already got a woman an' a parcel o' children.

Simon had not got across th' Blue Ridge, though, before he met up with a man what told him that they was having trouble with th' Indians who were goin' to fight alongside of th' English. So instead of Simon goin' on t' see his kinfolk, he joined up with th' army. But th' Indian woman, thinkin' most likely she'd never see him again, kept right on, for she knew th' direction he said he'd come from.

Finally one day a strange Indian woman showed up here in th' mountains with a baby that wasn't like an Indian baby at all, for it had red hair and blue eyes. An' though folks were scared of her at first, after a while she got 'em to understand that Simon was her man an' that he'd gone off to the war. It was a powerful blow to his kinfolk to think as how he had an Indian wife, but lookin' at th' baby they couldn't help but know he was th' father of it. So they took her in an' treated her kind.

But she couldn't bide white man's ways, an' one morning she an' the baby were gone when th' March winds had melted the snows. Th' Kentons' never saw her again. And when Simon came to bring his family back to Kentucky where he'd got a powerful lot of land by that time, what for bein' such a fine soldier an' all, he wouldn't ever talk about it. 'Tis said, however, long after all th' Kenton family had gone away there was a tall young man with red hair living with some Indians way off in the back woods. An' 'tis though[t] as how it may have been th' son [of Simon Kenton and] that Indian squaw.

——— 106 ———

SIMON KENTON'S
INDIAN DISGUISE

Miss Flora Smith, interviewed by Susan R. Morton
in Waterfall, Prince William County, on August 11, 1941

Simon Kenton was always a fetching looking boy, so folks that knew him said, and after he had lived with the Indians for years and years and been out in the cold and heat, he had skin that was tanned and red-like both and could easy pass for an Indian. 'Cept he had blue eyes and sort of reddish hair. He got his red hair from his Irish ancestor all right, and you know the kind of skin goes with it. After he had gone from these mountains for some years he had a longing to see some of his kin-folks and the old home that was called "Devil's Bed." I never heard how it got that name. But he was afraid to appear here, thinking all the time that he had killed William Leachman in a fight. And while he had proved he was a brave and honest man, he didn't see the use of bringing disgrace on his family by bein' hung.

So he got hold of some kind of root or bark that he could dye his hair with, and he wore leather clothes anyhow, and moccasins. And he had a string of some kind of teeth around his neck and a tomahawk, and his own mother you wouldn't have thought could have told him from a Red Man, which were common to see those days, although the most of the fighting ones had been driven back to the wilder parts, for at that time there were houses pretty near all over the mountains.

He kept a-thinking of that girl he'd wanted to marry, and as he got near to where she lived he had a hankering to see her. He decided to go by her cabin, thinking he had made her a widow, and supposin' she'd got another man long before of course. He knew she wouldn't know him, and he thought he'd go on by and take a peep at her.

It was near dark when he got near White Rock, which was near the Leachman home, and he found there were cleared fields and fences up, and as he neared the house he heard children a-laughing and playing. Creepin' along still as he'd learned to do from living with the Indians so long, he saw a right good house, for the cabin had been added on to. An' standing in the door was a woman who was fat, and her apron was all dirty and her hair hangin' careless-like. And after he had looked at her a few minutes he saw that it was Ellen, the girl that had been the innocent cause of all his wanderings, but also what had made him famous and rich, for he had a powerful lot of land in Kentucky at that time. And then and there he decided that whoever married her, he was glad that it wasn't him. So, layin' still in the bushes, he waited for her to go on in. But just then a man came around the cabin from the fields, and who was it but William Leachman himself, grown fat an' old-looking, while he, Simon, had grown to be handsome and a man everybody was sure to turn to look at.

The dogs then began to sniff and growl and William said to his wife that there must be some kind of varmint a-lurkin' in the woods, and to give him his gun, which made Simon think he had better show himself, or else git away. So he got up and moved out of the brush and one of the children saw him and started to scream and yell—"Indian!" An' William came a-runnin' out of the house with his gun.

Simon then walked up to the yard and made gestures that he meant no harm and talked in the Indian language and made out he wanted something to eat. When they handed him a big piece of pone and a hunk of bacon, they all watched him while he ate it, the children a-hanging on to their mother's skirts so scared they didn't dare to move. After he ate it he thanked them in Indian fashion and went off. And he told afterwards that when he got from in sight of the cabin he lay down on the ground and rolled over and laughed and laughed—he was so glad to know he was not a murderer, and he was glad too that he wasn't in William's shoes, for he had seen prettier girls in Kentucky and he was a-goin' to go back there an' marry one of them.

He went on to his father's house and he fooled some of them there, but not his old father, who said he reckoned he'd know his children even if they were Red.

———— 107 ————

SIMON KENTON
TRAPS A
BRANDY THIEF

John Peake, interviewed by Susan R. Morton
in Waterfall, Prince William County, on August 15, 1941

This Simon Kenton was th' laziest, orneriest boy you ever did see, from what my granpappy tells as he heerd it. There were a lot o' work on a farm in those days; th' land had t' be grubbed all th' time t' keep th' forest from a-takin' back what it once had. An' there had t' be 'nough tobacca raised t' pay th' rent an' git what things they had t' get that couldn't be growed at home. An' corn t' make th' hominy an' feed th' critter, and firewood t' cut an' an' fence rails t' cut t' cure, 'sides all th' work th' women folks had to do. And Simon's pappy had more girls than boys, an' after William [the oldest] took a wife they were short-handed. But Simon could work right enough when he had a min' t', but jes' as he'd be settled down t' a piece o' real work, off'n he'd go again a-huntin' or trappin', or huntin' bee trees. An' 'tis said he were th' best in the whole mountain fer that.

Thar were plenty o' varmints in the mountains in those days, an' from his talks with th' trappers an' Indians that he would a-meet with, he got learned in th' ways o' th' woods. An' he brought in plenty o' game, b'ars included. He had some kind o' b'ar trap that he claimed were th' best that could be made, but he wouldn't tell nobody how he made it.

Well, one day he heerd one o' th' neighbors say—fer in them days there were right smart of cabins about, as yo' can see now by th' stones and volu[n]teer fruit trees that keep a-comin up long where thar were once a house—this man, he kep' a-tellin' as how as some varmint upset all his brandy what he had stored in a cave back right back o' Whippoorwill; yo' can see th' very place now. Simon said as how he reckoned it were a b'ar a-nosin' 'round t' find some sweet an' upsot it. An' he'd set one o' his b'ar traps th' nex' night, he said.

Sure 'nough, come dusky time Simon fixed his trap all neat an' proper an' then he hides in th' bushes t' wait fer th' b'ar. When it come black dark an' he were a-dozin' off, come th' greatest screachin' an' cussin' as yo ever heerd. So he jump up quick an' run t' see what were th' matter. An' thar fast in his b'ar trap, an' a-kickin' an' a-cussin' an' a-yellin', what with th' hurt an' bein' caught makin' him so all-fired mad, were th' thief. An weren' no b'ar, nothin' but th' ole granpappy o' th' man what was complainin', all tight an' fast in Simon's b'ar trap.

SPIRIT DOGS

According to ancient mythology, spirit dogs guarded the gates of the afterworld. The Egyptians deified their dog god Anubis in the form of the dog-star Sirius, whose Roman counterpart was Cerberus, a three-headed dog-monster who was chained outside the gates of Hades.[1] As Barbara Allen Woods's monograph *The Devil in Dog Form: A Partial Type-Index of Devil Legends* has amply shown, this ancient association between dogs and the underworld is extremely widespread in folklore and has continued into modern times.[2] The Virginia Writers' Project workers gathered twenty-one narratives of supernatural and/or "devil" dogs in their collecting, most of them from Appalachia and all of them from the mountainous regions of the state.

There are three types of spirit dog stories in the WPA collection. In the most common type, a ghost dog simply appears. These narratives do not connect the dog's appearance to any sort of omen or make any moral or ethical point. "A Spirit Dog Causes a Broken Toe" (legend 112) is representative of this type. It reports the incident, gives a few details, and closes by commenting on its possible meaning. For no reason that is apparent in the story, the dog is assumed to be associated with the devil. "The Ghost on Chinquapin Hill" (legend 116) is another example of this type, and while it does not explicitly connect the ghostly dog with the devil, it suggests some relationship by having the apparition disappear when it comes near a church.

In his notes to "A Devil Dog Comes for a Slave Owner" (legend 108), James Taylor Adams described the second type of ghost dog legend, the moral tale. Adams wrote: "I have heard my parents, grand-parents, and other older people tell of the devil visiting people in the form of a dog. These visits were usually paid to dying men who had lived a notoriously wicked life." The cruel slave owner in the story Mary Carter told to Adams had escaped human justice for his murderous deeds all his life. The ghost dog's deathbed visit served to reassure his neighbors that he would not escape the final judgment of damnation. And the story itself reassured its audience that the wicked eventually do get what they deserve. "The Black Cat" in the Supernatural Events section, except for the specifics of the person's crimes and the species of the ghostly animal, is identical to the story of the slave owner. "A Devil Dog in the Path" (legend 113) is an interesting variation of the moral ghost dog narrative. Rather than confirming a person's wickedness at his death and escorting him off to hellfire, the dog in this story serves to redirect sinful behavior (in this case drinking) while the sinners are still alive, which casts the devil in the unusual role of moral agent. In "The Warning Dog" (legend 111) the spirit dog takes this role one step further. Not only does the dog discourage the immoral behavior of cruelty to Stella, the young stepdaughter, but it actually physically protects her.

The third type of spirit dog narrative is represented here by "The Death Dog" (legend 110). This type of story is associated with the folk motifs D1812.5.1.12.1, "Howling of dog as bad omen," and (Baughman) E574 (ia), "Ghost dog appears as death omen." In Europe during the Middle Ages, dogs howling at the moon were said to mean ill fortune because they sensed the angel of death approaching.[3] Also, the dog as an omen of death harks back to the concept of a dog guarding the gates of the afterworld. "The Death Dog" story given here suggests that the dog is more than merely an omen. It is termed a "carrier," implying that it actually causes the deaths which occur when it appears.

One striking aspect of the stories, no matter which type they are, is how similar their descriptions of the ghostly dogs are. The dogs are always large and black, and they all have remarkable eyes, which are variously described as being red, "as big as saucers," and "shining like balls of fire." It should be noted that these particular descriptions themselves are traditional. The motif index includes such entries as "giant dog," "spirit as black dog," "dog with glowing tongues and eyes," "dog with fire in eyes," and "dog with eyes as big as plates, tea-cups, etc." Also, Jamaican duppies, the returned souls of the dead, are said to take the form of black dogs with large red eyes.[4] And, as childhood readers of Hans Christian Anderson's "The Tinderbox" will recall, the treasure-guarding dog in that famous story was said to have "eyes as big as saucers." Several of the tales describe the dogs as shaggy, and a number note that the animals prove insubstantial when touched or kicked.

All but two of the collection's spirit dog stories were collected from white informants, refuting Texas folklorist J. Mason Brewer's contention that ghost dog tales are exclusively African American. In the introduction to his *Dog Ghosts and Other Texas Negro Folk Tales* he wrote, "As far as I have been able to ascertain, the dog spirit tale is not a part of any oral American tradition except that of the Negro."[5] Apparently, he did little research before making this pronouncement; he failed to note, for instance, that the *Journal of American Folklore* had printed a dog ghost tale from a white informant in Virginia's Blue Ridge Mountains in 1907.[6]

NOTES

1. Susan Lewis, *Major Arcana of the Ancient Tarot Cards* (State College, Pa.: A Hypercard Stack/Shareware, 1988), animal symbols stack.

2. Barbara Allen Woods, *The Devil in Dog Form: A Partial Type-Index of Devil Legends*, Univ. of California Folklore Studies no. 11 (Berkeley: Univ. of California Press, 1959).

3. Susan Lewis, *Major Arcana of the Ancient Tarot Cards*, animal symbols stack.

4. MacEdward Leach, "Jamaican Duppy Lore," *Journal of American Folklore* 74 (1961): 207.

5. J. Mason Brewer, *Dog Ghosts and Other Texas Negro Folk Tales* (Austin: Univ. of Texas Press, 1958), p. 3.

6. Mrs. R. F. Herrick, "The Black Dog of the Blue Ridge," *Journal of American Folklore* 20 (1907): 151–52.

A DEVIL DOG
COMES FOR A
SLAVE OWNER

Mrs. Mary Carter, interviewed by James Taylor Adams
in Glamorgan, Wise County, on March 17, 1941

One time there was an old man. He was a rich old man and owned a whole passel of slaves. I think he lived in Kentucky. Maybe it was North Carolina, I don't remember. He was awful wicked. They said he'd been married four or five times an' all his wives took sudden sick an' died, or was found dead. All of his wives had had a lot of money an' when they died he got it.

Well I've heard Pa say that when this ol' man's slaves died he wouldn't let nobody come an help bury 'em. It was thought he killed his slaves. Well, when he come to die a passel of his neighbors gathered in to set up with him. It was about midnight an' he'uz awful low. Expectin' him to die any minute. All at once they heard a noise at the door. Somebody opened the door an' there stood a big black dog. It had eyes as big as saucers, an' they looked like balls of fire. The dog jes walked right in an' reared up on the foot of the bed an' looked at the ol' man. He screamed an' tried to get out of bed. He said it was the devil come after him. He jes fell back an' was dead in a minute. The dog then jes turned and walked out, an' nobody ever seed hit again.

———— 109 ————

TWO MORE
DEVIL DOGS

Lenore C. Kilgore, interviewed by James Taylor Adams
in Big Laurel, Wise County, no date given

Jim Banks had been killed by a neighbor in an election fight. Soon thereafter Jim's wife and children began hearing things at night. Sometimes it would be one thing, sometimes another. Every few nights they would hear something in the room at back of the main house which Jim had called his granary, that is, he used it to keep shelled corn, wheat, oats and other grain stored in. He also kept his gears [equipment] there. They would hear something just like somebody was rattling the chains, and then it would go like somebody pouring the grain into measures. One night Mrs. Banks took a light and went out to see what was going on in the room. She kept the door fastened so nothing could get in. The door was fastened then, but she could hear the noise like wheat being poured from one tub or barrel into another. And the gears were rattling and somebody seemed [to be] walking around. So she eased the door open and stepped inside. Just as she did so, a big black dog with eyes as big as saucers and shining like coals of fire ran out by her. She never knew what it was. She saw the same thing many times.

She told this story to her brother-in-law, Sol Banks, and his wife, Celia Ann Banks. I heard it from them. She also told this one. She had a whole gang of children, boys and girls. She would send them after the cows late in the evening. They usually had to go to a field in which the graveyard was and where her husband was buried. Every time they went up on the graveyard hill they would see a big brown dog with eyes that shone like fire. He would suddenly come on them from the direction of the graveyard. They would run down the hill toward the house. The dog would run after them to where the trail turned down the hill. Then he would turn into something that looked like a barrel and roll down the hill after them. Mrs. Banks said that one evening she looked out and saw the children coming, running hard as they could and screaming every breath. And right behind them was something that looked like a barrel rolling after them. It came right up to the yard fence and just disappeared.

THE DEATH DOG

Mrs. Dicy Adams, interviewed by James Taylor Adams
in Big Laurel, Wise County, on March 24, 1941

One time long ago there was a neighborhood away back in the mountains that was visited by a big dog which seemed to be the carrier of death into the community. One day this dog showed up at a house and undertook to take up, but seeming to be vicious, the folks wouldn't let him stay. But he stayed in spite of them. Nearly every day they would see him sneaking around in the bushes and at night they would hear him howling around the house. Then one day one of the children of the family took sick. Nobody knew what was wrong with the child. Just sick. And it got worse and worse, and the more sick the child grew the more the strange dog would howl. Then one night the child was mighty bad off and the dog would come to the door and scratched on the shutter. They would run him away, but he came right back. Then the child died about midnight as the dog was howling outside. And the very minute the child breathed its last, the dog stopped howling and was not seen around that house again.

Time went on and the dog showed up at another house in the neighborhood and tried to take up. These folks had heard of its strange behavior at the other place and the death of the child, and they decided to humor it, thinking by so doing they might ward off its evil influence. But not so. The dog was petted and allowed the range of the premises, but he would howl through the night and slink about in the woods in the day time. It wasn't long 'till the man of the house was coming home from his work one night when he saw the dog coming towards him from a patch of bushes. The man told later that as the dog neared him that he seemed to become weak and sick and it was with much difficulty that he reached home, the dog following after him howling. So he took [to] his bed and everything known by friends and doctors was done for him, but he died one night as the big dog sat on his haunches in the yard and howled. Immediately after the man died the dog disappeared from that farm.

A few days later he showed up at another clearing. By this time the beast was held in deadly fear. The man at this house loaded his gun and took a shot at him. Even at a distance of only a few yards the shot seemed to have no effect on him. So it went until one day this man's little boy was sent to the field to drive home the cows. Soon after the boy passed out of sight they heard the dog howling in the direction in which he had gone. The parents became uneasy and went to look for the child. They didn't find him. He was never seen again. And the dog was not seen again.

——— 111 ———

THE WARNING DOG

Mrs. Emily Thompson, interviewed by James M. Hylton
in Big Stone Gap, Wise County, on March 31, 1941

This tale was told to me by Stella Sizemore, twenty-eight years old, who is now living in Benham, Kentucky, who married a man by the name of Clark. She is the daughter of Hiram Sizemore, Big Stone Gap, Virginia, aged forty, who is the man involved in this tale. He is the son of old Ned Sizemore of Big Stone Gap also. Stella's mother died when she was two years old, and soon after her father married another woman by the name of Mumpower and who is the woman involved. Well, when she went to the house after she married this Sizemore she had two children of her own and she never did like Stella. She made her do all the house drudge and other kinds of work and the washing for the whole family. She (Stella) was trying to go to school at the same time and do the work, and everybody talked how bad they treated her. Anyway, they got so mean to her that life was one battle after another, but there was nothing she could do as there was no other place for her to go and live.

She said that the man (Hiram) and the woman who he married got so they thought they saw a big shaggy dog in the swing on the porch every day or night when they came back from going out somewhere after leaving her there by herself and with all of the work to do. She said they would yell for her when they got to the porch and tell her to come and open the door for them and go in and light the lamp, that they were afraid of the big dog in the swing. But they said that when she opened the door the dog would jump down from the swing and go in the house, but that she herself never saw any such thing and knew there was none there, at least as far as she could see. Anyway they would go in when she had lit the lamp and later that night when they all went to bed the woman would get up and go to Stella's bed and make her move over and said that the dog would come around and lick her hands and growl around her bed when she tried to sleep in her own bed and she would make her move over and sleep with her the rest of the night. Hiram also thought the same thing at the same time, or soon later, and could not sleep for the dog bothering him and growling near his bed; and [he] lost lots of sleep over it. The woman (the mother or step-mother) got worried and lost a lot of weight over it and spent lots of sleepless nights over it. Well the dog appeared to them every time they went anywhere and came back home and they would not try to get into the house if there was not somebody with them to open the door or Stella wasn't there to do it for them.

It soon got to be the general talk of the section of town where they lived and everybody has heard about the dog at Sizemore's. Anyway that lasted 'till the girl grew up and it like to worried the man and woman to death. The woman was ill and the man a nervous wreck during the time. Later, Stella got married and moved away, but everybody knew of the dog they had seen which seemed to be a warning to them not to be so mean to the little motherless girl. After she married and moved they claim they never saw the dog any more.

——— 112 ———

A SPIRIT DOG CAUSES A BROKEN TOE

Findlay Adams, interviewed by James Taylor Adams
in Big Laurel, Wise County, on May 12, 1941

Talkin' 'bout ghost dogs. I guess you've heard about the dog ol' Si Collins seed. Well, their kitchen stood off from the house about twenty-five or thirty yards. You had to go out o' the main house an' across an open space to get in the kitchen. Used to be a whole lot of the houses built that way.

One night Si was out in the yard between the house an' kitchen an' he noticed the kitchen door was a-standin' open, an' he looked in an' seed a big, black, shaggy-haired dog standin' in there by the table. Strange dog to him. He scolded him, but he never let on. Never moved. He scolded him several times, but he didn't pay no attention. He ventured in. He spoke to the dog an' tried to mutch [soothe] 'im out, but he wouldn't move. Si got mad. He drawed back an' kicked at him. His foot went right on through it an' struck the table leg an' broke his big toe. I seed it. He couldn't wear his shoe for a month or two an' hobbled around on a cane with his toe all swelled up an' turned blue.

But after he broke his toe he run out o' the kitchen an' hollered for Aunt Peggy to go fetch a light. She brought a light an' they sarched all over the place an' couldn't find hide nor hair of any dog. He believed as long as he lived that it was the devil he seed like a dog.

—————— 113 ——————

A DEVIL DOG
IN THE PATH

Findlay Adams, interviewed by James Taylor Adams
in Big Laurel, Wise County, on May 12, 1941

One time, oh it's been forty years ago I guess, Buck Gibson lived down there on Smoot [Mountain]. Si Adams and Rob Holcomb got together and made up [their minds] to go an' get some liquor an' go down to Buck's an' get him drunk an' have a big time. So they kotch their nags an' pulled out right up the head of Smoot, goin' through by Sandlick Gap. Si told me all about it. He said they was goin' ridin' along, the path jes wide enough for one hoss. Rob was in front an' they'd got right up there above Pole Cat Hollow when all at once Si seed Rob's hoss rare up on his hind feet. An' he heard Rob holler out sumpin'. He looked an' jes ahead of 'em, there right in the middle of the path was the awfullest lookin' thing he'd ever seed. Hit looked like a dog, but hit was bigger than any cow he ever seed. Big as a hoss. Hit was sittin' back on hits hind parts in the road, an' hits eyes was as big as plates an' shone jes like fire. His hoss seed it too an' began to rare an' pitch. Rob's hoss wouldn't go another step. So there they was; they tried to go round hit, but the hosses wouldn't go. The thing opened hits mouth an' Si said he could see down hits throat. An' it looked like a roarin' furnace of fire. They decided hit was the devil an' that hit was there to turn 'em back from goin' after liquor. So they jes turned round an' went back home an' left hit settin' there in the road.

───────── 114 ─────────

THE GHOST DOG
ON INDIAN CREEK

Patrick Henry Addington, interviewed by James Taylor Adams
in Big Laurel, Wise County, on June 9, 1941

I remember that way back yonder when I was a boy [the informant was seventy-five at the time of this interview] they was somethin' to be seen on Indian Creek just like a big black dog. Hit was over there at the old school house just above the old Jerry Chase place. A lot of the school children seed it in broad daylight, but I never seen it. People passing there of a night would see something just like a big black long-haired dog come out of the bushes. The school children said it run them in when they'd get out in the bushes playin'. Hit got so bad that they gathered up hounds and went all through the woods tryin' to bounce it out. But they never could. An' the very next night somebody passin' there would see it.

They told about Jerry Chase bein' off up there one night an' it come out on him. He said that all at once it walked out of the bushes right behind him with its tongue lolling out and eyes as big as his fist an' shinin' like balls of fire. He started to the house and it started after him. He begin to runnin' an' hit started runnin'. Hit was gainin' on him. He come to the house an' the door was fastened. He didn't take time to holler for 'em to open it. He just broke it down and landed right in the middle of the floor. About that time he caught his breath and said, "Wah!" They looked out and seen the dog going back up the creek.

Oh, lots and lots of people have seen it. The big road goes right along where the school house stood then. I hain't heard of hit bein' seed in several years. You know they said they was some soldiers wounded at Gladeville and left near there and died durin' the Old War [the Civil War]. Some thought it was that that caused that to be seed there.

—————— 115 ——————

THE DOG THAT
TURNED TO RAGS

Silas Craft, interviewed by James Taylor Adams
in Big Laurel, Wise County, on June 16, 1941

One time, hit's been fifty years or more ago, I was workin' for a feller on Cumberland named Lewis. A wealthy feller. Had lots of money. Loggin' man. Me an' Melvin Brown. Brother Johnny was sparkin' Melvin's sister an' him an' John Pres Bolling was makin' likker for Thurston Banner. He'd wrote me or sent me word that he was comin' over Christmas, an' bring some brandy an' we'd have a good time. I sent back word for 'im to come on.

So him an' John Pres got 'em a keg of brandy two or three days before Christmas and started out walkin' up Pound. They both told me this. Said they was comin' 'long right there about the Jane Short mulberry [on the south fork of the Pound], when all at once somethin' that looked like a big dog raised up right in front of 'em. They stopped an' looked at it an' hit would turn hits head an' look at them. Had little teeny eyes, but they looked like blazes of fire. Seemed like hits neck was stiff an' [it] had to turn hit[s] whole body. One of 'em said to the other, "Here, hold this keg; I'm goin' to see what hit is." The hair on hit hung plum down to the ground, they said, and looked right shaggy. They thought maybe hit was a donkey. They scolded [shooed] hit, but hit jes stood there an' looked at 'em. Hit was way in the night, an' they was makin' for Uncle John Bolling's to stay all night. John Pres, I believe hit was, picked up a rock he'd kicked loose from the frozen ground an' cut loose at hit. But hit didn't move. He ventured up an' stuck out his hand to feel of it an' couldn't feel a thing, an' at the same time they could see hit an' hit turned an' looked him in the face. He grabbed up another rock and let go an' the rock didn't seem to hit anything. But they said that then whatever hit was jes seemed to tear all to pieces an turned into a great big bundle [of] rags and strings an' started windin' right round and round an' goin' right up. When hit was up in the air a little piece hit all seemed to gather back together ag'in an' turned into something that looked like an eagle, but big as a cow, an' went sailin' off over the timber.

———— 116 ————

THE
GHOST DOG ON
CHINQUAPIN HILL

Susie Murray, interviewed by Susan R. Morton
in Antioch, Fluvanna County, on February 24, 1942

Chinquapin Hill is a steep rise in the road known as the old Mountain Road between Hopewell Gap Road and Jackson Hollow Road. At the time the following story took place there were several homes—humble log cabins belonging mostly to negroes at that time. With the exception of [one] that is still standing, though long unoccupied, they are all gone, the sites marked by a few garden strays persevering in the encroaching woods. About a mile beyond the crest of Chinquapin Hill is Mount Olivet, the negro church, so that the road is more traveled than many in this section. In spite of the general serenity of the scene today, drama and tragedy have made it their home—Aged Sally Bowers, gathering lightwood before a threatening storm, fell a few rods from her door and perished in the fierce storm that came that night. A neighbor from the Jackson Hollow neighborhood, returning late from a trip to the village some twelve miles distant, was robbed and left dying by the roadside. One of the local belles was shot by her jealous lover as he came upon her and his rival at their trysting place under the massive chestnut (the stump of which is still seen) near the top of the hill.

[There is] hardly a bit of ground but what is the scene of some exciting episode, and therefore it [is] but little wonder that some of these unhappy souls return to the scene of their tragic ending. One late Fall night some fifty years ago there was a revival being held at Mount Olivet Church and two young women and a man were hastening from Antioch to church. As they reached the foot of the hill a dark object appeared directly in front of them. One of the women screamed at the big black dog, for such it appeared to be, but it paid no heed but kept in front of them jogging along easily. The man picked up a stone, which he threw, and was sure that it hit the creature; yet it seemed to go right *through* it, landing to the side of the road with a thud. Neither did the "dog" show any sign of having noticed it.

The women were in favor of turning back, but [they] finally decided *it* was likely to follow them in that direction as well, and [they] thought when they got to the church they could borrow a lantern and get a good look at it. However, when they were within about a quarter of a mile of the church, *it* simply disappeared. There were woods on both sides of the road, but no one saw it turn off, for it had kept within a few feet of them directly in the center of the road—then just vanished. After that it was seen by several others at the same place, and with never any further explanation of it.

SUPERNATURAL
EVENTS

These stories are much like the ghost and haunted house tales, except that no actual ghosts appear in them. They feature more mysterious and fleeting evidences of the supernatural—strange music in a cave, unusual markings on a hat, a certain spot where snow always melts, and lights, noises, and visible or invisible "somethings" in the woods. Also, except for the spirit dogs, which rated their own category, this section is home to the tales of supernatural animals. Many of the things said about the ghost and spirit dog narratives apply to these tales as well. Some of them contain blatant moral messages, such as "The Black Cat" (legend 127) and "The Boat That Would Not Move" (legend 118), which condemn infanticide and selling slaves "down the river" respectively. Others are more subtle. "The Disappearing Old Gray Horse" (legend 123), for instance, while it doesn't say so directly, warns against stopping by a still to drink whiskey.

In general, however, there is less of a moral thrust to these stories than to those in which ghosts actually appear. More often they simply assert the existence of a supernatural realm and its convergence with the natural one. The story of the "Jack-ma-Lanterns: Lights in the Woods" (legend 120), for instance, only describes the phenomenon and gives practical advice in case one encounters it. A ghost, although dead, was once a human being; its presence would be almost reassuring, indicating that the other world is to some degree like this one and that it is populated by beings not unlike ourselves. These vaguer stories of the unknown, on the other hand, offer no such assurance. The supernatural world either remains entirely mysterious or is revealed to contain malevolent lights, invisible forces with great physical power, and shape-shifting animals. The point of the tales is often simply that the world is strange and unknowable to humans.

One especially puzzling supernatural event is the poltergeist phenomenon. "The Shower of Stones" (legend 128) is the only description in the WPA collection of such an event. The Puritan writer and minister Cotton Mather recorded an account of a similar occurrence in 1682, describing how stones began pelting the house of George Walton of Portsmouth, New Hampshire. Furniture began moving around, flying rocks broke things inside the house, and food from the kitchen was found outside the house in trees.[1] The legend collector Charles Skinner noted a similar event in New Haven, Connecticut, in the 1760s. In his account stones came down the chimney of the house and children of the family complained of being stuck with pins. Skinner's version, like the one given here, offered an angered witch as an explanation of the strange happenings.[2]

NOTES

1. Cotton Mather, *Magnalia Christi Americana* (Cambridge: Belknap, 1977), 2:450–52.

2. Charles M. Skinner, *Myths and Legends of Our Own Land* (Philadelphia: J. B. Lippincott, 1896), 1:237.

DOGS CHASE AN
INVISIBLE CREATURE

Leslie Bolling, interviewed by Francis V. Green
in Richmond, on July 12, 1941

My two brothers and sister had a pet dog named Jack. As all kids, we loved the ground this dog walked on. Most of the time he slept with us, until mother and dad discovered our secret. Then we built a little house for him, and just before going to bed, we would put Jack to bed. He began making so much noise after midnight until dad stopped us from fastening him up. But he would still make this unusual noise. Then other people who had dogs in the neighborhood began observing [the] strange behavior of their dogs. It was also noted that the dogs were meeting after midnight at a certain place, as if by appointment. Then a chase would start and go over a definite course. Some of the old huntsmen thought it was an opossum or coon, so they decided to catch it. But when they went to get their dogs they were already in the chase or on their way to the meeting place.

This event cause[d] the little town of Dendron to sit up and take notice, especially in the mill lot around which section this story took place. People began talking about getting rid of their dogs because they just could not get any rest. And these events took place on summer nights, just at the time when the heat had cooled off and when the most desired thing was sleep.

Groups of men and boys formed all along the line of chase so they [that], if one group missed [it] the other would be certain to catch the hant. But in spite of torches carried by the group, no one saw the chase or what it was the dogs were running. This did get everybody up in the air. One night near daybreak the dogs must have gotten too close, and the invisible, what shall it be called?, turned on the dogs and all the men agree[d] to a man that this thing fought the dogs like a wild cat. But nothing in the form of an animal was seen. And the men all agreed that it must have been a hant or a ghost.

———— 118 ————

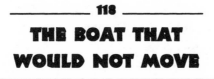

THE BOAT THAT WOULD NOT MOVE

Elizabeth Kilgore Carter, interviewed by James Taylor Adams
in Norton, Wise County, on August 4, 1941

One time, they said, there was a colored girl who was a slave an' she was a pretty girl. Everybody liked her. But her master lost a lot of money gamblin' an' he had to raise some more, so he sold this girl to a slave trader from way down south. They loaded her on the boat with some other slaves the trader had bought an' got ready to sail down the river, but the boat wouldn't budge. They worked at it for several days, but it wouldn't go. At last they took the girl off an' the boat went off without any trouble. But the trader was determined he'd have this pretty girl. She'd bring a lot of money down the river. So he put her in a carriage an' was going to drive through. But the horses wouldn't budge an inch. Beat 'em as he might, they jes wouldn't move. So he finally had to jes give up an' let the girl go free. I don't know what become of her.

—————— 119 ——————

THE WHITE DOVE: A DEAD WIFE RETURNS

Melviny Brown, interviewed by Bessie A. Scales
in Danville, on December 16, 1940

When I was er young gal long time ago, de big house, where we-alls lived in de yard of, had so many big rooms an' winders [that] we-all niggers what work in dis house were 'feared ter walk 'round in it by ourselfes when night come. We-all sho' did luv our young mistress, kase she were that pretty an' real smart. She sho' love her flower garden, an' she jes' set in it when the flowers were a-smelling sweet all de time. De young marster, he jes' luv her more'n enything, an' everybody talk 'bout how happy them two was.

One night, when de moon was a-shinin' bright, look lak dat moon was de biggest an' de brightest moon we-uns ebber did see, an' all we niggers were a-settin' out in front o' de cabin, when all at one'st a ole screech owl began ter holler an' ter screech an' make er terrible noise. An' dat ole owl he were a-settin' right up in a big tree over de big house. My mammy she begin ter turn de pocket ob her a'prin inside out, an' den she tie er knot in de a'prin string. But dat ole owl he keep on hollerin' an' er screechin', an' my mammy she say "Somebody in dat big house is sho' gwine die."

Well, sho' 'nuff, in 'bout er week, one day when de young miss' an' de young marster was a-walkin' in de gartin, she seed a new kin' er flower er bloomin', an' when she lent over ter smell it, she fell ober in er faint, an' de young marster he taken her up in his'n arms an' carried her in de house an' lay her on de bed. An' when she come to she say she knew she was a-goin' ter die. But she say she would come back ter her home, an' she say she would come back as er white dove an' set on de sno'-ball bush in de gartin.

And sho' 'nuff she did die. An' we-uns all grief an' be sorry, an' miss her so much. We-all's feel sorry fer de young marster, 'case he grief hisself 'most ter death, too. An' den de close up de big house an' say he was a-goin' 'way ter de fur parts ob de worl'. An' he lef' we-uns ter keep on livin' in de cabin an' ter take care ob de home fer him. I wuks in dat gartin, tends dem flowers myse'f. An' ebery day I look fer de white dove in de sno'ball bush. But so many years pass an' de dove didn't come. An' de marster didn't come back neither.

But one day, arter many years, come er letter from de marster say he done got married agin, an' dat he would be home in de spring an' bring de new mistress. We-uns busied ourse'fs an' clean up dat 'hole house an' eberywhar 'round, an' when I went out ter clean up de gartin, I noticed de sno'-ball bush was in full bloom. I jes' neber did see so many bloom on dat bush befo'. On de day de marster come an' bring de new mistress, we-uns was all dress up an' stan' 'round to tell 'em howdy. An' jes' as de marster an' de new mistress step up ter de do' ter go inside de house, er low griefin' were heard in de gartin, an' right on de limb ob de sno'-ball bush mid de blossoms sat de white dove.

Ebery ev'ning at de same time arter dat de white dove come an' sat on dat bush an' moan an' moan. We-uns all got scade, 'case we knew'd our first mistress had kep' her word an' come back. All de peoples 'round got 'cited an' come ter look ober de gartin wall ter see de dove. De new mistress she felt so bad she jes' set an' cried, an' neber would go out in de gartin. But de marster he got worryin' an' frettin' at de people comin' an' makin' such er stir. So on one evenin', jes' befo' twilight, de marster he tooken his'n gun an' went out de house in er great rage, an' when he come near de sno'-ball bush de dove riz' up in de air an' fluttered to him; an' he raise de gun an' fired. A woman's scream sounded ober de gartin an' de dove flew 'way wid er red stain in her white heart. Dat night as de marster lay in his bed, he died, an' no one is eber knowed de cause ob his'n death. De new mistress lef'. An' dat ole house is still a-sittin' thar, winders all broken out. An' white doves jest fly in an' out all de time. It sho' is de ole hanted house.

JACK-MA-LANTERNS: LIGHTS IN THE WOODS

Catherine Newman, interviewed by Laura Virginia Hale
in Front Royal, Warren County, on June 29, 1942

I used to know a lot of that stuff you axin' about, but I reckon I done forgot most of it, or jist can't rek'lect it offhand. I remember how the ol' folks used to tell 'bout Jack-ma-Lanterns (My informant insisted that the middle syllable was "ma.") that 'ud lead you off at night. You know, back in those days there wasn't lights ever'where to guide a body like 'tis today. If you started out to go somewhere at night, you'd try to spot a light in some neighbor's house and foller that. On real dark, foggy nights one of them Jack-ma-Lanterns would appear in front of someone trav'lin' along a lonely road or path, a-lookin' jist lak a light way off in somebody's winder, so as to make that person foller it. Then it'd lead him off into the thickets or swamps somewhere. Why, I've heard of folks bein' lost all night follerin' one of them Jack-ma-Lanterns. So if a body had to go somewhere at night and didn' want to be led off by a Jack-ma-Lantern, he'd turn his pockets wrong side out. That'd keep 'em away, they said.

THE CAT WOMAN

Aunt Sudie, interviewed by an unknown female worker
in an unknown location in Smyth County, no date given (late fall)

Nigh 'bout er hundred years agone, a hard working young man come an' settled in Smythe County. He'd done saved his yearnin's an' bought er pa'cel o' land. He had er big house-raisin', and him an' th' neighbors built er good house an' barns. He bought horses, cows, sheep, an' pigs. He lived by hisself, lonesome like, doing his own work.

One powerful stormy night when he was settin' by his fireplace feelin' low in his mind, a pretty spotted cat come through ah cat hole cut in th' corner o' the door. Hit begun singin' [purring] an' bowin' itself up, sullen-like, 'round his laig fer er spell. Then hit went away sudden-like through th' hole in th' door. After that, every night 'bout dark hit 'ud come and go. He got ter studyin' 'bout how he wanted the critter fer comp'ny. So the next night when she come in, he stopped up the cat hole, caught a-holt of hit, and began rubbin' its back.

All of er sudden that spotted cat turned inter the purtiest young woman you'd want ter see. She stood ag'in his sides a-smilin' devilish-like an' lookin' up in his face. Nacherly, being er single man, and good-looking, he begun talkin' to her right then an' tha.

Soon he give out th' noration [narration] that he war goin' to get marr'ed. She made him a whopper of er wife, an' soon two mighty sweet little child'en come ter cheer 'n' brighten tha home.

One night in late fall, just 'bout like 'tis now, dampish and th' wind a-howlin', some neighbors came ter set 'till bedtime. Th' wind riz an' screeched 'round th' house like all the hants an' witches from Hell wus turned a-loose. Th' cabin scrooched 'round on th' hilltop like th' old Devil hisself had a-holt of hit by one corner. But them as was inside didn' pay no pertic'lar 'tention. They'd done got uster winds roarin' an howlin'. The talk jus' nacherly turned inter th' different ways of how each of um had done got marr'ed ter tha mates.

Each of 'em told about tha 'talkin' days' an' how they got their mates. Last of all, th' man o' th' house begun ter tell how he met his purty wife. He'd no more'n begun his tale, when his wife gethered her two child'en tight in her arms an' set there a-smilin' strange-like as his story went on.

Th' man riz up from his cheer [chair] ter show th' comp'ny how th' cat come through th' door. Ah mighty blast o' wind shuck th' house 'till it rocked like er cradle. Hit howled so loud nobody heared th' man's last words. But th' minute he moved th' block from the cat hole, a pretty spotted cat an' two kittens darted through th' hole. Th' man's wife an' child'en wan't never seed ner hearn tell of after that.

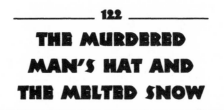

—————— 122 ——————
THE MURDERED
MAN'S HAT AND
THE MELTED SNOW

P. T. Sloan, interviewed by Raymond Sloan
in an unknown location in Floyd County, no date given

Being a school boy on his father's farm and greatly interested in listening to stories told by visitors, he [the informant] was particularly interested in a story told by a man named Bailey Thomas of Floyd County who came to pay his family a visit. About a year before this, a man by the name of Brogan had killed a man named Agee near old Silver Leaf (now a discontinued post office) in Floyd County. This may be easily located at this time by saying that it was near Old Payne's Creek Church on the Skyline Drive.

Thomas had on a black hat of the style of the day and told that this hat was the "Sunday Hat" of the murdered man, and gave the details of the murder. The story is well known by residents of both Franklin and Floyd Counties. Brogan had beaten Agee about the head with a rock and went away leaving him for dead under an old pine tree. But Agee had apparently lived some time, and when he was found dead later, the spot where he lay under the tree had been worn smooth by his death struggles.

Thomas, who spoke with a slight lisp and an Irish accent, said, "You can see by the style and quality of this hat that it is of good material, and you can see also that it is as good as it ever was, except these spots where I now put my finger. Everywhere you see a hole in this hat is where there was a wound on the murdered man's head." Sure enough, the hat that seemed fashioned of the finest felt had flaws in several spots, and these were identical with the wounds on the dead man's head, although the hat was not on his head when he was murdered.

Following this well-illustrated story, Mr. Thomas said that many people had noticed that grass never grew under the pine tree and that snow melted as soon as it fell on the spot worn smooth by Agee's death struggles. Soon afterward, Mr. Sloan said, he had occasion to make a trip to the neighborhood where the murder was committed. This was when his father, Sam Henry Sloan, swapped a yoke of oxen for a horse owned by a man named Ed Sweeney. Sweeney had been Agee's father-in-law, and Mr. Sloan said that when he went into Floyd County to bring home the horse, he and Sweeney's son Walter stopped by the murder tree. Snow was on the ground all around, but the spot where the dying man had struggled was clean and bare.

––––––––– **123** –––––––––

THE DISAPPEARING
OLD GRAY HORSE

Mr. Butler, interviewed by Gertrude Blair
in Amsterdam, Botetourt County, on July 12, 1939

Old man Linkenhoker had a still in that hollow and Squire John Etzler lived on a farm not far away. The squire said every time he passed through there with a load of hay going to his barn and halted for a moment at the still, when he came out, an old gray horse would be standing there, eating hay out of the back of his wagon. When he threw a rock or a stone at the horse he would disappear. Nobody could tell which way he went, or see anything of that horse, until a wagon or load of hay passed by. Squire Etzler said "I bet I'll fix him. When I have hay again I will have a gun too."

So the next time he passed through he kept close watch for the old gray horse. And sure enough, no sooner had he stopped and gone into the still house, when he looked out and there stood the old horse eating his hay. He stepped out and leveled his gun at him and fired away. But just as before, the horse vanished and nobody ever seen him come or go.

—————— 124 ——————

THE HAUNTED WOODS

Mrs. R. V. Brayhill, interviewed by John W. Garrett
in Hopewell, no date given

My grandfather Pernell had a large farm and in those days the farms all had to be fenced and the cattle run outside [the fence]. And between his farm and the Crysel farm was a haunted woods. The road was a narrow wagon road going through a thick pine forest between the two farms, and often people had seen and heard things as they pass[ed] through this pine thicket. My mother and my Aunt Bittish said that often as they went over this road at night that they would hear the most pitiful cry, as if someone were in distress, and then an animal that resembled a big black bear would brush by them and then it would suddenly vanish.

And one time the fence around the farm caught fire about three o'clock in the morning. And Aunt Bitty saw the fence burning and she come running over to my father's to get him and my brothers to go help put the fire out. And as she was coming through the pine forest there was something that looked like two men came running behind her, and as they passed her they suddenly disappeared. Bitty said she was scared almost to death, but it was closer to my father's than it was back home, and she was through the haunted woods. So she came running to my father's for help. The family left the haunted farm and went to another community.

_____ **125** _____

THE FIDDLER
OF PETER CAVE

W. Scott Powers, interviewed by James Taylor Adams
in Wise, Wise County, on January 12, 1942

Over close to Dungannon is a round hill overlooking Clinch River. They call it Powers Hill because some of the old Powers's used to own it and live there. Under that hill is one of the biggest caves in the country. It is a salt petre cave and has been called "Peter Cave." I remember when I was a boy going in this cave and hearing the strangest sounds. Went like somebody playin' the fiddle. It seemed like I could almost make out the tunes. I know I got excited and come out and never went in again. I told some of the old people about what I'd heard and they said that the cave was haunted.

Said that a long, long time ago an early settler took in a traveler one night and that the man was a fiddler. He was telling the stranger about the big cave, and he said he'd like to go in it. So the next day he took him to it and their voices resounded so sharp against the walls that the stranger said he'd bring his fiddle the next day and play and see the effects. So the next day they went again to the cave and the traveler took along his fiddle. They went away back in the cave and he played and the man said it made the prettiest music he had ever heard.

Then somehow they got separated and he could not find the stranger. He could hear him fiddling, but he could never come up with him. He hollered and screamed at him, but if the stranger heard, he never let on, just kept sawing away on his fiddle. Then at last the fiddling ceased and he couldn't hear anything. So he gave up and come out and put out the alarm that the stranger was lost in the cave. People gathered in and hunted all through the cave. They could hear what they took to be the music of the fiddle, but they could never find the fiddler. And another thing, they could travel, it seemed, for miles and find no end to the cave. They would go in what they thought was a straight line and first thing they knew they'd be right back at the mouth of the cave. They carried lights, of course, and could see dozens of passageways leading off in all directions. Some would go one way, others another, but they always turned up at the mouth of the cave. And no matter where they went they could always hear the music, but could never seem to get any nearer to it. When they were near the mouth of the cave the fiddler seemed to be far back in the cave. When they were far back it seemed still farther, and, following it, they would soon reach the entrance, still hearing it.

So they say that ever since then you can go in the cave and hear the fiddler playing his fiddle. I know I heard something like fiddle music, but I don't know what it was.

———— 126 ————

THE SHOWER
OF STONES

William Steele, interviewed by I. M. Warren
in Newport, Augusta County, on April 11, 1939

Dr. McChesney's household consisted of his wife and four young children, together with several Negro servants. One of the latter was a girl named Maria, who was probably eight years old. One evening in January, 1825, while the family was at supper, Maria ran in from the kitchen, which was some thirty feet from the main house, very much scared, and said that an old woman with her head tied up was chasing her. Little attention was given to this incident, but for days Maria complained of being afraid to be alone and her strange actions attracted the notice of the family. One day a shower of stones fell on the roof of the dwelling house, and afterwards stones continued to fall at intervals both day and night. The average size of the stones was about the size of a man's fist, but some were too heavy to be thrown by a person of ordinary strength. Occasionally some were so hot that the dry grass on which they fell was scorched.

Reports of the stone showers spread through the country and people came from miles around to gaze on the curious spectacle. On some days the yard was crowded. The showers did not occur everyday, and off-day visitors generally went away doubting the whole queer business.

Maria's complaints of being chased by the old woman continued, and as she was suspected of being the cause of the disturbance, Dr. McChesney sent her to the home of his brother-in-law, Thomas Steele. While Maria was on her way across the hill to the Steele's home, Mrs. Steele and her children (including her son William), a young white woman, and a Negro woman and her children were sitting under a tree in the yard. Mrs. Steele was knitting and the Negro woman was washing clothes. Mr. Steele was not at home. Suddenly they heard a loud noise in the house as if it were full of frightened horses. The white woman ran to the house first, followed by Mrs. Steele. The furniture of the large front room—bed, bureau, chairs, andirons, etc.—had been piled up in a big heap in the middle of the floor, and while the frightened women looked on stones began to shower down on the house. Soon Maria was seen coming and she told that she had again been chased by the old woman, and was in a state of evident terror.

The Steele's sent Maria back home but stones continued to fall on the roof. They even got into the house, how and from where, no one could discover. Glass in the cupboard doors and plates and dishes were broken and the furniture was severely pelted. Some of the articles still preserved show the marks to this day.

The jinx was still on at the McChesney place too. One day in the spring, the weather being still cool, the family was sitting around the fire. Those present were Dr. and Mrs. McChesney, Mrs. Mary Steele, Mr. and Mrs. Thomas Steele, their son William (the author of this story), and others. The doors were closed and the windows were down, when a stone seeming to come from a corner of the room near the ceiling struck Mrs. Thomas Steele on the head. A lock of her hair was cut off as if done by scissors, and her scalp [was] cut to the bone. Mr. Steele, enraged, denounced the evil doer for "taking its spite on a woman" and not on him. Afterwards, as he sat at the front door, he was pelted with clods of sod and earth that seemed to come from inside the house. The missiles piled around him, until, at the entreaties of his mother, who cried that "the thing" would kill him, he left the spot and was not pursued.

To remove the McChesney and Steele children from danger, they were sent with Maria to their Grandmother Steele's home near Midway. Soon things began to happen there—stones fell about, furniture in the kitchen moved around of its own accord, and a large kitchen bench one day pranced about the floor like a horse. The children at first were amused, and young John Steele (afterwards Dr. Steele, now dead) proposed to bridle the bench and ride him. Mounted on the bench it capered about so that young Steele fainted. During this time also the farm servants found that food and tools they had taken to the fields disappeared and later turned up at the house.

All this time Maria kept complaining of being beaten. One day Mrs. Steele took the Negro girl between her knees, drew her skirts about her, and with a stick struck around as if beating off something invisible. Maria cried out that she was being beaten and stuck with pins. These "slaps" on Maria, said William Steele, were heard distinctly but nothing could be seen. At last Maria fell to the floor exhausted and apparently dead. She was soon revived, but for weeks continued her complaints of being punished.

Worn out with these troubles, Dr. McChesney, as a last resort, sold Maria and she was taken south. As soon as she went away the disturbances stopped. An old Negro woman living in the neighborhood was reputed to be a witch. She walked about with a stick and chewed tobacco. Dr. McChesney in his boyhood says he always "gave her the road" when they met. It was said that the Negro girl, Maria, had been impudent to this old crone and had been threatened with punishment.

127

THE BLACK CAT

Woodrow Sexton, interviewed by James Taylor Adams
in Big Laurel, Wise County, on March 24, 1941

One time there was a woman who had several children but was never married. All of her children died from some strange disease. People got suspicious and they took up one of the babies and found a pin sticking in the top of its head. They then went and took up all of them and found pins in all of their heads. She'd stuck pins right in the tops of their heads to kill 'em, but they couldn't prove she done it. So it went on and it wasn't long 'till she took down sick. She got worse and worse and one night they knew she was dying. All of the neighbors was there setting up with her. About midnight they heard a cat squalling up the hollow from the house. They didn't pay much attention at the start, but [it] kept coming closer and closer. At last it started squalling and scratching on the door shutter. They wouldn't open the door and all at once it come right through the door. It was a big black cat, bigger than any cat they'd ever seen and its eyes shone like balls of fire. It squalled and walked to the bed and rared up on it and looked the sick woman square in the face. She screamed out that it was the devil come to get her for killing her children, and she wheeled over with her face to the wall and never drawed another breath. The cat slid out through the closed door and went squalling back up the hollow.

TREASURE

Mel Fisher, the famous treasure hunter, has been in Bedford County recently, searching for the horde of silver, gold, and jewels that Thomas Jefferson Beale supposedly buried near a creek in Montvale in the early 1820s.[1] He spent several weeks digging around the area in the fall of 1989, and although he didn't find anything, he told a local newspaper reporter that he still believes Beale's Treasure is there. The reporter suggested that it was all a hoax, though, and that Fisher would have more luck if he went back to raising sunken ships.[2] The local people I talked to said he'll never find anything. In fact, they seem put off by the idea that this professional might win the prize that has eluded so many others in the past. The connection between this newspaper story and the treasure legends collected by VWP workers fifty years ago is this: basically, people want buried treasure to stay buried.

In his article "Buried Treasure Tales in America," Gerald Hurley has noted that American treasure narratives "usually end with the treasure not being found."[3] This is the case in all but one of the twenty-nine treasure tales in the WPA collection. The folklorist Alan Dundes has suggested that treasure tales reinforce the folk idea of "unlimited good," the unspoken assumption that there is no real limit to how much of anything exists or can be produced. He said the idea of unfound treasure indicates "that boundless wealth is still available to anyone with the energy and initiative to go dig for it."[4] But, as Patrick Mullen found in his work on legends from the Texas Gulf Coast, treasure tales are seldom about energy and initiative; they are about quick and easy money. Furthermore, some physical or supernatural blocking force is almost always an element of the story. So while the unlimited good is there, it is also not there, or at least it is not usually obtainable.[5] Both Dundes and Mullen are right in a sense—buried treasure does represent the possibility of unlimited good, but it is a good which must remain forever unfound to continue as a possibility. Treasure tales are more about hope and the future than they are about actual material wealth. To actually locate a legendary treasure would be to cancel hope and spoil the future.

So, some blocking force is essential to the treasure legend's structure. In "A Gold Hunter Finds a Ghost" (legend 130), the one WPA treasure legend that ends in success, the hunters are initially blocked, until they obey the spirit that protects the gold. The purpose of the ghost in this tale is to direct the treasure's proper distribution, a common ghostly motif. In "Ocean-Born Mary" (legend 128) the ghost does not reveal the treasure, but the story ends with the hope that she will in the future. But these are atypical; a more common scenario of ghostly treasure stories has the ghost itself serve as the blocking agent. In the two cases given here, the treasure-guarding ghost appears as a black dog and a mysterious human hand.

Like other kinds of legends, treasure tales often make moral points. A common one is that finding treasure is "too easy," that it is illegitimate wealth because it is not earned by work or effort. A corollary is that the search for it is a waste of time—"A Spirit Dog Guards Swift's Mine" (legend 134) even suggests that searching for treasure caused a man's death. Also, immoral behavior in itself can block one from finding treasure. "The Story of Swift and His Compass" (legend 133) is an example. Structurally it manipulates several polar oppositions—dead versus alive, Indian versus white (standing for wild versus "civilized" in an ironic sense), and lost versus found—along with the primary one, the moral opposition of good versus evil. The mine is found initially through contact with Indians. Swift and his partner Monday engage in counterfeiting money, minting currency illegally from the silver. At this point they also become criminals. When they are attacked by the Indians, they run for their lives, abandoning the mine and the silver. As he escapes, Swift kills his partner and buries some silver with him, compounding the seriousness of his evil doings. At this point he has also unwittingly created a treasure-guarding ghost. When he returns to retrieve the silver, Monday's ghostly hand appears over the dial of Swift's compass so he can never find his way back. Swift's silver may be hidden somewhere, but a "bad" person like Swift will never find it. The element of the Indians using the silver to shoe their horses also suggests that the treasure may be accessible only to those who are in a natural state and innocent of its (unnatural) cultural value as money.

While three regions—the Chesapeake Bay, the Shenandoah Valley, and the Appalachian Plateau—turned up treasure legends, stories of Swift's Silver Mine in Wise County dominated the WPA collection treasure material, so much so that the collection organizers created a separate file for it. Containing field-collected anecdotes, legends, and beliefs, as well as extensive background research, the file amounts to over fifty typed pages.[6] It is a wealth of folklore that deserves extensive exploration.

NOTES

1. Peter Viemeister's *The Beale Treasure: A History of a Mystery* (Bedford, Va.: Hamilton's, 1987) recounts the history and folklore associated with this famous Virginia treasure story.

2. "Treasure Hunter Believes Beale's Treasure Story Hoax," Charlottesville, Va., *Daily Progress*, April 7, 1990, p. C12.

3. Gerald T. Hurley, "Buried Treasure Tales in America," *Western Folklore* 10 (1951): 197.

4. Alan Dundes, "Folk Ideas as Units of Worldview," *Journal of American Folklore* 84 (1971): 96–97.

5. Mullen, *I Heard the Old Fishermen Say*, p. 106.

6. The Swift's Silver Mine material is in box 3, folder 2, item 62 and box 5, folder 6, WPA collection.

128

OCEAN-
BORN MARY

Mrs. Nancy C. Wooding, interviewed by Bessie A. Scales
in Danville, on April 14, 1941

Legend says that many years ago the seas were filled with pirates, and sailors sang of Captain Kidd, who was the greatest
pirate of them all. But finally he was hanged, and one of his men
took his place as the King of the Pirates, but he was murdered by
his own men so that his ghost might guard their treasure which
was supposed to have been buried somewhere on the shores of
Chesapeake Bay in Virginia, and if this is true the ghost is still
there, because a pirate's ghost could not desert his gold if he
wanted to.

Once a crowd of emigrants on their passage from Ireland were
captured by pirates, and while these pirates were on board this
immigrant ship, a baby girl was born. The King of the Pirates,
when he saw the baby, was touched by its tiny helplessness and
he asked the mother if she wouldn't name the child for his wife—
whom he had loved and lost many years ago. The mother promised
she would, and the King of the Pirates sent one of his men back
to his ship for a bolt of Chinese brocade silk, delicate green and
shimmering like the sea in the sun. He gave it to the child's
mother and told her to save it for the little girl's wedding gown,
and to name her Ocean Born Mary. Then the pirates left the boat
without harming anybody or taking anything. As they rowed away,
the King of the Pirates stood in the boat and called back, "Tell
Ocean Born Mary I'll see her again."

When at the age of twenty Ocean Born Mary was married, her wedding dress was made of the green brocade, soft and green as moss and shimmering like the sea in the sun. Ocean Born Mary was a lovely Irish girl. Six feet tall. She had four great sons, the tallest being six feet six inches tall.

When the King of the Pirates grew old and tired of a pirate's life, he built a large square house overlooking the Bay, and as Ocean Born Mary's husband had died, he brought her and her four sons to live in this house. Of course she brought her sea-green wedding gown, which never wore out. After a time the King of the Pirates grew restless and decided to again go to sea. But he was murdered by one of his own men and his body was brought back to the big square house overlooking the Bay. Ocean Born Mary carried out the request he had always made of her that he be buried on the highest point overlooking the Bay. He always told her he wanted to be buried on this high spot so as to watch over his buried treasure and see all the ships coming in and going out of the Bay.

Ocean Born Mary lived to be a hundred and two. When she died she was buried by the side of the King of the Pirates on the highest spot over the Chesapeake Bay. Ocean Born Mary still haunts the scene of this big square house. On moonlit nights a very tall woman flits through the shadows and those who have been there feel her presence always. On windy nights a ghost can be heard wailing on the wind. For many centuries men have dug along these shores hoping to find the Pirates' buried gold. To this day nobody has found it, but the fishing folk say—some of these days the ghost of Ocean Born Mary will lead them to the spot where the treasure is buried.

129

THE TWO PINE TREES

Mrs. Robert Edwards, interviewed by Cornelia Berry
in Fleeton, Northumberland County, no date given

On the tip end of the peninsula where Fleeton is now located, stood two large pine trees. Under these pine trees the children of the neighborhood used to go to play. As this neighborhood was sparsely settled about a hundred years ago, most of the land was covered with woods at this time.

One day while George Edwards and some other children were playing under the two pines, they saw a big black ship come in the river and anchor off the point where the two pines stood. In those days ships of this type were seldom seen, so this ship attracted everyone's attention. As night came on the children forgot about the ship and hurried home to supper.

The next day when the children went back to the two pine trees to play, they found their play house scattered and a deep hole dug out of the earth. Upon close examination rust was found all around the hole. And a chest of gold was believed to have been removed.

130

A GOLD HUNTER
FINDS A GHOST

Charles Patton, interviewed by John W. Garrett
in Buckingham, Buckingham County, on May 24, 1941

Charlie Patton said that his grandfather was a man that made his living by hunting gold. He had a needle that would point out where there was gold. So he went out one evening in the mountains, had his helper with him, to dig. When he found a place where it was gold, and while searching, he came to a rock pile and decided to stop there and rest for a while. And, his needle pointed down in that rock pile [and] indicated that there was gold. So he said to his helper, "It is gold in this rock pile," said, "Dig here and pull back those rocks and see if we can find any gold."

So the helper went to work digging and pulled back several rocks. And as he was getting clost to the gold, there was something caught his trousers and pulled him back. The helper said to the boss, "Did you see anything?" He said, "No, I didn't see anything." He said, "I didn't either, but something pulled me back!" His boss laughed at him and said, "That's nothing but imagination, go on and dig."

So he started to dig another rock up and something got hold of his trousers again and pulled him back. So he made another attempt to dig and the same thing got a hold of him and threw him head over heels off the rock pile. And the helper got up and started back to the boss and felt the same thing again getting a hold on him. He said "What is that and what have I done that you're doing me this way?" The boss laughing at him didn't think nothing about it, supposing he just fell off the rocks and fell backward. But a voice spoke out and said, "This gold is mine and I left it here for another person!" Called the man's name and said, "You go and get this man and I will let you get it and divide it up." They knew the man well, went and got this man and went back and dug under the next rock and found the gold and divided it up without any more trouble. It was several thousand dollars in gold.

131

THE SIGN THAT
POINTED TO GOLD

Taylor Nash, interviewed by James M. Hylton
in Wise, Wise County, on July 2, 1941

I'se goin' up through the Hurricane country once an' old J. W. Crabtree, a man of many years an' life long residenter of that section, told me he'd go 'long too, if'en I didn't care. Well, I'se allus glad to have company on my long galavants in the hills, an' [so] he up an' went 'long too. He knowed a right smart 'bout the ole places in thar, an' as we'd pass some ole house er tree he'd pint an' say, "Thar's where so an' so kilt a bear, er so an' so had a big fight with some Injun er wildcat thet had sidled off from the hills up on above us. Once we passed a big rock in the bend uv a ole road an' he pinted an' showed me a great big mark on hit. An' when we got a little closer up we could see thet hit wuz a big long arrer [arrow] with uh shaft pintin' right 'round towards the top uh the hill up from us a little ways.

"Thet," said ol' man J. W., "is whar some Injuns hid some gold er other stuff uh some kind back when they's prowlin' 'round in this country. My Pap tole me thet one time they's a squad uh Reds come through hyar an' all uh 'em wuz lo[a]ded down an' with skin sacks hung crost their backs. They's some whites got atter 'em, an' they let a few uh 'em hole 'em offen 'till the others buried the stuff they had on 'em. They's many a man hunted fer hit atterds [afterwards], but never found hit yet. I've hunted fer hit myself, tho' I'd ruther nobody but you'd know 'bout hit fer the time bein'."

Well, we could see thet arrer wuz plain an' pinted plimeblank [exactly] to the top uh the hill. We both made uh bargin to come back sometime en' hunt some more fer hit later, but we never did. He said "They allus left uh sign uh some kind er other fer to tell where they's somethin' hid, but [they] knowed the whites couldn't find hit fer they's no way [of] readin' their signs." To be ruther trueful though, hit looked lack hit'd been dug in the rock with a tomahawk er somethin' lack thet. I'd heerd sech a tale 'bout a rock lack thet before but I'd never seed hit myself 'till then. He said his Pap'd tole him 'bout hit a good many years 'fore then. They's supposed to be plenty uh gold in them hills. An' iffen a man'd only spend enough time he'd be 'most shore to find hit some time er other.

———— 132 ————

THE BEVERLY DIAMONDS

Mrs. Minnie Collins, interviewed by James Taylor Adams
in Glamorgan, Wise County, on September 30, 1941

Down here at Relm between Norton and Coeburn's a big flat rock, or used to be, called the Beverly Rock. I've played on it when I'uz a child an' sot on [it] since I've been grown. They said that's where some of the old Beverly's lived—old Freeman Beverly, I believe. Here about forty years ago hit got norated [narrated] aroun' that old Beverly, whatever his name was, had brought a fortune in diamonds into this country with 'im an' hid 'em up the holler there before he died. People believed in [that] so much that a lot of 'em hunted and hunted fer 'em. I remember that an old man named Cavendish put in one whole summer diggin' here an' thar up that holler. I lived right at the mouth of the holler, an' would see him go up the holler with tools of a mornin' an' come out of a night. I don't rec[k]on he ever found anything, but some folks think he did. I remember he got worked up over hit so strong that he bought an' paid a big price fer some sort of rod or contraption that would lead 'im to the diamonds. Then I've heard hit said that old Beverly didn't bring the diamonds in here with 'im, but that he found a diamond mine in that holler, an' hit was the mine old Cavendish was huntin' fer. I know I've heard 'em tell that old Beverly showed sumpin' he'd found near thar an' that old Pat Hagan took 'em to send off an' see what they was an' that he never heard from 'em anymore. I don't know about that, but I do know old Cavendish, Bill's an' Harry's daddy, put in one summer diggin' up that holler.

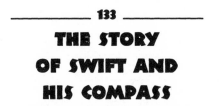

133

THE STORY
OF SWIFT AND
HIS COMPASS

Mrs. Clara Bozarth, interviewed by Emory L. Hamilton
in Josephine, Wise County, July 19, 1939

Mr. Swift came down to Virginia from Pennsylvania a long time ago, while the Indians were still here. He got acquainted with a white man that was raised by the Indians who was called Monday [another version says he was French and named Monde]. Monday showed Mr. Swift where a silver mine was that the Indians had found. 'Tis said that the Indians shod their horses with the silver. They [Swift and Monday] went to counterfeiting money that was pure silver, without alloy. One day the Indians attacked them and Swift killed Monday for fear he would tell where their mine was; he buried him in what is known as Pickum [southeast of Norton]. They buried a lot of coined money along their route as they fled from the Indians.

Swift was gone for several years then returned to get some of the money he buried, and maybe coin some more. He knew they had went up Ice Plant Hollow [named for the Norton Ice Works] to the High Knob. When he came back he would go that way by a "rock man" that stood near the road. The men working with him used to say "Good morning" to the rock man when they passed it on their way to work.

When Swift reached the High Knob he would try to set his compass, and Monday's hand would appear over it, so he could never determine the direction of the mine. For several years he hunted, but could never find any of the money, nor the mine.

——— 134 ———

A SPIRIT DOG
GUARDS SWIFT'S MINE

W. Patton Beverly, interviewed by James Taylor Adams
in Norton, Wise County, on March 17, 1941

I'm not sayin' this is so. My father in his old age married a woman who put in all her life huntin' for Swift's mine, an' I honestly believe she drug poor old pap around over the mountains so much that it caused his death. She told of finding some silver way back in the mountains somewhere an' she had pap to go with her. When they got there a big black dog come out of the laurel an' growled and looked like it was goin' to jump on them. Now pap never told me this, but his wife did after he was dead. She said the dog was big as a yearlin' an' that its eyes was as big as saucers and shone like balls of fire. It wouldn't let them go near the place where she had found what she thought was Swift's silver mine.

——— 135 ———

THE OLD
WOMAN WHO
FOUND THE SILVER

Taylor Nash, interviewed by James M. Hylton
in Wise, Wise County, on April 9, 1941

All this I am telling you about Swift's silver was before the [Civil] War, but my mother knew my father's business and Uncle Jessie's business better than I did I guess. And when they would sit and tell the tales of Swift and the silver he was supposed to have hidden it was something to interest anyone, and I listened to all that I heard them say. Everyone knows I am interested in this and have been for some years and I have traced down every bit of evidence I have heard of about Swift being in this part of the country.

I went to see a woman down at Coeburn, or rather, between Flatwoods and Coeburn, and she told me this tale of his [her?] mother who she said found some silver that had been melted and the slag and dirt had held to one end of the cinder-like [cylinder?] formation, and she thought that it was some kind of old iron that had been left there in the hills. But, as she was picking blackberries at the time, she never said anything about it to anyone for years. Then when she did think of it she told her family about it, and they, having heard of Swift's silver, went in search for it.

The old lady had grown feeble by this time, and almost blind herself. So some of her sons carried her all the way into the mountains and she tried to point out to them where she had thrown the stuff she had found the few years before. It was a place where nobody would have been apt to find it, but they hunted high and low. They could not find the big piece she said she had found and thrown there; however, they did find some silver ore with some slag and rust-like dirt or sand hung onto it. It was a good deal smaller than she said she had found, and they thought that someone had more than likely found it and had broken it on a rock to see what it was and when it broke and they saw the silver part of it they took it along with them after being unable to find the other piece they had broken off on the rock.

They carried the old lady back and she tried to draw a map and show them where she found the metal, but all searches wound up a failure, and it was not so long after that she died. However, her relatives have hunted time and again for trace of it, and every time any of them go into that section of the hills they make a brief search, hoping they will at last find where she found it.

—————— 136 ——————

SWIFT'S SILVER MINE

Tom Hale, interviewed by Emory L. Hamilton
in Wise, Wise County, on August 13, 1940

The Swift mine, I've been told, was seven mile from the "burning spring" [a lit natural gas well] in the Nettle Patch. Near here was where the gun was buried with the barrel pointing toward the entrance to the mine. Uncle John Powers and some others were in there hunting and found a kit of tools in a hole in a rock in the Nettle Patch country. Another rock had been set over the opening where the tools were hidden. This was up a branch from the old Smith place in the Nettle Patch; they called it Laurel Branch. He said they went up the left side of the branch in a laurel thicket. The hole in the rock, he said, looked like it had been cut out and a flat rock laid over the hole to cover it up. They found a hammer, a crucible, and a pair of moulds. He had the hammer when he died, I've been told. He told me and Emmet White, here at my house one Sunday, the directions to take to find the hole. And we went there and searched, but couldn't find anything. I've heard that Swift and them lived in Tennessee. I believe I heard old Isaac Willis say this. When I was a kid they told me that a lot of counterfeit money had been passed in Tennessee. It was silver dollars and half dollars. Finally the counterfeiters were caught and sent to the pen. Everybody believed that the counterfeiters mined their silver in this section out of Swift's mine to make the money.

UNUSUAL EVENTS

The legends in this section touch upon a variety of subjects. The one thing they have in common is an absence of supernatural elements. Not every legend moves from the real world into another realm; sometimes the movement is simply from the ordinary to the extraordinary, the striking, or the grotesque. Some of the stories resemble supernatural ones, but with natural forces replacing spiritual agents. Two, for example, depict an epidemic of disease and a devastating blizzard meting out punishments for immoral behavior. These may be seen as indirectly supernatural, however; while plagues and storms are natural phenomena, they are considered in both these stories as instruments of God, who is, after all, a supernatural being. Both have directly stated moral messages, and both also have clear undercurrents of racial tension. Narrated by African American informants, they depict punishments that are occasioned by the cruelty and meanness of whites toward blacks.

Like the forces of nature, chance sometimes replaces the supernatural element in these tales. When a boy decides to skip church to swim on a hot summer morning in "The Naked Bull Ride" (legend 148), it is not a dragon or some invisible power from the moon which punishes him but a swarm of bees which happens to be in the tree he climbs to get away from a bull which happens to chase him. When he falls onto the bull's back, it happens to head straight for the church and dump him at the feet of the people coming out of the service. We sense the hand of fate, or at least poetic justice, at work here. The same is true of the migratory legend "Caught in the Graveyard" (legend 149). The young woman who has gone to the graveyard to learn who her future husband will be just happens to plunge her knife into the folds of her skirt as well as the ground. Both stories have moral points to make. The first, though comic, is a distinct reminder to keep the Sabbath day holy, and the second a serious and forceful warning against defiling graves and delving into occult matters.

But stories such as these are by no means simply the sum of their moral points. In fact, their moral impact depends on their dramatic impact. The image of a naked youth surrounded by well-dressed churchgoers is striking. The image of a dead man, frozen stiff, still sitting in his buggy holding the reins, commands our attention. The image of children playing a macabre game of leap-frog over stacks of dead bodies sticks in the mind's eye. Like motorists who slow down to stare at a highway accident, we are drawn to them. We may make certain connections later, as the motorists may suddenly decide to buckle their seatbelts a few miles down the road. But the image precedes the idea; the anxiety precedes the moral. Furthermore, there need not be a moral at all. There is no point to be drawn from "Dick the Slave Boy and the Wolves" (legend 141). It is simply an edge-of-the-seat story of a brush with a horrible death. If any moral lesson about the basic evil of slavery occurs to us concerning "A Scar Identifies a Slave Woman's Husband as Her Son" (legend 139), it arrives later, after the primary shock of the idea of mother-son incest.

Several of the stories in this section are predecessors of what are sometimes termed "modern urban belief" tales. A modernized version of the "Roast Cat for Breakfast" tale (legend 147), which involves a wood-burning stove, has been widely collected as "The Cat in the Microwave." Also, "A Man Dies of Earwigs" (legend 150) is an ancestor of "The Beehive Hairdo" and its variants, which depict dreadful cranial contaminations. And "The Naked Bull Ride" is related to a broad range of narratives about being caught naked.[1] Since these legends are often said to reflect the concerns of modern urbanites—the anxiety and stress of coping with technological devices, corporate food distribution, the dictates of fashion, overcrowding, etc.—it is important to note that the core stories themselves are not necessarily modern or urban. What is clear is that they concern people's deep-seated concerns and fears, such as sex, death, and suffering, and these concerns are not new or unique to modern urban life.

NOTES

1. The most extensive discussion of these and other contemporary belief tales is in Jan Harold Brunvand, *The Vanishing Hitchhiker* (1981), *The Choking Doberman and Other "New" Urban Legends* (New York: Norton, 1984), *The Mexican Pet: More "New" Urban Legends and Some Old Favorites* (New York: Norton, 1986), and *Curses! Broiled Again!* (New York: Norton, 1989).

A SMALLPOX EPIDEMIC:
A CURSE ON WHITES

Virginia Hayes Shepherd, interviewed by an unknown worker
in Norfolk, no date given

I usta hear my mother an' grandma sit an' talk 'bout things that happened durin' pestilence days. They all said the white folks treated the niggers so mean that God made up his mind to punish them, killin' off the cruelest. Fever come an' it killed all de white folks. They say ain' nary a single nigger die from de disease. Some ornery nigger[s] took sick, but God didn't kill 'em. Jus' scared 'em to death. My mother said it killed mos' o' her white folks. On a lot o' plantations every single white person died, but not a single slave. The colored people was jus' havin' a big time. Everywhere you went, the slaves was sittin' on the front porches jes' a rockin' and the white folks stretched out inside, all dead. Was good times after that for the Negroes. Wouldn't any white folks dare treat 'em mean no more.

We come to Norfolk durin' the war. Come for freedom an' be safe. When the war was goin' on, Norfolk was full of soldiers, an' everythin' else. They either come to Norfolk or Hampton. That's why the Hampton school started. Slaves wasn't quite free. Abe Lincoln said they was, but Lee hadn't surrendered yet. Mos' o' them thought they was free.

People wasn't so quick 'gainst catchin' things then. I went to school. There was a pest house 'tween school an' home. They was a lot of smallpox there. One day a lady died of black smallpox. All of us from school stopped by an' had a good look at her. Then my

baby brother got sick an' was down in bed nine days. He was room-
ing with L. P. Robinson's mother. She said brother had smallpox.
Mother got worried and called a doctor. He lied; told mother it
was black measles and told Mrs. Robinson that it was black smallpox. Mother went on to work and left me to look after brother.
But when she was gone Mrs. Robinson and the doctor had a man
come from the pest house to get brother. I wouldn't let the man
in; I locked the door and kept it locked. When mother came, we
all went to the pest house. Everybody fussed because she took me.
She said we might as well die along with the others and if she died
she didn't want to leave me behind. We all lived there a month
and none of us died. More white folks died than Negroes. Negroes
somehow seemed to get well.

There was a big snow on the ground. Snow was deep everywhere. We played leap-frog and a game we made up for using dead
bodies. White people died so fast and the snow froze the ground
so hard that funerals and burying wasn't possible. They held the
funerals, I guess, but they couldn't bury the bodies. Bodies were
stacked on the snow between the sidewalks and gutters. They
were stacked pretty high. This game was a dare game of jumping
over these dead bodies. One child would say, "See that big one
there? Bet you can't jump over it." Sometimes I'd jump over 'em
and sometimes I'd jump right smack on 'em. Didn't make no difference. They was froze stiff. It certainly was cold. I expect everyone would have died if it hadn't been for the Yankee soldiers takin'
care of everybody. They gave us plenty of good food and clothes.
You could go to them and get anything you needed.

————— 138 —————

HOW COX'S SNOW
GOT ITS NAME

Mrs. Jennie Patterson, interviewed by Susie R. C. Byrd
at Clover Hill, Chesterfield County, on May 14, 1937

Do I 'member Cox's snow? Oh yes when dat man freeze to death. I was up yonder in de big house settin' knittin' socks fer my marster. Dr. Cox was de name of de man dat got frez. He had bin drinkin' heavy dat day when he came from Petersburg. When he got most to de house, we heard him callin' but thought t'was some of de t'other folks 'round dar. His daughter (Mrs. Grimes), wouldn't git up to open de do' 'cause we all was gittin' ready fer to go to bed. I seed him dar when dey all went out. Fus' seed dis horse an' buggy comin' to de house dout [without] nobody in it. All got scared an' went a searchin' an' callin' him. An' lo an' behold, dar was Marse Cox stiff in de snow. Chile, I'se bin feard to tell all I know 'bout dis here thing. Dar's been all kinds of tales de white folks bin all kiverin' hit over. Marse Cox liked his liquors so he was drunk an' couldn' make hit, not bein' of his self. I bet you ain' heard dat. Yes, yes, dar was a big botheration at de big house.

Mrs. Sis Shackelford, interviewed by Claude W. Anderson
in Hampton, no date given

I wan' to tell you 'bout dat snow 'cause I don't t'ink hit's written anywhar. Hit come in 1857, yessuh, on de ninth day of February. Mama had a stack o' pies wrapped up in a table cloth underneaf de table. She had jus' made 'em for de quiltin' spree which was to be held Saday night. Didn' get to have nuffin'. Anyway, de snow it started Friday mornin'. Snowed all day Friday, all night Friday, all day Saday, all night Sunday, all day Monday, an' all day long Tuesday. When it stop, you couldn't git out, an' couldn't see out. Snow was way up lebel wid de do' top. Twarn' no blo' snow an' it twarn' no drif' snow, t'was jes' plain lebel snow.

My father couldn't git to his marsa so he put on some ole boots an' gloves an' push de snow from de back do' an' start making a path to de animals. Mama, she put on a ole hat an' pants an' help him. Yessuh! She was de chambermaid slave, an' she knowed she better git to de white folk's house. After dey git de animals, dey went an' got hosses an' steers an' hitched 'em up an' move dat snow offen de roads.

'Twas de coldest night I 'bout ever seed. Ole Phillip Cox, he was a great drinkin' white man. Some said he was drunk dat night. Anyway, he frez to def. Yessuh! Foun' him sittin' up in his buggy, jes' holdin' de reins lak he was drivin'. God knows he was so mean, God had to do suppin' to him. So He jes' let him git drunk an' den frez him to def. 'Twas col' 'nough to freeze anybody. The news dat ole Cox was daid went 'roun' like a win'. After dat dey call dat snow Cox's Snow.

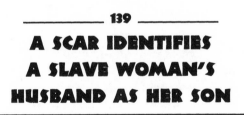

——— 139 ———

A SCAR IDENTIFIES
A SLAVE WOMAN'S
HUSBAND AS HER SON

Georgiana Gibbs, interviewed by an unknown worker
in Portsmouth, no date given

My father told me dere was once a mastah who sold off a slave woman and her son. Many years after dis, de woman married. One day when she was washing her husband's back she seen a scar on his back. De woman 'membered de scar. It was de scar her mastah had put on her son. 'Course, dey didn't stay married, but de woman wouldn't ever let her son leave her.

—— 140 ——

THE OLD NEGRO
THAT FLAGGED
THE TRAIN

Charles Patton, interviewed by John W. Garrett
in Manteo, Buckingham County, on May 26, 1941

Charlie Patton said that there was a colored man that lived in the state of Tennessee. He had a hard time in his life; would work around at different places for a small wage and he had to walk everywhere he went. As he was walking one day along the railroad track he began to think, as he looked at the tracks. He said, "It is a strange thing how that a big thing like a train can run on these little rails and they can hold the train and it run at a rapid speed and those men set up there and ride. Seems they have such a nice time, and they get big pay. Here I am walking out here in the hot sun and my feet is sore. And when I work all day I get just a little money and have to live so hard. It is not fair. The people don't care anything about me no how. All they care for me is what they get out of me. And I believe I have as much right to ride that train as anybody."

He walked along with his feet sore and paining him. He come to the conclusion that he was going to make an attempt to ride. Now he thought serious and said, "I can flag dat train when it come. I will tell the man the truth." He was determined to carry out his thought. He felt he would have to ride, as he had never had the opportunity to ride a train. It was a hot day. He was a little nervous about it, not knowing what would happen. He walked along and was about three miles from the station. All at once he heard a passenger train blowing. Oh, it sounded lonesome to him. But he wanted to ride so bad. And as the train pulled around the curve in sight, the Negro with his wide brim straw hat began to wave it. He stood in the middle of the track. He heard the blow from the engine and saw her begin to slow down. He said, "I got her stopping. I wonder what they are going to say." The engine rolled up and came to a dead stand[still]. The conductor stepped off wondering if the track had given away, and he said in a rough voice—"What's the trouble old man?"

"Boss, I was just tired and worn out, and I see you fellows having it so easy, and I want a ride on this train."

The conductor flew mad and began to curse him. He said, "Dat alright, Boss, but please give me a ride as I am so tired." The conductor said in an angry tone, "Get on here." He carried him to the station. Cursing at him and said "Get off of here, and don't do this any more." The poor old Negro said, "Yessir Boss, and thank you for the ride. I would be willing to take a cursing anytime for a ride."

He went on for a few days and caught himself a possum. As he was walking along the railroad track he said [to himself], "I might be able to sell the man on the next train my opossum and get more money for him. He studied about it and said to himself, "Yes'is, I will do dat." So in a little while he heard a train blowing. He got his old wide brim straw hat off and began to wave it. The train blew and began to slow down, rolled up and stopped. The train man said, "What's the matter, old man?"

"Nothing," he said. "But I got a nice opossum here for to sell. Won't you buy him?" He cursed him out. The old Negro said as he laughed "I don't mind that just so you buy my opossum." He made the sale and went on happy.

——— 141 ———

DICK THE SLAVE BOY
AND THE WOLVES

Harold Pugh, interviewed by Susie Sproles
in Grant, Grayson County, no date given

In early pioneer days the people would gather together for house raisings and things of that kind. In this instance the house raising was on Smythe County side of Iron Mountain, while the family to whom the slave boy belonged lived on the Grayson County side. The entire family had been invited, so they had gone on in the early morning leaving Dick to care for things during the day and to lock up that night before he came on. The reason for his going was that at night after the work of the day had been completed, the host gave the participants a party, or frolic, as they were called in those days. Dick was one of the best fiddlers in the country, so of course he had to go over to help make the music.

He started out in the early afternoon to complete his work so that he might be able to start on his journey before nightfall. As the cows had strayed away, he had to spend some time hunting them. Finally, however, they were found and safely housed.

After seeing that everything was safe under lock and key he snatched up his violin and started on his way. He traveled rapidly for he was fleet of foot and covered much ground in just a short time. But before he could reach the mountaintop dark overtook him. He was growing tired because of the mountain climb, but he knew he must press onward because the people would be waiting for him to come. And then he also knew there were many wolves on the mountain, and if they were to get on his track that he might perish before he could get assistance or before he could reach his destination.

Just as he was reaching the top of the mountain he heard behind him the long drawn out howl of a wolf. Then, on the opposite side, he heard the howl of a fellow creature and in a second he heard the howl of two or three of the beasts on the other side of the mountain. He knew by instinct that they were on his track, and that they would gather in force as they came on after him.

He started in a run down the mountain, but he could tell by their howls they were gaining on him. He knew of an abandoned house not far down the mountain that if he could reach he might thereby save his life. He was by this time very tired, but his seeing the house revived him, and with the wolves close behind him he made one last effort to get there before they could overtake him.

The door had rubbish piled up against it from the inside, but with one superhuman effort he pushed the door open, all the time clinging to his violin. Then he slammed the door shut just as the wolves came up. He laid his violin upon some planks that lay across the joists of the house and then he barricaded the door as best he could.

By this time the pack of wolves had surrounded the house and he knew if they found the door they could with their strength soon push it open. So as soon as possible he climbed to the top of the joists and, settling himself in on the planks with his feet hanging down he tremblingly waited.

It was not long before the leader found the door and, aided by his followers, they soon pushed it open. It made the pack angry when they saw their prey just out of reach. They commenced jumping up, but could not reach him. Finally one of the beasts jumped up and landed on the back of another of the pack, and in that way bit at Dick's trousers, which nearly pulled him off into the midst of the howling wolves. This frightened Dick very much, and he quickly pulled his legs up and crouched in a sitting position on the planks.

The animals were making fearful leaps now and were about to get to him when suddenly he picked up his violin and drew the bow sharply across the strings. This frightened the beasts away for the time being. He succeeded with this stratagem but a few times, for they soon got used to the noise and would not leave. Suddenly one of the beasts jumped up so high that he caught with one paw on the plank. But he could not hold on. This was very serious for Dick, and he racked his brain to find some device to drive the animals away.

Presently he thought of the way wolves would jump on anything when it was covered with blood. Taking out his knife, he opened it and held it in readiness to cut the next wolf that had the audacity to put his paw on the plank. He soon had this opportunity and the beast fell back among his fellow creatures. They, seeing the blood, turned on the one that had been cut and soon had him torn to pieces. In the melee another of the pack was hurt and his companions jumped on him as soon as they had finished the first one.

By this time the day was beginning to break into the darkness, and just at that moment Dick heard someone calling, "Dick, oh Dick!" This was a crowd of men who were hunting for him. Dick's heart beat with joy and gladness as he answered, "Heah I is, boss! In the old cabin, an' ah is powerful glad yuh is come!"

This conversation caused the wolves to run out of the cabin and away into the woods. Many of them were killed by the men who were hunting Dick. And then they came on to the cabin where they found Dick, who had just climbed down from the joists. When he told them of his adventure, they all exclaimed in unison, "You have had a narrow escape, Dick, a narrow escape!"

142

MURDER AT THE COUNTY LINE

Henry Bridgett, interviewed by Susan R. Morton
in Antioch, Fluvanna County, on February 6, 1942

"**T**imes ain't what they us't t' be," said Henry, changing the quid of tobacco from the right to the left cheek and expectorating thoughtfully into a puddle from the night before's rain that stood in front of the store. "Now thar's thet murder at the county line—couldn't get by wi' sech these a-days, wi' telephone an' sech, but in them days th' won't no truck with sech. Ain't never heerd o' th' killin' at the old Stillman place? Well, reckon 'is [this] was 'fore yo' day, an' folks hev so much t' think 'bout now, [they] don't go back t' th' ole days like we use' t'."

"Yes, it were at the Stillman place whar th' ole chimbly stand thar in th' cleared spot. Somepin' funny 'bout thet too. Never no kind of trees grewed up thar same as mos' places what ain't ever worked, but all 'round the house site it's as bare as it ever were. All those flower plants yer see come Spring be what some o' th' women folk planted thar. And thet were a long while back, fer the house has been gone fer nigh seventy year."

"Ol man Stillman bore th' name o' hevin' a powerful quick temper, an' when he'd git an idee thet someone were a-workin' again' him, twere sure t' be trouble."

"When Si Stillman's pappy built th' house 'twere all in th' one county, though part o' his lot were in Fauquier. Then they up an' change th' county line, an' what did hit do but go clean in th' middle o' th' house so they cooked and sat in Prince William, an' slept in Fauquier. The house were log, and it hed one big room with a fireplace, powerful big, as you kin still see, even if it has fallen in some. The other room pappy and his woman slep' in and the least one too. Th' other young-uns slept in th' loft, an' they were hardy in them days fer I've heard tell as how they'd wake up in the mornin' wi' th' snow on their kivvers. But they all grewed up, 'leven of 'em. After a while they all married an' th' ole folks died and thar were no one lef' but Silas."

"Silas never got him a wife. [The] gal he courted ran off wi' some other man an' he grew ole 'fore his time. He jes grew grabbeder an' grabbeder [crabbier?] all th' time. But he liked a good game o' cards, an' anyone were always welcome t' spend an evenin' an' play, 'specially if he thought he'd be able t' lick 'im good an' proper."

"Ol' man Stillman—he got t' be called ol' long 'fore he was ol', jes nat'ully looked thet way—used t' make right smart o' likker, an' he come near t' gittin' in trouble too. But he were pretty slick, an' no one could ever prove nothin' again' him."

"Wal, this night he an' 'nother man who lived over th' mountain, Bill Reilly, agreed they'd hev a little game. An' 'bout midnight a young feller coming 'long th' trail from a-seein' his gal passed the house an' saw a light thar. He hed a min' t' go in, but it were so late an' he wanted t' git home, so he went on. But he recalled, when they asked him, as how he hed heerd someone a-talkin' angry-like."

"Bill Reilly didn't come home th' nex' day, an' then his folks started to look fer him. And when they come nigh th' Stillman place they didn't see no smoke, an' when they knocked at th' door no one come. So they went in an' thar everythin' were in a mess, th' chairs knocked over and th' table turn[ed] upside down and cards all over th' floor. An' thar in a corner were Bill, still an' dead, an' a hole in his head whar th' shot had entered. Thar weren't no sign o' Stillman."

"Arter a while people said they seed smoke comin' from the

chimbly, an' then he got so bol' as t' come out right out in the yard in th' daytime. An' pretty soon the sheriff come t' 'rest him. But he went into the sleepin' room and laughed at him an' tol' him as how he could[n't] cross the county line. Then, when th' sheriff from Fauquier come, he stayed right in th' kitchen an' tol' 'em if they tried to cross th' line he'd shoot, an' they knew he would too. So after a lot of foolin' 'round, the two sheriffs come at th' same time, but somehow the ol' man hed got wind o' what were up an' when they both got thar t'gether he were nowhar t' be foun'."

"But [I] reckon thet he knew his end were come, fer they'd git him sooner or later; an' it were th' next night an' when they looked over there they saw it were th' Stillman place afire; 'twere burned mos' to th' groun' when they got thar, th' house were almos' gone, an' th' nex' day they foun' all thet were lef' o' Ole Man Stillman. Most people were of th' 'pinion he killed hisself 'fore th' fire burned him up. Most likely [he] set the house afire then shot hisself. No one could ever know, but 'tweren't likely as how he couldn't a got out hed he a mind t'."

"No, ain't one ever tried to live at thet place, even if hit were sech a nice spot t' hev a house. Ever go thar at night and you'll likely hear a houn' dawg a-howlin'. An' some as says they seed th' ol' man a-walkin' 'round. Somepin' funny too 'bout good land as thet is thet won't let a tree or nothin' grow thar. Murder's a funny thing; blood puts a spell on a place, hit seems like.

143

THE WOMAN
DRESSED IN BLACK

Miss Molly Crews, interviewed by John W. Garrett
in an unknown location in Amherst County, on December 14, 1940

A Mr. Webb told me, said Molly. A family bought a farm in Amherst, and they lived there peacefully until they started to plow up a twenty acre lot. En [and] he would git up early and go to plowin' and his wife would do the milking. En when she would come in with the milk she would see a woman dressed in black standing at the basement door crying. She went on fer three days and saw her every morning. But she didn't tell anybody. Said the fourth morning she told her husband, "We'll just hafta move, I can't stay here." And he told her the next time she saw the woman to speak to her. So the next morning she come up with the milk and she saw the woman and she spoke to her en said "What's the matter?" En she told her that out in that field where her husband was plowing she had two children buried, and he was goin' to plow the graves up. En she told her she had money hid in the basement en to git it en to fix those two graves and keep the rest for herself, but to never tell anyone how much she got. En said that they went out and found the two little graves out in the middle of the lot; and they put a nice iron fence around it, put two little stones [up]. En they never saw the woman again. But they are wealthy now. They were poor people before that, and after that they were considered wealthy in the community where they live.

───────── 144 ─────────

THE BOY WHO
TURNED WILD
IN THE WOODS

Goldie Hamilton, interviewed by Emory L. Hamilton
in Esserville, Wise County, September 3, 1940

I've heard my daddy tell this. There was a little boy. His father lived close to the woods. He was just two years old. He went out to play one day and got lost in the woods. He wandered off so far from the house that he couldn't find his way back. They searched the woods far and near and couldn't find him.

Years later there was some people in the woods a-huntin' and they saw a man. He acted like he was wild and he run from them.

The hunters reported it and a crowd went and surrounded him and caught him. And it was that same child that was lost when it was a kid. He was a grown man and he had worn his clothes all off him and never could get any more clothes. Hair had growed all over him just like a varmint or animal and all the food he had ever had to eat was just nuts and berries and things he could find in the woods. They had to keep him confined to a room 'till they tamed him. He'd gone wild.

145

THE WILD GIRL

Mrs. Dicy Adams, interviewed by James Taylor Adams
in Big Laurel, Wise County, on August 19, 1940

One time the smallpox was a-ragin' in the country, and there was a man and his wife had one little baby and they was afraid of getting the smallpox, and they took their baby and went away off in the woods and built a little cabin and lived there. But they took them anyway and both died.

The baby didn't die and several years after that some hunters was in that country and run up on the cabin and found the skeletons of the man and woman lying in the old broke down bed. They noticed that something had been there not long before, so they watched the cabin and after a while they seen a young girl, start-naked come out of the woods and go in the cabin.

The men went back and told what they had found and a whole lot of men from the settlement got together and went back to the cabin. They watched and they saw the girl come out and go off in the woods. They slipped along behind her and watched to see what she done. She went to a patch of berries and picked and eat some of them. Then she scratched up some roots and gnawed them. They followed her back to the cabin and when she went in they all rushed up and caught her.

She fit and scratched and screamed like a wild cat, but they finally got her tied up and took her back to the settlement with them. They couldn't get her to eat and at last they turned her loose. And she went straight back to the cabin in the woods, and when they followed her they found her huddled up between the two skeletons.

They caught her again and brought the skeletons out with them and burnt the house down. They buried the skeletons. Then they put clothes on the girl, but she would tear them off just as fast as they could put them on.

As time went on they got her so she would eat and wear clothes as long as there was nobody around but the family she was staying with. But every time a stranger come she would tear every rag she had on off and run up on the hill and set on a certain big rock up there and scream, like at the very top of her voice, until the strangers left. Then she would come back to the house and let them put clothes on her again.

——— **146** ———

THE MAN WHO
ATE LIVE MEAT

Howard Roy Pegram, interviewed by James Taylor Adams
in an unknown location in Tazewell County, on March 17, 1941

I heard Jose tell about a man down in Tennessee, where he was raised, going to a neighbor's hog pen one night when the people were away from home and cutting off one of the fattening hog's hams and carrying it off and cooking and eating it and leaving the hog standing there on three legs. She said the people lived right close to her folks, and that they found out who done this and arrested the fellow and sent him to the penitentiary for two years. When he got out and started home he stopped at a farm before he got home and stole some chickens. They arrested him and sent him back to jail before he reached home.

And about what Winfred Kilgore told you about the man eating what he cut off the hogs [items 11, 18, 1690, WPA collection], they say there is a feller, I won't mention no names, right a-here at Wise that does that. I've heard people say that he told them that hog seeds [testicles] was the best meat he ever eat in his life.

147

ROAST CAT
FOR BREAKFAST

Mrs. Cornelia Ann Robbins, interviewed by James M. Hylton
in Wise, Wise County, on March 23, 1942

Old lady Gordon who lives below us here told me that at one time she had a big tom cat that they had reared up from a kitten and that they all around the place thought a good deal of it and would pet it a lot. On cold winter nights they felt sorry for the fellow as he grew older and would let him in the house and put him in the kitchen to warm. That later, however, they would put him out on the back porch where they had placed an old sack for him to sleep on where it would be better than out in the open air and cold.

In one cold spell they had one winter it was very cold for several weeks without an end and they got into the habit of letting the cat in every night, more so as the days and nights wore on. The cat would be at the door after the supper meal was over and they had fed him, with his meowing and scratching at the wooden back door, to be let in to the warm house. Some of the family would always go and let him in.

It so happened that one night they had let the cat in and it had as usual walked over near the stove where it would find warmth. Some neighbors came in later and they were all busy in conversation and never noticed when the cat got up and crawled into the big oven of the range stove as they still sat talking and the night grew colder. Later they never thought of it when the company left and they all retired for bed, as they had to get up early next morning to see that the grandson was up and ready to go to work by a certain time. Mrs. Gordon had gotten into the habit of opening the oven door to take the supper bread out, and she would lift the bread out and leave the oven open with the door down and then would place the empty bread pans on this open door. When the company left that night she moved the dishes to the sink and shut the door back just before going to bed.

The next morning she made her fire and made her bread dough and in a hurry jerked open the oven and shoved in the dough in the pan. The fire grew hotter and she called her grandson to breakfast. And as he walked into the kitchen putting on his shirt, she reached down and opened the door to withdraw hot biscuits as usual. When the door was opened an awful smelling cloud of smoke floated up into her eyes and she almost fainted on the spot, whereupon the grandson saw that something was amiss and went to the door of the oven; and inside he found the biscuits brown in front and just below them and in the far corner, a fine roasted tom cat. She has the stove to this day, cooking on it as usual and says it cooks as good as ever.

——————— 148 ———————

THE NAKED BULL RIDE

Mrs. Berry, interviewed by Susan R. Morton
in Luray, Page County, on April 8, 1942

The following story, told by some of the old folks of Page County, was recalled by Mrs. Berry: It was a hot Sunday, and to a young boy of the neighborhood, the prospect of sitting in the old Lutheran church through a long sermon seemed pretty tough compared with the delights of the cool swimming hole on Deacon Smith's place not far from the church. Slipping away from the family, he proceeded to Deacon Smith's knowing that everyone there would be at the Baptist church some distance away. Herman went across the field and to the pleasant coolness of the creekside where he took off his clothes and was just about to plunge in when he heard a roar behind him, and turning, [he] saw the deacon's bull charging toward him. This particular animal was known as being very vicious, but it was not usually kept in that field.

Herman started to run and dodged the bull just as he was about to hit him. He grabbed his tail, keeping a grip on it while they raced around the field until the bull was tired and went under a large white oak that stood near the center of the field, to rest. Once he came to a stop in the shade of the tree, Herman quickly grabbed a low hanging branch and swung himself up, then on to another where he paused to get his breath before ascending any higher where he thought he could stay in safety until the bull tired of standing there and he could then [get] his clothes and make his escape.

But in a moment a buzzing sound reached his ears and, looking up, he saw there was a large hornet's nest just a few feet above him. And at that very same time there was a sharp sting on his shoulder while dozens of angry hornets seemed to be flying all about. The bull was still standing quietly beneath the tree. To stay up in those branches meant he would be stung still more, so he lithely gave a swing and landed on the back of the bull grabbing his horns tightly and digging his toes into the animal's sides. They started their mad race about the the field, and then, heading towards the road not very far away, they broke through a rail fence and made straight for the church!

The boy clung close and the bull, finding that he could [not] get rid of him, kept on; and to Herman's horror he saw that they would soon be in sight of the congregation that he knew must soon be coming out. And all his clothes [were] laying far back by the creekside. But nothing he could do would make the bull change his course. Herman wondered if punishment often came so quickly, and he vowed if he lived that he would never start swimming again on Sunday. But he did not think that he would live, and he almost hoped that he couldn't, if it meant facing all those people in his present condition. If he had to die, though, he wished it could be with his clothes on.

Then things began to happen fast. He could hardly remember how it all came about, but he saw the people coming out of church, and someone screamed at the sight of the approaching bull and its rider, so that when they reached the picket fence that surrounded the churchyard, the animal bounded off in the other direction, throwing Herman clear over the fence. He was not hurt, for he landed in a deep bed of myrtle, but he felt that bruises, or even a broken bone, would be better, as nothing in fact compared to the sight of all those people running towards him, and his clothes, all of them, several hundred rods away.

—— 149 ——

CAUGHT IN
THE GRAVEYARD

Clinton H. Gregory, interviewed by John W. Garrett
in Manteo, Buckingham County, on January 1, 1941

My grandfather and grandmother told me this, said Mr. Gregory, and they said it was a true story. They said there was a girl, and she wanted a sweetheart, and she wanted to know who she was going to marry. And the people told her, if you will go to the graveyard some night by yourself, and not tell nobody where you are going, and take a table fork with you and stick it down in a grave, you will see the man who you will marry. And in olden times the woman wore long dresses, you know. So, she was afraid to go, but she kept thinking about it. So after a while she decided to go. So she went, and as she stooped down to stick the fork in the grave she stuck it through her dress. And she thought it was something pulling her down, and it scared her to death, and she died right there.

Charlie Carter, interviewed by John W. Garrett
in Norwood, Nelson County, on March 15, 1941

Charlie Carter said that his father lived in the days of the Civil War. He said that there was a thief that caused much trouble and could not be caught up on. There was a very wealthy man that died and he had some very expensive jewelry and the man requested that this jewelry be buried with him, so his request was granted. There was no thought of anything or anybody, depredation of the grave, but just a short time later someone went to the grave, and when they got there, they found the grave opened. The corpse [coffin] had been opened and all of the jewelry [was] out. A man was laying across the box which had contained the corpse. His coat was fastened to the box with the screw that fastened the top on the box. He was dead. Apparently he was scared to death. So this was thought to be the thief that was causing the trouble in the community.

150
A MAN DIES
OF EARWIGS

Samuel Simpson Adams, interviewed by James Taylor Adams
in Big Laurel, Wise County, on September 9, 1940

You know these little old earwigs that you see crawling around, mostly find them under bark of dead trees and on old rotten logs. Look sorty like a thousand leg; them old hardshelled kind. Well, sir, them things will sure get in a body's ears. Or that's what I've allus been told.

I've heard pap and mother tell a tale about one time there was a man in the neighborhood that got to complaining with the headache. He done everything he could for it, but it just got worse and worse. They even got a doctor, and he couldn't do nothing for him. He just kept gettin' worse and worse; got so he just went into fits nearly. Said it just felt plimeblank like there was something crawling in his head all the time. He couldn't sleep, and it got so he was in such misery that he couldn't eat. And he finally died. The doctor wanted to know what was the matter with him. So he begged his folks to let him cut his head open to see what was the matter with him. They didn't want to, but he kept on until at last they said, "all right." Well, sir, when he cut that man's head open they was a measured pint of earwigs in his head. They allus 'low'd that one had crawl'd in his ear when he was asleep and had young'ns in there and they just kept breedin' an' increasin' 'till they was that many. My Lord, that man must a-suffered a sight in this world!

NOTES
TO THE LEGENDS

APPENDIXES

NOTES
TO THE LEGENDS

The numbers in parentheses after each legend title form the file number for that item in the WPA Virginia Writers' Project Folklore Collection, accession no. 1547, Manuscript Division, Special Collections Department, University of Virginia Library, Charlottesville, Virginia 22903. These numbers, which are also given for WPA collection items not included in this volume, consist of a box number, a file folder number, and an item number. An asterisk (*) after a legend title indicates that it is from the African American portion of the WPA collection, which was filed separately in boxes 1 and 2.

The motif and tale type numbers noted are from (1) Stith Thompson's *Motif-Index of Folk Literature*, 6 vols., rev. ed. (Bloomington: Indiana Univ. Press, 1955–58); (2) Baughman's *Type and Motif-Index of the Folktales of England and North America*; and (3) Antti Aarne's *The Types of the Folktale*, tr. and enlarged by Stith Thompson, Folklore Fellows Communication no. 184 (Helsinki, 1961).

1. A Horn Snake Kills a Cruel Mistress* (1.2.15). Motifs B91.3, "The horned snake," and D1563.2.2.2, "Snake's venom poisons tree." This narrative is closely related to accounts of the hoop snake (motifs B765.1, "Snake takes tail in mouth and rolls like wheel," and X1321.3.1, "The hoop snake"). Versions of the latter can be found in Vance Randolph, *We Always Lie to Strangers: Tall Tales from the Ozarks* (rpt. Westport, Conn: Greenwood, 1974), pp. 132–36; Richard M. Dorson, *American Negro Tales* (Greenwich, Conn.: Fawcett, 1968), no. 143, pp. 272–73; Burrison, *Storytellers*, p. 173; the *Frank C. Brown Collection of North Carolina Folklore*, 1: 637 (hereafter cited as Brown, *North Carolina Folklore*); and other regional collections. This is the only horn snake narrative in the WPA collection; there are, however, three hoop snake tales (5.2.609–11). None of the latter, which are all Anglo-American, contain the element of a punishment for a cruel mistress. Note that the informant named her father as her source, making this a family legend, and not one which was necessarily at large in her community.

2. The Child and the Snake* (1.4.40). This narrative, given here as factual, is a variant of an international tale, type 285, "The Child and the Snake." The central motif is B765.6, "Snake eats milk and bread with child." The story in the Grimm brothers' collection, with a toad rather than a snake, is märchen no. 105. Charles and Mary Lamb wrote a literary version of this legend, and Butler H. Waugh, Jr., wrote a dissertation on it titled "'The Child and the Snake,' Aarne-Thompson 285, 782C, and Related Forms in Europe and America: A Comparative Folklore Study" (Ph.D. diss., Indiana Univ., 1959). Waugh studied the American versions, both in folktale and legend form, in "The Child and the Snake in North America," *Norveg* 7 (1960): 153–82. There are thirteen versions in the WPA collection (5.2.596–608). Several of these include motif F1041.1.1, "Death from broken heart," in which the child sickens and dies after

the snake is killed. I have found no motif listing for the idea that certain people have "snake-charming blood," but motif B765.14, "Snake has hypnotic stare: person cannot move," should be noted as related.

3. A Black Snake Chokes an Infant (5.2.615). (*Worker note:* The above is a very old folk tale that is pretty widely known in the Cumberland back hills. I've heard it told since I was a child. I think it merely a tale and not an authenticated happening.) I found no motifs precisely corresponding to this, but two approximate it: Baughman B765.5, "Snake crawls out of sleeper's mouth," and B784.1.7, "Scaly lizard jumps into sleeper's mouth." For several variants of narratives relating these motifs, see J. Frank Dobie's *Publications of the Texas Folklore Society* 5 (1926): 65. It is also somewhat related to the "Bosom Serpent" narratives, motif B784, "Animal lives in person's stomach," except that the snake doesn't get all the way inside the infant. Note that while the informant gave her source as a family member, the worker note indicates wider regional circulation for the narrative.

4. A Black Snake Squeezes a Girl's Body (5.2.614). (*Worker note:* The belief around in this section is very common that blacksnakes will coil around human beings and eventually squeeze the life out if not disengaged. A specie of black-snake, very long and slender, is called the "racer" and are feared as the ones that coil around human beings. The term *racer* of course is applied because the snakes glide over the ground with astonishing speed.) This belief is not in Newbell Niles Puckett's *Popular Beliefs and Superstitions: A Compendium of American Folklore*, ed. Wayland D. Hand et al. (Boston: G. K. Hall, 1981). Note that while the source of this narrative was the informant's grandmother, the worker note indicates widespread group acceptance of the animal behavior belief underlying it. This tale gives a glimpse of the fellowship and courtship that occurred during group walks home from church.

5. The Walking Rattlesnake (5.2.719). (*Worker note:* Told by Craft at his place of employment on State Highway 626.) Baughman B765.15, "Snake stands up, whistles," and B875.1, "Giant reptile." See Chapman J. Milling's "Is the Serpent Tale an Indian Survival," in *Southern Folklore Quarterly* 1 (1937): 45, for a discussion of various southern snake belief narratives. Note that this is a first-person account of an event and therefore technically a personal experience story rather than a legend, even though it contains traditional motifs. The culture of homemade whiskey and music as an integral part of the social scene in the region is notable in this tale as well.

6. A Race with a Panther (5.2.668). Item (5.2.671) is a variant of this legend by the same informant in which a woman removes her clothing to stall the panther. Burrison's *Storytellers*, p. 226, prints a version of this variant which was collected in the Florida Panhandle in 1974. A version of the "meat-throwing" variant (with a female protagonist) titled "The Last Chase" (no. 88a), is given in Leonard Roberts's *South from Hell-fer-Sartin: Kentucky Mountain Folktales* (Lexington: Univ. of Kentucky Press, 1955), pp. 175–76. It was collected in 1950 in Mercer County, West Virginia. A New England version in Richard Dorson's *Jonathan Draws the Longbow* (Cambridge: Harvard Univ. Press, 1949) has a wolf pack as the animal and bluefish as the meat; this was rendered as a ballad-stanza poem by Robert P. Tristram Coffin in his *Maine Ballads* (Cambridge: Harvard Univ. Press, 1957). An Irish version is given in John F. Campbell's *Popular*

Tales from the West Highlands (Edinburgh: Edmonston and Douglas, 1860), no. 26, in which a woman takes a pot from the fairies; it has meat scraps in it, and when they loose dogs on her, she drops the scraps to delay the dogs. Vance Randolph's *The Devil's Pretty Daughter and Other Ozark Folktales* (New York: Columbia University Press, 1955), pp. 11–13, 139–40, prints two Ozark versions, one involving a monster who stops to eat meat and the other a rapist who stops to pick up money a young girl drops as she escapes. The following related tale is also from Burrison, *Storytellers*, p. 105: "Older people believes in Ha'nts and so forth. Long time ago, they said, when they be walkin' at night, if they thought it was a haunted trail they was on they would carry whiskey along. If a ha'nt would get after 'em, they would pour it in the tracks, y'know. So, he would stop and drink, and finally [they'd] get home, y'know."

7. The Bear and the Panther (5.2.657). A version from Breathitt County, Kentucky, has the witness named James Vicars, the animals fighting, the bear saying "Oh Lord," and Vicars killing the panther. It is printed in E. L. Noble's *Bloody Breathitt* (Lexington, Ky., 1920), p. 95. Although no motifs exactly correspond to this narrative, A2494, "Enmity between tiger and bear" (from India), and B211.2.3, "Speaking bear," are related. Note that while it is a family story, the first paragraph indicates wide circulation among the "old people." There are eighteen narratives altogether in the WPA collection that involve bears. They range from legends to place-name stories, such as "How Haddix's Branch Got Its Name" (legend 98), to jokes, such as "What Darkens the Hole" (5.2.661), in which a bear enters a cave where two men are hiding.

8. The Eagle and the Baby (5.2.690). Motifs B552, "Man carried by bird," and F1021, "Extraordinary flight through the air," though not exact, are related. The informant was seven years old at the time of this interview. Note that it is a family legend with no substantiable wider circulation.

9. Cats Feed on a Corpse (5.2.39). Motif B766.1, "Cat mutilates corpses." In the *Journal of American Folklore* 54 (1941): 54, Grace Partridge Smith published samplings from a collection of folklore from the "Egypt" region of southern Illinois which included a narrative titled "The Cat Witch." It states that the cat caught on a corpse "was unusually large and not at all like an ordinary house cat, for it was unusually long-bodied. This cat was crouched on the window sill ready to spring on the body. . . . After that the family was careful to keep the window closed. They felt the cat was supernatural and had come to get the soul of the dead person." There is a related belief that cats will suck breath out of infants (motif B766.2). Note the burial customs depicted in this narrative.

10. Daniel Boone's Dog Thrasher (5.2.637). Motif B421, "Helpful dog." Note the reference in the first paragraph to the value judgment by the informant's grandfather in rejecting all narratives except those from "very truthful sources." The worker noted that Nash was seventy-six years old and "a man who has delved into the early history of the country in his own interests." For more on Boone, see legend 78, "Daniel Boone's Tricks on Indians"; for more on Indians and the war between them and the settlers, see the Indians and Simon Kenton sections.

11. The Faithful Dog (5.2.631). (*Worker note:* Carter says he heard this from his grandfather Samuel Simpson Adams and also his father Leonard Carter.)

This narrative, given here as factual, is a variant of an international tale, type 178A, "Llewellyn and His Dog." The central motifs are B331.2, "Llewellyn and his dog," and B524.1.4.1, "Dog defends master's child against animal assailant." A recent version of the narrative is found in Brunvand's *The Choking Doberman*, pp. 31–34. A variation was employed in Walt Disney's animated film classic *Lady and the Tramp*.

12. The Good Watchdog (5.2.617). (*Worker note:* Mr. Carter heard this from his grandmother, Elizabeth (Roberts) Adams, twenty-five years ago. She told it as a true tale.) Motif K1600, "Deceiver falls in his own trap," applies to this narrative in a general sense. Motif K1651, "Woman bitten by own fierce watchdog," is the closest specific motif corresponding to it. A version is given in Roberts's *South from Hell-fer-Sartin*, pp. 195–96. It is titled "Watching Bulldog" (no. 102) and attributes the conflict to neighbors rather than a mother and son. Unlike the informant here, Roberts's narrator insists his tale is true.

13. Solomon the Wise Horse (5.2.704). Motif B120, "Wise animal." J. Frank Dobie, in *The Mustang* (Boston: Little, Brown, 1952), pp. 58–64, depicted a horse of similar intelligence and humanlike characteristics in a legend titled "The White Steed of the Prairies," but it is a wild rather than a domestic animal.

14. Why Negroes' Hands Have White Palms* (1.3.25). (*Informant note:* Why dey was a time when ev'ybody was black. Dat was 'long time back; you see, my hand sho' is white for de rest of my body to be so black, an' my feets is de same way, but I ain't gonna show em to you. Couse I reckon de sun done played wid me too, but I has always been black. But dey was a time when all de white folks was blacker dan me.) Motifs A1614.6, "Origin of light and dark skin color," and A1614.9, "Origin of white man." Joel Chandler Harris's collection *Uncle Remus: His Songs and His Sayings* (New York: Appleton, 1908), pp. 166–68, contains a version of this legend. It is reprinted in J. Mason Brewer's *American Negro Folklore* (Chicago: Quadrangle, 1968), pp. 20–21. A version collected by the Mississippi Writers' Project was printed in *American Stuff: An Anthology of Prose and Verse by Members of the Federal Writers' Project* (New York: Viking, 1937), pp. 150–51. It is reprinted in Botkin's *A Treasury of American Folklore*, pp. 428–29. The text given here was previously published in Perdue, Barden, and Phillips, *Weevils in the Wheat*, p. 233.

15. Why Butterflies Was Made* (2.9.43). Motifs A2041, "Creation of butterfly," and A830, "Creation of earth by creator." A version of this narrative, in thick black dialect, is in the University of Detroit's Student folklore archive, New D File, no. 2, collected in November 1972.

16. Why Colored People Work for the Whites* (2.3.306). (*Worker note:* Mrs. Carter learned this from her parents, the late Mr. and Mrs. Stanton Kilgore, who were slaves and were born in Scott County.) Motifs A1671.1, "Why the negro works," and A1440.1, "Assignment of crafts and professions." The narrative element of a choice between two (or three) bundles is widespread; see tale type 480 and motifs J260, "Choice between worth and appearance," and L212.4, "Modest choice proves good." Two versions of the motif "Why the negro works" that are close to the one given here are in Brown, *North Carolina Folklore*, 1:633, and Zora Neale Hurston, *Mules and Men*, p. 102. Hurston's version includes the folk rhyme that ends the one given here. The "Assignment of crafts" motif, from

Hindu sources, has the Creator open a shop and distribute various items to various groups, such as plows for the farmers, nets for the fishermen, and pens for the scribes and bankers. Dance's *Shuckin' and Jivin'*, p. 9, prints a Richmond version which reverses the sizes of the bags. As in the Hindu tale, God distributes the bags; a white man gets the big bag (of money) and the black man gets the little bag (of nothing). Dance noted that both versions give blacks the losing proposition.

17. The Man in the Moon (5.4.737). (*Worker note:* This short legend about the man in the moon is widely known in the Cumberlands. I have searched and checked every reference on mythology and ancient beliefs I have had access to, but have not been able to find where this belief started. It seems to be local here and very little known, if any, elsewhere.) Motifs A751.1.1, "Man in the moon as punishment for burning brush on Sunday," A751.2, "Man in the moon a rabbit," and C631, "Tabu: breaking the sabbath." A version is given in Brown, *North Carolina Folklore*, 1:631.

18. The Origin of Gypsies (5.4.740). (*Informant comment:* This is a true legend. It happened when the Gypsies were in Spain, when they were birds together, before they spread out all over the world. Now Gypsies are living in all parts of the world, since they let their stomachs get the best of them and were turned from birds into human beings. This true Gypsy legend is taught the little children at the time they are taught to dance and sing.) Motif A1611.2, "Origin of Gypsies." For close Scandinavian and Irish versions, see Antti Aarne, *Folklore Fellows Communication* 8, no. 12 (1940): 104, and the *Journal of the Folklore of Ireland Society* 21 (1938): 304, 325.

19. Disobedient Sammy (5.4.748). (*Worker note:* Simpson Randolph Adams learned this from his brother Spencer Greenfield Adams. *Pencil note reads*: Legend (the black gum tree).) Motifs B211.5, "Speaking fish," D1556, "Self-opening tree trunk," D1610.2, "Speaking tree," K714.3, "Dupe tricked into entering hollow tree," and Q551.3.5.2, "Punishment: transformation into tree." I have found no motif for a tree opening in order to lure its victim in, but motif K714.3, "Dupe tricked into entering hollow tree," is related.

20. How Vote Buying Started in Wise County (5.1.573). Motif K2368.3, "Enemy tricked into fleeing plague," applies to the last sequence of this text, if voters of the opposing party are seen as the enemy. The trick is reminiscent of Huck's ploy to keep Jim from being discovered as a runaway slave in the "A White Lie" section of chapter 16 of Twain's *The Adventures of Huckleberry Finn*. Fieldworker Adams titled this narrative "Ginger Bread and Politics."

21. Why the Buzzard Is Bald (5.4.725). (*Worker note:* This story of why a buzzard has so few feathers on his head was told to children to amuse them.) Motif A2317.3, "Why the buzzard is bald." See *Journal of American Folklore* 32 (1920): 282, for an Ojibwa Indian version. Note that this narrative, while etiological, is also a fictive animal tale, featuring animals that speak and act in human ways.

22. The Legend of the Dogwood Tree (5.4.732). Motifs A2711.2, "Tree blessed that made the cross," and A2751.3.2, "Cross on certain trees." The special accord given the dogwood as the state tree of the Commonwealth of Virginia reinforces its particular significance.

23. James Bowser, Emancipation Hero* (1.11.229). Motif Q421, "Beheading as punishment." The opening sentences indicate the informant was telling an event which was not in common circulation in her community. In fact, they show that the grandson of the hero of her tale does not know the story she relates. This puts the classification of her narrative as a legend in question. But her mention of the surname Hale at the opening and her conclusion that Bowser should be equated with Nathan Hale indicate her conscious attempt to create legendary status for Bowser. The text given here was previously published in Perdue, Barden, and Phillips, *Weevils in the Wheat*, pp. 259–60.

24. Henry ("Box") Brown: Mailed to Freedom* (1.10.196). Motif F1088, "Extraordinary escape." A fuller account of this event and its circumstances can be found in Brown's autobiography, *Narrative of the Life of Henry Box Brown* (Boston: Brown and Sterns, 1849). Note the formal language of the tale. The informant, as a minister, probably chose this rhetoric as suitable for a formal interview and for relating an event of significance to the history of the black struggle for freedom.

25. A Confederate Spy (10.4.1570). The man's name was actually John Yates Beall, not Bell. Otto Eisenschiml's *Why Lincoln Was Murdered* (Boston: Little, Brown, 1937), pp. 373–76, gives an account of John Beall's wartime activities in Virginia and elsewhere and relates the history of the widespread story that Lincoln was assassinated to avenge Beall's execution. Beall, who had been a schoolmate of John Wilkes Booth, was a captain in the Virginia fleet of the Confederate navy. He served with distinction. He spied for the Confederacy, captured several Union ships in the Chesapeake Bay, secured the release of many southern prisoners, and partially destroyed the Cape Charles lighthouse. He was finally captured, convicted by a court-martial, and sentenced to hang on February 24, 1865. Many powerful and influential people, including James A. Garfield and Thaddeus Stevens, as well as Booth, petitioned President Lincoln to commute his sentence. Lincoln ignored these calls, however, and Beall was executed. Soon after Lincoln's assassination, a story arose connecting his death with Beall's. It was rumored that Booth had extracted a promise from Lincoln that he would spare his friend, and that when Lincoln broke his promise and let Beall hang, Booth swore to avenge him at the first possible opportunity. Eisenschiml's book says there is no foundation to the story. He traced it to a sensationalist weekly magazine published in Richmond shortly after the war by Mark M. Pomeroy. What is remarkable is that this tale from the popular press of the 1860s was found in oral circulation in Virginia in the late 1930s.

26. A Premonition of Death (3.3.154). Motif D1812.5.1.2.1, "Vision as bad omen." Note that the narrative as given here was maintained through family members of the informant, although presumably the others who saw the apparition also would have given it circulation.

27. The Curse of the Carbine (3.3.98). Motif Q211, "Murder punished." Home Guard militia units were organized by both Northern and Southern sympathizers. A number of WPA collection narratives make note of Home Guards and their Union and Confederate activities. And one VWP social history essay titled "The Home Guard" gives many details of this aspect of the war; worker: Berry, informant: Mrs. Bertram Hayne (10.4.1563).

28. A Yankee Drinks from a "Poisoned" Well (10.3.1533). The depiction of

the Southern reaction to invading Yankee soldiers is interesting in this narrative, which is more of an anecdote than a proper legend. Note the quick wit of the slave woman and her abhorrence of the soldiers who are theoretically her benefactors. See "A Smallpox Epidemic: A Curse on Whites" (legend 137) in the Unusual Events section for a more positive reaction by a slave to the presence of Union soldiers in Virginia.

29. A Young Girl Shoots a Yankee (10.4.1566). The scene depicted here is reminiscent of chapter 26 of Margaret Mitchell's *Gone with the Wind*, in which Scarlett O'Hara gets a gun from an upstairs room at Tara and shoots a Yankee soldier who has come into the big house. Not believing a woman would shoot him, the soldier calmly looks up at her and says, "All alone, little lady?" Scarlett, an embodiment of the delicate but courageous Southern lady archetype, pulls the trigger. Since Mitchell's intruder was alone, there was no need for Scarlett to hide as this narrative's Aunt Clarcy was forced to.

30. A Conjuror's Revenge* (2.2.271). Motifs D1274.1, "Magic conjuring bag," D1814.1, "Advice from magician (fortune-teller, etc.)," G263.4, "Witch causes sickness," and Q551.6, "Magic sickness as punishment." As the opening sentence indicates, this narrative was part of a longer interview in which Rev. P. L. Harvey described several other cases of conjure. These are found in the WPA collection at file nos. 1.2.15 and 2.2.279. In *Dog Ghosts and Other Texas Negro Folk Tales*, p. 106, Brewer printed a folk rhyme which indicates how African American lore associates conjure with religion and sees it as comparable to and apart from the powers of white society: "White man got de money an' education / De Nigguh got Gawd an' conjuration."

31. A Slave with a Magic Hoe* (1.6.48). Motifs D1204, "Magic hoe," and D1601.16.1, "Self-digging hoe." For a North African version, see R. S. Rattray's *Hausa African Folklore* (Oxford: Clarendon, 1913), 2:74. The text given here was previously published in Perdue, Barden, and Phillips, *Weevils in the Wheat*, pp. 347–48.

32. The Conjuror's Beck* (2.2.280). Motifs D1711, "Magician," and Baughman D2072, "Magic paralysis. Person rendered magically helpless." In *Black Culture and Black Consciousness*, p. 73, Levine notes an account which states that "hoodoo Niggers . . . couldn't make old master stop whipping him with his hoodooism, but could make other Negroes crawl to him."

33. A Witch Rode a Girl to Riceville, Virginia* (2.2.267). Motif G241.2, "Witch rides a person." Four versions of this legend are given in Brown, *North Carolina Folklore*, 1:649–50. One, like the version here, is a first-person account; the other three are attributed, believed, third-person narratives. In Emelyn Gardner's *Folklore from the Schoharie Hills, New York* (Ann Arbor: Univ. of Michigan Press, 1937), p. 65, a witch-riding tale is given in which the rider turns the tables on the witch. Her intended victim rides her all night and even has her hooves shod. When she returns to her normal form the next day, her family finds iron horseshoes nailed to her hands.

34. Devil Bill Boggs (3.1.1). See "The Witch Tree" (legend 35) for more on Boggs. Motifs D2086.2, "Guns rendered ineffective by witch," G211.2.4, "Witch in the form of a deer," and G265.8.3, "Witch bewitches gun."

35. The Witch Tree (3.1.28). Motifs C510, "Tabu: touching tree," D630.1, "Power of self-transformation received from wood spirit," D950, "Magic tree,"

G211, "Witch takes animal forms," Baughman G262.4, "Witch kills with aid of witch ball (hair rolled in beeswax)," and, perhaps, G265.10, "Witch bewitches tree"; I give this last motif because it is not clear in the legend if Boggs got power from the tree or gave power to it. The motif of the witch tree killing all other trees around it is notable; I could not locate it in any motif listing.

36. Montague and Duck Moore (3.1.46). Motifs G263.4, "Witch causes sickness," G263.7, "Witch causes insanity," G265.4.1, "Witch causes death of animals," and, in regard to the counterconjuring of Montague, G271.6, "Exorcism of witch by counter-charm."

37. A Silver Bullet for a Witch (3.1.45). Motifs D1385.4, "Silver bullet to ward off witches," Baughman G271.5(e), "Shooting witch in person with silver bullet breaks spell," and Baughman G271.4.2(ba), "Shooting witch picture or symbol with silver bullet breaks spell." The version here differs from those noted in Baughman in that they omit reference to a sore which never heals; this element is found, however, in a witch tale from Gardner, *Folklore from the Schoharie Hills*, p. 75. This tale, which relates the shooting of bewitched partridges with a bent silver coin, concludes that the partridges disappeared, but "ever after that old Mrs. Schermerhorn had wounds in her wrists which never healed."

38. Witch Mountain (3.1.5). Motifs C784.1, "Tabu: lending to witch," and G271.6, "Exorcism of witch by counter-charm." Baughman motifs G224.13.2*, "Initiation: person kneels, puts one hand on head one hand under feet, says 'All that lies between my two hands I consign to the Devil.'" and G265.4.2.4*(a), "Witch causes illness in sheep." Concerning the element of heating a plow in the fire, I found two motifs which, when combined, approximate this counter-charm: G271.4.1(lh), "Breaking spell by heating iron in fire," and G271.4.1(kb), "Breaking spell on cream by putting a heated plow in it."

39. A Witch's Gun Charms the Woods (3.1.29). Motifs C784.1, "Tabu: lending to witch," D1741.2.1, "Drawing a witch's blood breaks spell," D2086.2, "Guns rendered ineffective by witch," G265.8.3.1, "Witch bewitches gun," G271.2.3, "Name of deity breaks witch's spell," and Baughman G271.4.2(b), "Shooting picture or symbol of witch breaks spell (usually injuring or killing the witch)." I have not located a motif for "ringing the woods" with the sound of a gunshot as a spell. The text given here has been published in McNeil's *Ghost Stories from the American South*, pp. 113–14.

40. Aunt Lucy's Bewitched Cow (3.1.50). Motifs D2083.2.1, "Witches make cows give bloody milk," G271.6, "Exorcism of witch by counter-charm," and Baughman G271.4.2(ba), "Shooting witch picture or symbol with silver bullet breaks spell."

41. Cooking a Witch's Shoulder (3.3.31). Motifs C784.1, "Tabu: lending to witch," G265.4.1.4*, "Witch causes death of sheep," G271.6, "Exorcism of witch by counter-charm," and Baughman G257.1(a), "Burning heart of animal, usually one of victims of witch, brings witch to scene to stop burning"; see also Baughman G271.4.1(a), "Exorcism by burning heart of animal." The version here is unusual in its use of shoulder meat rather than the sheep's heart. This detail adds credibility to the narrative's assertion that the woman recovered. Baughman's note states that in some versions the witch dies from the sympathetic magic burning. Note that while this tale is drawn from family material,

it is also stated as being at large in the community. McNeil's *Ghost Stories from the American South*, which prints this legend on pp. 120–21, attributes it to Burkett Casteel, a fifty-five-year-old white male from Bristol, Virginia, and states that it was collected by Gail Ogle in 1981.

42. A Conjured Girl Tries to Jump into the Fire (3.1.13). Motifs D847, "Magic object found in chimney," D1274.1, "Magic conjure bag (filled with nail pairings, hair, feet of toads, etc.)," G263.7, "Witch causes insanity," G269.14(a), "Witch causes child to jump (or fall) into fire," and G271.6, "Exorcism of witch by counter-charm." Hurston's *Mules and Men*, p. 233, gives a hoodoo ritual to make a person leave town which involves throwing a conjure bag into a river at noon and saying, "Go, and go quick in the name of the Lord."

43. A Witch Gets Caught in a Store (3.1.5). (*Worker note:* The old lady that told this story told it in such a way that you could see she really believed it, to a certain extent anyway. There was a young girl in the room when she was telling it, and she made some laughing remarks, in a good-natured way, about it. And the old lady said, "Believe it or not, but I know my mother and my grandmother told it, and they were truthful women.") Motifs Baughman D1531.8, "Witch flies with aid of word charm," G249.7, "Witches go through keyholes," and Baughman G242.7, "Mistakes made by person traveling with witches." Baughman G242.7(b) adds the element of the whiskey as motivation for the night party. Baughman also noted that in England this narrative is often told involving the fairies rather than witches. A North Carolina version very similar to the text given here is found in *Journal of American Folklore* 47 (1934): 268. Gardner, *Folklore from the Schoharie Hills*, p. 63, printed a narrative in which the person attempting to travel with witches says, not the wrong thing, but something in addition to the charm words. This breaks the spell immediately, and he is left behind.

44. The Quaker's Gold* (2.1.257). Motifs E371, "Return from dead to reveal hidden treasure," and E545.19.2, "Proper means of addressing ghost." Note that the young Quaker, in line with the tradition of the Society of Friends' ministry of all believers, fills a role which ghost narratives typically give to professional ministers. Also, the Quaker second person familiar pronouns function as the proper form of address to this "Friendly" ghost.

45. Midnight Annie* (1.5.41). Baughman E589.5, "Ghost walks at midnight," and motif F411.2, "Spirit floats in air." While there is little narrative content here, the effect of the apparition on the community shows widespread circulation of the legend. A version of "Mary the Wanderer," a ghost legend from black informants on Georgia's St. Simons Island, printed in Burrison's *Storytellers*, p. 207, has a similar feel and mood.

46. A Ghost Voice Makes a Couple Argue (3.3.153). Motifs E236.4, "Return from dead because last will was not fulfilled," and E402.1.5, "Invisible ghost makes knocking noise." Note that though the informant called his narrative a "tale," he went to some length to give specific details of place and people before beginning to tell the events.

47. The Headless Ghost of Griffith's Wife (3.3.151). (*Worker note:* Carter says he heard it from people who had seen the ghost.) Motifs E334.1, "Non-malevolent ghost haunts scene of former crime or sin," E422.1.1(b), "Headless woman

revenant," and Baughman E530.1, "Ghost-like light." The small town of West
Point between Richmond and Williamsburg is the locale of another narrative
about a ghostly light along a railroad track. In this tale (from the editor's personal
recollection), the light is said to be carried by a headless brakeman searching
for his head which was severed in an accident.

48. Nancy Loveall's Ghost Pounds Coffee (3.4.204). (*Worker note:* This was
told to Dr. Hill by his father who lived in the vicinity of this happening at the
time. It is supposed to be an unquestioned truth.) Motifs E334.1, "Non-malevolent ghost haunts scene of former crime or sin," and E545.19.2, "Proper means
of addressing ghost."

49. The Old Plantation Master's Ghost (3.3.109). Motif E338.1, "Non-malevolent ghost haunts house or castle," and Baughman E542.1, "Ghostly fingers
leave mark on person's body." The WPA collection sheet gave this text the sub-
title "The Legend of the Pear Tree."

50. Converted by a Ghost (3.3.159). (*Worker note:* Fletcher Sulfridge is 47
years old, was born and raised in the Flatwoods section of Wise County. He is
now employed as a foreman on the WPA Sanitary Project.) Baughman motifs
E402.1.2.4, "Ghost sings," E530.1, "Ghost-like light," and E599.6, "Ghost
moves furniture."

51. The Old Woman of the Pies (3.3.105). Motifs E332.2(h), "Ghost seen
on road at night," E334.1, "Non-malevolent ghost haunts scene of former crime
or sin," E402.1.1.2, "Ghost moans," and E425.1, "Revenant as woman."

52. The Ghost That Squeaked the Door (3.3.197). Motifs E281, "Ghosts
haunt house," E334.1, "Non-malevolent ghost haunts scene of former crime or
sin," E402.1.1.6, "Ghost sobs," E402.1.7, "Ghost slams door," and E402.1.8,
"Miscellaneous sounds made by ghost of human being."

53. The Ghost's Little Finger Bone (3.4.221). Motifs E231, "Return from
dead to reveal murder," E235.2, "Ghost returns to demand proper burial," E281,
"Ghosts haunt house," E334.1, "Non-malevolent ghost haunts scene of former
crime or sin," E371, "Return from dead to reveal hidden treasure,"
E545.19.2(e), "Proper means of addressing ghost, must name the Holy Spirit,"
and D1007, "Magic human bone." The element of the finger bone sticking to
its murderer combines Q551.2.4, "Corpse sticks to its murderer," and
H251.3.8, "Magic object clings to hand of guilty person."

54. The Ficklin Field Haunted House* (1.10.211). This narrative, with the
central motif B210.1, "Person frightened by animal successively replying to his
remarks," is usually given as a fictive tale rather than a legend. Botkin, *A Treasury of American Folklore*, p. 421, gives a standard humorous version. Note the
element of a test of bravery here. Although this motif, H1411, "Fear test: staying
in a haunted house," appears rarely in the WPA collection, it is a very common
aspect of haunted house narratives, both fictive/comic and believed. Motif E281,
"Ghosts haunt house." The rhyme at the close is a variant of a verse from "New
Dirty Dozen," recorded by Memphis Minnie on Vocalion records, July 1930 (no.
1618). In this blues song the rhyme goes, "Now the funniest thing I ever seen
/ Tom cat jumpin' on a sewing' machine / Sewin' machine, run so fast / Took
ninety-nine stitches in his yas, yas, yas."

55. A Civil War Haunt in an Old Log House (3.4.261). Motifs E279.1, "Ghost haunts outside at night in human shape," E281, "Ghosts haunt house," E334.1, "Non-malevolent ghost haunts scene of former crime or sin," E422.1.1(b), "Headless woman revenant," E425.1.1, "Revenant as lady in white," and E439.1, "Revenant forced away by shooting." Note that while the informant gave a family member as his source, it is indicated within the narrative that there was wider circulation in the community.

56. The Dancing Couple (3.4.212). Baughman motif E530.1.0.1(c), "Building lights up strangely at night when unoccupied," and motifs E281, "Ghosts haunt house," E421.3, "Luminous ghosts," and F470.2, "Night-spirits dance." While the informant gave her source as a family member, the narrative also had wider community circulation.

57. Ghost Chains from a Logging Accident (3.4.225). Motifs E281, "Ghosts haunt house," E334, "Non-malevolent ghost haunts site of former misfortune, crime, or tragedy," E337.1.2, "Sounds of accident re-enact tragedy," and E402.1.4, "Invisible ghost jingles chain." Note how the fact of chains being involved in the accident dovetails with the common ghostly motif of chain-rattling to add credibility to the narrative and the motif.

58. A Confederate Soldier in a Haunted Room (3.4.265). Motifs E279.3, "Ghost pulls bedclothing from sleeper," E281, "Ghosts haunt house," and E281.3, "Ghost haunts particular room in house." Note the detail of the frequent leaves this Confederate soldier took from military duty during the Civil War.

59. The Haunted House of Saunders (3.4.253). Motifs E281, "Ghosts haunt house," E293, "Ghost frightens people (deliberately)," E334, "Non-malevolent ghost haunts site of former misfortune, crime, or tragedy," Baughman E338.1(i), "Ghost walks around grounds of house or castle," E402.1.2, "Footsteps of invisible ghost heard," and E402.1.7, "Ghost slams door."

60. The Praying Ghost of the Old Barlow Place (3.4.215). Motif E281, "Ghosts haunt house," and Baughman E402.1.1.3, "Ghost cries and screams." Note how the Catholicism of the subject makes him an outsider in what is apparently a Protestant community, and the connection between Catholicism and both "foreignness" and idolatrous rituals. I have found no motif of a ghost kneeling in prayer.

61. The Slave Trader's Haunted House (3.3.112). (Worker note: Rebecca Ashby and others.) Motifs E281, "Ghosts haunt house," E332.2(h), "Ghost seen on road at night," E334.1, "Non-malevolent ghost haunts scene of former crime or sin," E402.1.1.2, "Ghost moans," E402.1.1.6, "Ghost sobs," and F411.2, "Spirit floats in air." The impression the contextual information gives is that Morton pieced this text together using versions she collected from several informants.

62. The Ten Indians (5.5.763). (Worker note: This is an American folk tale. It is interesting chiefly in that it can be traced back through four generations. It was told me on July 21, 1940 by Spencer Greenfield Adams; he learned it from Leonard Erastus Carter; he learned it from his mother-in-law, Mrs. Robert Adams; and she learned it from her husband, Samuel Simpson Adams, who

learned it from his father Spencer Adams.) Note the text says there were six Indians, while the title indicates ten. The story structure of a suspected harmer turning out to be a savior appears in such modern legends as that of the truck driver following a woman home flashing his lights. For interpretations of this legend, see Carlos Drake, "The Killer in the Back Seat," *Indiana Folklore* 1, no. 1 (1968): 107–9, and Xenia E. Cord, "Further Notes on 'The Assailant in the Back Seat,'" ibid., 2, no. 2 (1969): 47–54. In the Indian and modern tales the killer persists under very unlikely conditions.

63. The Two Women Who Married Indians (5.5.767). Motif R227.2, "Wife flees from hated husband," is relevant to this tale, although there is some ambivalence about the women hating their Indian captors until the husband is overheard saying he will kill "Honey." With the appropriate substitution, motif R13.1.6, "Girl abducted by bear and made his wife," fits the given narrative. In Roberts's *South from Hell-fer-Sartin*, pp. 168–69, a narrative titled "Tommy and the Indians" (no. 83) tells of a young boy escaping from Indians in a similar manner. It contains the element of hiding in a hollow log as the chasing Indians pass by close enough to be heard. The next text in that collection, "Yansoo Po Shinie!" (no. 84), is close to the one given here. In it the two girls do not marry the Indians but simply work for them. It includes the element of one girl being happy with the situation and the other not liking it, and also the episode of hiding in the log. In this version two small dogs the Indians have with them discover one of the escaping girls; she feeds them scraps of meat she has taken with her. After the Indians leave to continue their search for her, she meets a white man hunting in the woods who helps her escape. Once they are back in civilization, she marries him.

64. Disturbing Indian Graves (4.1.299). Motifs E235.4.3, "Return from dead to punish theft of bone from grave," E235.6, "Return from dead to punish indignities to corpse or ghost," and D2148, "Earthquake magically caused." I have found no motif of Indian bone filings unspelling a gun. For more on "gun spelling," see "Devil Bill Boggs" (legend 34) and "A Witch's Gun Charms the Woods" (legend 39) in the Conjure and Witchcraft section.

65. Indians Kill a Pioneer Family (3.3.150). (*Worker note:* Told to me by Eva Fair Pegram, who learned it from her great-uncle, Samuel Simpson Adams, who had it from his mother, Celia Church Adams, seventy-five years ago. *Second worker note:* The foregoing tale may be based on the Hamlin family tragedy near the present village of Hamlin in Russell County. Mrs. Hamlin and her children were killed by Indians there. It also resembles a story in song (not traditional here) from Alabama, where a woman was drowned and her children burned in a house by Indians.) Motifs E334.1, "Non-malevolent ghost haunts scene of former crime or sin," and Baughman F974.1, "Grass will not grow where blood of murdered person has been shed." Note the detail of the narrative here is that nothing will grow from the ashes of the burned house, which Baughman did not list as a specific submotif. See "Murder at the County Line" (legend 142) for an example of this motif generalized from grass to all vegetation refusing to grow.

66. The Indian Who Lived in a Cave (6.1.833). Motifs F757, "Extraordinary cave," and R315, "Cave as refuge." This narrative gives a more sympathetic and humanized picture of the Indian than most in the WPA collection.

67. Two Indians Killed with a Boulder (5.5.760). Note the etiological element at the end of this narrative which explains the origin of an unusual pathway up the mountainside.

68. The Friendly Old Hog (5.5.781). This is structurally similar to several modern legends in which the danger is close but not realized until the last minute, as in "The Baby-Sitter and the Phone Caller"; see Sylvia Grider, "Dormitory Legend-Telling in Progress: Fall, 1971–Winter, 1973," *Indiana Folklore* 6, no. 1 (1973): 6–7. See also "The Ten Indians" (legend 62) for a similar case of an unbelievably insistent malefactor.

69. The Indian Boiling Pot (5.5.778). (*Worker note:* George's father was named Riley Mullins; the Mullins' live in the Birchfield section of Wise.) Like "The Indian Who Lived in a Cave" (legend 66), this narrative reveals an attitude that the Indian may be more than just a subhuman savage. Perhaps because both of these legends deal with concrete evidence of Indian culture, they take a more appreciative stance toward it.

70. Cry Baby and Your Mammy'll Come (5.5.782). The informant's final comment reflects a distinction between the fictive and the legendary genres of folk narrative. As much as the informant wanted the story to end happily, as märchen usually do, her grandmother kept its graphic brutality, even when telling the story to her grandchild.

71. Indians Come down the Chimney (5.5.771). Motifs K372, "Intruder captured in chimney, burned," and K912, "Robbers' (giants') heads cut off one by one as they enter house." Note how the Indians replace standard European badmen figures of either reality (robbers) or fantasy (giants). Cf. Aarne/Thompson tale type 956B, "The Clever Maid at Home Kills the Robbers." In *Our Western Border*, published in 1875, McKnight printed as historical fact the story of "Mrs. Merrill, the Terrible Long Knife Squaw," p. 698. This account of an Indian attack on a cabin in Nelson County, Kentucky, includes the element of the wife throwing feathers in the fire to choke her assailants in the chimney and her use of an axe to split heads in succession until a pile of dead Indians lay on the floor. Unlike the Virginia version, this account has her husband with her at the time of the attack; he is shot, however, so he cannot protect her, and she is left to defend herself.

72. Indians Capture a Bride on Her Wedding Day (5.5.773). Motif K1371, "Bride stealing." The fierce intensity of this brief narrative brings to mind García Lorca's folk-based drama *Blood Wedding*, which depicts a groom's intensity and great *tremendismo* over the theft of his bride. Note the poetic image of the horses "flying off the earth."

73. Henry Armstrong, de Forgin' Man* (1.6.47). Motifs K455.8, "Credit based on forgery," and K362.7, "Theft by forgery: signature forged to obtain money." Note the mention of Armstrong's war service as a possible cause of his mental disturbance. See "The Man Who Ate Live Meat" (legend 146) in the Unusual Events section for another case of a man whose obsession is so great he returns to it before he gets home from the penitentiary.

74. Bill Cabell, a Badman at de Bar* (1.5.45). Motifs J2353.1, "Foolish boasts bring trouble," and K2320, "Deception by frightening."

75. Judge John Crutchfield: "Justice John"* (1.1.15). Five texts about Judge Crutchfield are given in Dance's *Shuckin' and Jivin'*, pp. 169–70. Curiously, Dance, printing narratives from interviews conducted in 1975, gave the judge the fictitious name of Whitfield. It is clearly the same person, since she noted that there were narratives about him in the WPA collection. Dance's tales give the same picture of a judge who joked with the blacks who came before him (if they were sufficiently humble), sang sarcastic parodies of black songs, and gave out random and idiosyncratic sentences. Dance's texts reveal that in Richmond in the 1930s it was illegal to buck dance or to sing in public songs that the white population perceived as obscene. Aspects of black domestic life of the time are also revealed; one text has a man who is brought before the judge for beating his wife describe in detail how he slapped and kicked her before throwing and locking her out of the house. Expecting sympathy from another male, he is surprised at receiving a stiff fine for each act he has described. Whether Judge Crutchfield was considered hard or lenient varies from text to text.

76. How Railroad Bill Chased Himself to His Girl's House* (1.5.46). Motifs A527.3.1, "Culture hero can transform self," D135, "Transformation: man to sheep," D141, "Transformation: man to dog," and D313.1, "Transformation: fox to person." In discussing Railroad Bill in *Black Culture and Black Consciousness*, p. 415, Levine mentions both the canned food (which his sources said was sold by force to the poor shack dwellers along the railroad tracks!) and Railroad Bill's shape shifting to a sheep, dog, or fox. Any hint of Railroad Bill's kindness or nobility is missing from the folk-song texts. Folksinger Paul Clayton sings John Hooker's version of "Railroad Bill" from the WPA collection on *Folksongs and Ballads of Virginia*, Folkways Records no. FP 47/3.

77. William Wydeman: Peacock and the Soldiers* (1.5.43). Motifs F610, "Remarkably strong man," J642, "Foolishness of surrendering weapons," and K631, "Captors induced to disarm themselves."

78. Daniel Boone's Tricks on Indians (5.5.766). The trick of capturing the Indians by catching their hands in a split tree is a variant of an international tale, type 38, "Claw in Split Tree," in which Boone's role is attributed to a fox and the Indians' part to a bear. This motif is commonly applied to various pioneer Indian fighters. Harold Thompson, in *Body, Boots, and Britches: Folktales, Ballads, and Speech from Country New York* (Philadelphia: Lippincott, 1939), p. 51, attributes the trick to Tom Quick but noted that it is given to many other pioneers. He specifically mentions Boone. Baughman K551.29*, "Man asks captors to wait until he has split a log he is working on. He then asks them to pull the log apart by putting their hands in the crevice held open by a wedge. He then knocks the wedge out, catching their fingers in the crevice," and motif K1111, "Dupe puts hands (paws) into cleft tree (wedge, vise)." Boone's tobacco-throwing trick is a version of the Aarne/Thompson tale type 7, "Escape by Blinding the Guard." Motif K621, "Escape by blinding guard" also applies. Two versions of this tale are found in Joel Chandler Harris's *Nights with Uncle Remus: Myths and Legends of the Old Plantation* (Boston: Houghton Mifflin, 1911), pp. 95, 280. Concerning his rescue of the children stolen by Indians, motif R153, "Father rescues children" applies. The motif of children leaving bits of yarn to be followed is reminiscent of the attempt by Hansel and Gretel in the Grimms' tale no. 15 (Aarne/Thompson tale type 327) to leave first bread and then pebbles

as a trail marker. The closest listed motif to the yarn trail element is R135.0.5, "Trail of thread."

79. Ira Roberts, the Strongman (6.3.865). Motif F610, "Remarkably strong man." Note that the beginning of the narrative is a firsthand account, but the second portion never clarifies whether or not the informant witnessed the feat of strength.

80. Molly Mulhollun, the Cabin Builder (6.3.863). Motifs K1831, "Service under a false name," and K1837, "Disguise of woman in man's clothes." This is the only legend in the WPA collection that features a legendary female figure. Robert D. Mitchell's *Commercialism and Frontier: Perspectives on the Early Shenandoah Valley* (Charlottesville: Univ. Press of Virginia, 1977), pp. 30–34, gives some background on the entrepreneur Benjamin Borden. Borden, a New Jersey land agent, was granted a large tract of Shenandoah Valley land by Lord Fairfax under the condition that he attract a certain number of settlers on to it; according to Mitchell, he had some trouble and had to advertise as far away as his native New Jersey to meet the required numbers (Mitchell refers the reader to a larger study, "Benjamin Borden, Shenandoah Valley Pioneer," *William and Mary Quarterly*, 2d ser., 11 [1931]: 321–29).

81. Major Mike Wallace (5.4.749). (*Worker note:* The informant is a descendant of Wallace and a Commonwealth's Attorney for Stafford County. He is himself tall, broad, and strong and in his college days around 1900 was a famous full-back on the University of Virginia football team.) Motifs F556, "Remarkable voice," F610, "Remarkably strong man," F616, "Mighty pugilist," and N330, "Accidental killing or death."

82. Booker Mullins, the Bear Fighter (6.3.868). Motif F628.1.1.4, "Strong man kills bear." This is one of eighteen bear tales in the WPA collection. All are from the Anglo-American files. Note how wildness is pitted against civilization in this narrative in the overlay of human sporting rules on a struggle with a ferocious wild animal.

83. Thomas Jefferson's Manners (5.1.545). Motif J914, "King shows humility by mingling with common people." A minor democratic adjustment is needed to make this motif fit, but its applicability is clear. Jefferson, as only the third president after colonial rule by a king, and an elderly slave, as a "common person," translate reasonably well. During his administration many Federalists faulted Jefferson, a Virginia aristocrat, for exactly the type of "democratic pretensions" that this legend sympathetically depicts: see Dumas Malone's *Jefferson the President: First Term, 1801–1809* (Boston: Little, Brown, 1970), pp. 29ff. A version of this legend was printed by Booker T. Washington in his autobiography *Up from Slavery* (rpt. Garden City, N.Y.: Doubleday, 1963), pp. 101–2, but it involves only an exchange of tips of the hat and is attributed to Washington rather than Jefferson. Botkin printed this version in his *Treasury of Southern Folklore* (New York: Crown, 1949), p. 155, and noted that it was also told of Virginia governor William Gooch and of Robert E. Lee.

84. Johnny Appleseed (5.4.744). (*Worker note:* Mrs. Wooding, age 73, got this version of the legend from her grandmother when she was a young child. Her mother told it to her as well; she has passed it on to her own children and grandchildren.) Motifs A515.1, "Culture hero arrives in boat," A2602, "Planting the

earth," and F556, "Remarkable voice." The hero's oceanic origin and the Virginia setting are the two main variations of this text from most collected and literary versions of the legend. The phrase "news straight from heaven" is noted in "Johnny Appleseed: A Pioneer Hero," an article on John Chapman by W. D. Haley, *Harper's New Monthly Magazine* 43, no. 258 (Nov. 1871): 830–36, reprinted in Botkin's *A Treasury of American Folklore*, pp. 143–48.

85. Gowl James, the Human Ratter (6.3.873). (*Worker note:* Mrs. Tolliver said she learned this from a cousin who lives not far from the locality where this man James lives. She has also seen something about it in the newspaper. She is 32 years old.) Motifs F660, "Remarkable skill," and J2103, "Expensive extermination of rodents." Note the similarity to "Johnny Appleseed" (legend 84) in how a single obsession, though not so noble, is the crux of the person's legendary fame.

86. Doc Taylor's Walk with Riley Mullins (5.1.521). Doc Taylor, "The Red Fox of the Mountains," figures as a character in several of John Fox's novels of the Appalachian wilderness. Taylor's crime and trial make up a major portion of Fox's best-known novel, *The Trail of the Lonesome Pine* (New York: Scribner's, 1908). There is extensive background material (over forty typed pages) on Taylor's life and times in the WPA collection (items 305A, 518–21, 721, and 854 in boxes 4, 5, and 6, various folders). I should note that I read item 305A, "Doc Taylor's Boots," in 1972 and wrote the WPA collection index description: "Tale—two men fill Doc's boots with honey to detain him. He turns the trick on them," but the item was missing from the WPA collection when I inspected it in June 1990.

87. How Doc Taylor Got Named "The Red Fox" (6.3.854). (*Worker note:* Mullins was a deputy when Doc Taylor was the sheriff of Wise County.) Motifs F511.1, "Person unusual as to his face," and K534, "Escape by reversing shoes." See note to "Doc Taylor's Walk with Riley Mullins" (legend 86).

88. A Strange Light at a Murder Site (4.1.272). Motifs E334.1, "Non-malevolent ghost haunts scene of former crime or sin," E530.1, "Ghost-like lights," Q211, "Murder punished," and Q414, "Punishment: burning alive." While this legend does relate a supernatural occurrence, its main thrust is the murder and retribution.

89. The Murderous Tavern Keepers (5.1.560). Motif K911.3, "Sleep feigned to kill enemy." Three versions of this legend are given in Roberts's *South from Hell-fer-Sartin*, pp. 198–200; only one of these, "Guest Robbery" (no. 104b), involves the intended victim spending a night and overhearing that his hosts plan to rob and kill him. But all involve uncovering a murderous robbery plan and escaping. Vance Randolph's *Who Blowed Up the Church House? and Other Ozark Folk-tales* (New York: Columbia Univ. Press, 1952), pp. 62–63, contains a parallel narrative titled "The Woman and the Robber."

90. Killing an Unwanted Infant (5.1.542). (*Worker note:* In the early days of this county a pioneer family was supposed to have murdered one of their children in the manner above described. It was only suspicion and no one ever knew whether they really killed the child or not. Nevertheless, the tale has been told around the hearthsides in this county until it has become a widely told folk tale.) Motifs S10, "Cruel parents," S112.2, "Murder with hot iron," and S116.6,

"Murder by trampling of horses." The worker note, while calling the narrative a folk tale, indicates that the truth of the story was at issue in the group. This particularly grisly form of killing the infant was probably an attempt to leave no visible mark which could be traced to the family. According to *Holinshed's Chronicles of England, Scotland, and Ireland* (rpt. New York: AMS Press, 1965), 2:587–88, this was the motivation behind the murder of King Edward II in this manner by the earls of Lancaster and Kent in 1327. "A plumber's instrument was made very hot, the which passing up into his intrails, and being rolled to and fro, burnt the same but so as no appearance of any wound or hurt outwardlie might be perceived."

91. Scaring the Widow (5.1.559). For more on the treatment of widows and women without men on the frontier, see Julie Roy Jeffrey's *Frontier Women* (New York: Hill and Wang, 1979), pp. 25ff., and Joanna Stratton's *Pioneer Women: Voices from the Kansas Frontier* (New York: Simon and Schuster, 1981). For another case of a malefactor disguising himself as an animal, see "The Friendly Old Hog" (legend 68) in the Indians section.

92. The Robinett Death Hole (5.1.588). (*Worker note:* John is 31 yrs. old, the son of Willard Elkins, he owns the cafe in Jonesville. He heard this from his father who was also a Jonesville businessman. He said back when times were not so good they had many idle hours in his father's store and they would sit on the nail kegs day in and day out and relate yarns.) Motifs N387, "Feud starts over trifle," and D1812.3.3.11, "Death of another revealed in dream." (*A second worker note appears at the end of the narrative:* The two men were found there, but the investigation found they had died of too much moonshine. But folks are still afraid of the hole. They feel it is just a matter of time before some other of the older generation meets his death there. They all dodge it and never mention it at home where their children can hear of it.)

93. A Murder Belief Solves a Crime (5.1.544). (*Worker note:* Mrs. Johnson, Aunt Polly, learned this from her father, who was around when it happened. He died at 93 and has been dead many years. He said he was a young man when it happened. She says the old saying about murderers touching their victim's body was believed by all the older people in her dad's day, and it is still sometimes mentioned to this day.) Motif D1318.5.2, "Corpse bleeds when murderer touches it." In Brown, *North Carolina Folklore*, 1:639, a story from Wilmington involving this belief is given in which two suspected murderers were brought before a victim's body in 1875 by a local justice of the peace and told to touch the body to test their guilt or innocence. Other motifs in this narrative are Q211, "Murder punished," Q413.4, "Hanging as punishment for murder," and T612, "Child of slain mother cares for itself during infancy."

94. A Strange Funeral (10.5.1601). Motifs Q411.7, "Death as punishment for ravisher," Q411.10, "Death as punishment for impudence," Q413, "Punishment: hanging," and S113.1 "Murder by hanging." This last motif applies because the hanging was not official or legal.

95. How Dragon Run Got Its Name (6.1.818). Motifs B11.1.4, "Devil in the form of a dragon," B11.9, "Dragon as power of evil," C631, "Tabu: breaking the Sabbath," and D2125.3, "Crossing water in chariot." In the Grimm brothers' collection, tale no. 125, "The Devil and His Grandmother," depicts the devil as

a fiery dragon who appears suddenly. In that tale, however, he offers assistance rather than frightening and chasing the person to whom he appears.

96. How Bloody Branch Got Its Name (5.4.727). (*Worker note:* Mrs. Moore, 54 years old, was told about this incident soon after she moved into the Big Stone Gap area. She showed this writer the path to the bushes where it happened years ago.) Motif D474.2, "Transformation: water becomes bloody."

97. How Champion Swamp Got Its Name (6.1.819). (*Worker note:* Mr. Underwood, born in Smithfield in 1856, said he thought every citizen of Isle of Wight County would know at least something about this story. Mrs. Cofer, born in Smithfield in 1862, said she had heard it all her life.) Motifs E334.1, "Non-malevolent ghost haunts scene of former crime or sin," E422.1.1.3.1, "Headless ghost rides horse," and E581.2, "Ghost rides horse." In *Jonathan Draws the Longbow*, p. 169, Dorson cites several New England headless horseman tales that are associated with swamps.

98. How Haddix's Branch Got Its Name (5.2.658). (*Worker note:* Bond had this from his father who was born in 1810 in Scott County, Virginia, and died in 1883 in Big Laurel. He was among the first settlers here.) Motif B16.2.5, "Devastating bear killed."

99. How the Bull Run Mountains Got Named (6.1.823). (*Worker note:* This is how the tale was told to Miss Ewell by an old native of the Bull Run Mountains, some sixty years ago. It was told to me by several others, in almost the same version.) Motifs B16.1.5.3, "Devastating bull," B741.4.1, "Bellow of bull heard over great distance," and H1161.2.2, "Task: killing fierce bull."

100. How Mother Leather Coat Mountain Was Named (6.1.824). This place-name narrative, surprisingly, contains the only mention of George Washington in the entire WPA collection. There is a description in an oral history of how a group of Virginia Military Institute cadets removed a huge granite boulder from the Peaks of Otter and sent it to Washington, D.C., to be part of the Washington Monument as a way of honoring Virginia's greatest son (10.3.1533).

101. Hickory Gap and the Hickory Gap "Church" (6.2.842–43). (*Worker note:* Mr. Freeman gave me a hickory nut after this interview which I prize very much.) Similar to the Hickory Gap Church is a group in popular circulation called "The Turtles." As in the Hickory Gap Church, the only point of the organization is the solidarity created in belonging to it, as it has no apparent function. There is also a talisman of "The Turtles" which is to be carried at all times.

102. How Simon Kenton Left Home (5.4.746). Motifs M341.2.23, "Prophecy: death by hanging," and N770, "Experience leading to adventures."

103. Simon Kenton's Growing Tree (5.4.747). Motifs E765.3.3, "Life token, life bound up with tree," and T589.3, "Birth trees."

104. Simon Kenton's Exploits (5.4.746). Motifs F610, "Remarkably strong man," F628.1, "Strong man kills animal with own hands," and K540, "Escape by overawing captor."

105. Simon Kenton's Indian Wife and Family (5.4.745). (*Worker note:* There is, of course, no foundation for this, as historical facts have nothing that would coincide with it. It is evidently a fab[r]ic of the imagination told for the sole purpose of entertainment. Maggie Hensley told this some time ago to me before

I realized there were so many Simon Kenton stories afloat.) Motifs H20, "Recognition by resemblance," and R162, "Rescue by captor's daughter." The latter motif may be recognized as the "Pocahontas motif," famous in Virginia for its association with that Indian princess and Captain John Smith of the Jamestown colony.

106. Simon Kenton's Indian Disguise (5.4.747). (*Worker note:* This was told in all sincerity as to its truth. It is far from the actual facts of Simon's return as revealed by records. But it shows how an oft told story can in time be taken as truth. The narrator is a niece (great, great) of Simon Kenton; she is in her sixties and has always lived in the Bull Run Mountains.) Motif K1815.1, "Return home in humble disguise."

107. Simon Kenton Traps a Brandy Thief (5.4.746). Motif K730, "Victim trapped."

108. A Devil Dog Comes for a Slave Owner* (3.2.81). Motifs B15.4.2.1, "Dog with fire in eyes," B15.4.3, "Dog with eyes as big as plates, tea-cups, etc.," E421.3.6, "Ghosts as dogs with glowing tongues and eyes," Baughman E423.1.1(b), "Ghostly black dog," and G303.3.3.1.1, "Devil in the form of a dog." Brewer, in *Dog Ghosts and Other Texas Negro Folk Tales*, pp. 92–93, printed what amounts to an oppositional parallel of this narrative. A good black woman is visited on her deathbed by a white dog, which approaches the bed and gives her pills to nurse her back to health; the narrator of this tale concludes that the ghostly white dog is the spirit of the woman's mother, whom she had cared for in her old age. Interestingly, all the ghost dogs in Brewer's collection are both white and benevolent.

109. Two More Devil Dogs (3.2.85). Motifs B15.4.2.1, "Dog with fire in eyes," B15.4.3, "Dog with eyes as big as plates, tea-cups, etc.," E402.1.2, "Footsteps of invisible ghost heard," E402.1.4, "Invisible ghost jingles chains," Baughman E423.1.1(b), "Ghostly black dog," and G303.3.4.5, "Devil as rolling barrel." This last motif is somewhat of an extrapolation, as it is not clearly stated in the text that the apparition was a "devil." The title is the one the field-worker gave the narrative, however, and the motif index gives the rolling barrel motif as a satanic phenomenon only, with no ghostly dog connection. Also, note the violence associated with elections at this time.

110. The Death Dog (3.2.80). In the *Journal of American Folklore* 54 (1941): 55, Grace Partridge Smith published samplings from a collection of folklore from the "Egypt" region of southern Illinois which included a narrative titled "The Specter Hound" (text no. 2). Smith paraphrased the legend as follows: "A certain family was reported to have a superstition that a large black hound came scratching at the door when anyone was about to die. The belief had held for several generations. One day, a scratching and whining was heard at the kitchen door. The window was then raised to get a better view of what was going on outside. What should be seen but an enormous black dog at the back door. A short time later there was a death in the family, for their grandmother died." Motifs D1812.5.1.12.1 "Howling of dog as bad omen," Baughman E574(ia), "Ghost dog appears as death omen," and F401.3.3, "Spirit as black dog." Smith's collection gives numerous British references to this belief legend, and Randolph, in *Who Blowed Up the Church House?*, pp. 171–73n., gave several Ozark and Appalachian references.

111. The Warning Dog (3.2.87). Motif F401.3.3, "Spirit as black dog." Note the theme of the consequences of violating acceptable moral norms in this narrative. The spirit dog is an agent of punishment for the cruelty of the father and stepmother.

112. A Spirit Dog Causes a Broken Toe (3.2.77). Motifs E521.2, "Ghost of dog," and G303.3.3.1.1, "Devil in form of a dog."

113. A Devil Dog in the Path (3.2.67). Motifs B15.4.2.1, "Dog with fire in eyes," B15.4.3, "Dog with eyes as big as plates, tea-cups, etc.," B871.1.7, "Giant dog," and G303.3.3.1.1, "Devil in the form of a dog."

114. The Ghost Dog on Indian Creek (3.2.72). Motifs B15.4.2.1, "Dog with fire in eyes," E334.5, "Ghosts of soldiers haunt battlefield," and E423.1.1, "Revenant as dog." In Brown, *North Carolina Folklore*, 1:675ff., there are several ghostly black dog narratives which involve encounters on the road such as the one described here.

115. The Dog That Turned to Rags (3.2.66). Motifs B15.4.2.1, "Dog with fire in eyes," B15.4.3, "Dog with eyes as big as plates, tea-cups, etc.," B871.1.7, "Giant dog," D412.5, "Transformation: dog to another animal." In Brown, *North Carolina Folklore*, 1:675, a ghost dog narrative relates two consecutive transformations: "There is another man who had a very strange experience with a ghost or hant. When he was going along the woods one night, he came to an old cemetery. In the road lay something white about the size of an opossum. When he came near it, he kicked it and it became as large as a dog. He kicked it again and it became the size of a calf. The man then became frightened and ran away."

116. The Ghost Dog on Chinquapin Hill (3.2.75). Motifs E423.1.1, "Revenant as dog," and E334.1, "Ghost haunts scene of former crime or sin."

117. Dogs Chase an Invisible Creature* (2.1.246). (*Worker note:* This story is known by many of the old people who lived around the mill lot in Dendron.) Motifs E421.1, "Invisible ghost," E421.1.3, "Ghost visible to dogs only," and, possibly, F4013, "Spirit in animal form." I posit the invisible creature to be an animal spirit since the narrator says it fought "like a wild cat." Although it was told as a firsthand account, the worker note attributes wider community circulation to it.

118. The Boat That Would Not Move* (2.2.282). Motifs D2072.0.2.1, "Horse enchanted so that he stands still," and D2072.0.3, "Ship held back by magic." A literary legend by George S. Wasson, which Dorson described in his *Jonathan Draws the Long Bow*, pp. 243–46, includes the motif of a boat refusing to move. And Gardner, *Folklore from the Schoharie Hills*, p. 79, gave a narrative which attributes a boat being stilled in the water to a witch. Here a witch doctor breaks the spell with a countercharm made of witch hazel and elder bushes.

119. The White Dove: A Dead Wife Returns* (2.1.249). Motifs E221.1, "Husband haunted by dead wife on second marriage," and E322.4, "Dead wife returns in the form of a bird."

120. Jack-ma-Lanterns: Lights in the Woods* (2.2.262). Motif F491.1, "Will-o'-the-Wisp (Jack-o'-Lantern)," and F491.3.1, "Person led astray by Will-o'-the-Wisp turns one of his garments inside out to end its power."

121. The Cat Woman (3.1.58). Motifs B601.12, "Marriage to cat," B651, "Marriage to beast in human form," C35.1, "Tabu: mentioning origin of animal wife," D142.0.1, "Woman transformed to cat," and D342, "Transformation: cat to person." A long literary version of this well-known European legend is found in Brown, *North Carolina Folklore*, 1:660.

122. The Murdered Man's Hat and the Melted Snow (3.3.94). Baughman motif F974.1, "Grass will not grow where blood of murdered person has been shed," and motif F159.3, "Hill on which snow always melts."

123. The Disappearing Old Gray Horse (3.2.70). Motifs E439.1, "Revenant forced away by shooting," and E521.1, "Ghost of horse."

124. The Haunted Woods (3.3.119). Baughman motif E402.1.1.3, "Ghost cries and screams," motifs E522, "Ghost of wild beast," and, perhaps, G303.8.13, "Devil in the woods": there is no motif for ghosts or spirits in the woods except this satanic one. There are several motifs for wood spirits, which are fairies or "little people," but they do not apply to the phenomenon described in this narrative.

125. The Fiddler of Peter Cave (3.3.196). (*Worker note*: This legend is not well known and certainly has not gone out of the mountains of SW Virginia. Oldest people in the section say it was told by their parents *and* grandparents. Perhaps it was an interesting topic before there was the Civil War to talk about and after the Indian tales had grown stale.) Baughman motif E402.1.3(a), "Ghost plays violin," and motif E402.4, "Ethereal music." J. Frank Dobie's *Legends of Texas*, Publications of the Texas Folklore Society, 3 (1922), pp. 137–41, prints eight texts of a "mysterious music" legend from the San Bernard River at Music Bend, Texas. These have some elements of the version given here, but none mentions a lost fiddler as the origin of the music.

126. The Shower of Stones (3.1.48). (*Worker note*: The informant is the son of Thomas Steele and was about six years old when the events took place.) The event's date is given as 1825, much too early for the informant to relate the story from personal experience in 1939. Baughman motifs E281.0.3*, "Ghost haunts house, damaging property or annoying inhabitants," and F473.1(a), "Spirits throw stones (at individual houses)." Baughman commented that "it is hard to tell whether the haunters under this category are ghosts, witches, or familiar spirits." Motifs D2136.1, "Rocks move by magic," E599.6, "Ghost moves furniture," G269.10, "Witch punishes person who incurs her ill will," and G269.17, "Invisible witch sticks victim with pins."

127. The Black Cat (3.2.69). Motifs B721, "Cat's luminous eyes," B871.1.6, "Giant cat," C867, "Tabu: unusual cruelty," G303.3.3.1.2, "Devil in the form of a cat," S12.2, "Cruel mother kills child," and S115.2, "Murder by sticking needle through head." The theme of guilt is evident here. The woman had already violated the moral norms of her group by having illegitimate children, and her grizzly crimes make her ripe for punishment, which, coming from a supernatural agency, reinforces the norms. In the *Journal of American Folklore* 54 (1941): 202–3, James Travis printed an Irish-American tale in which a priest visiting the home of a Protestant family perceives that their curiously intelligent and talented cat is the devil in disguise. After a strenuous exorcism struggle,

the priest vanquishes the satanic feline, which flies out the window in a ball of flame.

128. Ocean-Born Mary (5.4.739). (*Worker note:* Mrs. Wooding said she was first told this story by her grandmother in about the year 1867.) The obviously literary tone of this narrative is probably the creation of the VWP worker. It seems to be field-derived material, though obviously not given in its field-collected form. Motifs E291.1, "Person burying treasure kills person to supply guardian ghost," E425.1, "Revenant as woman," E545.12, "Ghost directs men to hidden treasure," N572, "Woman as guardian of treasure," and R12, "Abduction by pirates."

129. The Two Pine Trees (5.4.743). Motif D2157.3.2, "Treasure hidden in trees' roots."

130. A Gold Hunter Finds a Ghost (3.3.102). Motifs D1181, "Magic needle," D1314.2, "Magic wand locates hidden treasure," E291, "Ghost protects hidden treasure," E451.5, "Ghost laid when treasure is unearthed," E545, "The dead speak," N533, "Treasures discovered by magic object," N576, "Ghost prevents men from raising treasure." In *Jonathan Draws the Longbow*, pp. 179–82, Dorson gives numerous New England accounts of rods and other devices for finding precious metals. In the *Journal of American Folklore* 51 (1938): 92–93, Helen Louise Taylor prints an account of a divining rod which detected treasure in New Castle, Delaware.

131. The Sign That Pointed to Gold (5.5.752). Note how the narrative focuses more on hearing about the treasure and the pact to hunt for it than on the treasure itself.

132. The Beverly Diamonds (5.1.589). As in "The Sign That Pointed to Gold" (legend 131), the subject is the hunt rather than the treasure or any belief narrative about it. Motifs D1314.2, "Magic wand locates hidden treasure," and N533, "Treasures discovered by magic object." For more on this theme, see "A Gold Hunter Finds a Ghost" (legend 130).

133. The Story of Swift and His Compass (5.6.784). (*Worker note:* Mrs. Bozarth believes this legend to be true and that the mine is somewhere in the High Knob section of Wise County. This version is in her own words. She says the oldest people in the area remember their grandparents' talk about the mine.) Motif E422.1.11.4, "Ghost as hand or hands." Dobie's *Legends of Texas*, pp. 3–104, gives numerous texts of legends of lost mines similar to Swift's in a chapter titled "Legends of Buried Treasure and Lost Mines." One in particular, "The Silver Ledge on the Frio," pp. 60–62, is similar to the one given here. It includes Indians who know the treasure's location and attack whites who get too close to finding it.

134. Spirit Dog Guards Swift's Mine (3.2.62). Motifs B15.4.2.1, "Dog with fire in eyes," B15.4.3, "Dog with eyes as big as plates, tea-cups, etc.," and B871.1.7, "Giant dog." Baughman motif B576.2.1*, "Dog as guardian of treasure." For similar narratives, see the Spirit Dogs section.

135. The Old Woman Who Found the Silver (5.6.785). (*Worker note:* Mr. Nash is 76.) Note that the thrust of this narrative is a failed attempt to locate the treasure and a connection of the community legend to the informant's family history and experience.

136. Swift's Silver Mine (5.6.802). The connection between the Swift Silver Mine and a counterfeiting scheme is mentioned in several WPA collection narratives not given here; see boxes 5 and 6, files 790–94, 808, and 811.

137. A Smallpox Epidemic: A Curse on Whites* (1.2.15). Motifs F493.3, "Protection against pestilence spirit," and Q552.10, "Plague as punishment." Much of this text is a personal account, but the assertion that the epidemic was a curse on whites for their cruelty makes it a belief legend. H. W. Burton's *The History of Norfolk, Virginia* (Norfolk, 1877), indicates that there was no smallpox outbreak during this period. There was, however, a yellow fever epidemic in August–December 1855. Even though the Civil War was over five years away, many U.S. soldiers were in the city during this period, helping to fight the pestilence. Burton (on p. 23) substantiates Shepherd's assertion that blacks had a much lower morbidity rate than whites. This probably involved both susceptibility and exposure factors. At this time it was unlikely for blacks to live near the water where the disease-bearing *Aedes aegypti* mosquito had been brought in on a ship from the Virgin Islands. Further, Burton notes that, besides along the waterfront, the outbreak was concentrated in the poor Irish section of the city, a population less likely than most to own slaves. Dr. Grayson Miller of the Virginia Department of Health's Epidemiology Office told me that "once a person survives yellow fever infection, he is immune from the disease for the rest of his life. Some of the black population may have been exposed to yellow fever earlier in life and therefore been immune, especially those who had been in Africa or some other area in which yellow fever is common." He also noted that, unlike smallpox, yellow fever is not contact contagious; the mosquito must bite an ill person and then bite others for the disease to occur, so anyone could have safely walked around the pestilence houses and even played on the bodies of the dead.

138. How Cox's Snow Got Its Name* (1.9.91–92). Motifs, for the second version only, Q552.14, "Storm as punishment," and Q558, "Mysterious death as punishment." Cox's snow is recorded historical fact; it was a major blizzard which struck eastern Virginia in the winter of 1857.

139. A Scar Identifies a Slave Woman's Husband as Her Son* (1.9.91). There is a handwritten note on the page: "Where from? Superstition?" Motifs N365.1, "Incest unwittingly committed," and T412, "Mother-son incest." Note the motif, from *Oedipus Rex* and elsewhere, of recognition by a physical marking.

140. The Old Negro That Flagged the Train* (1.10.217). In *Dog Ghosts and Other Texas Negro Folk Tales*, p. 30, Brewer printed a version of this legend under the category of "Carefree Tales." Collected from R. A. Atkinson in 1952, it is titled "Uncle Aaron Peddles a Possum." In this story Uncle Aaron has a farm right by the tracks and doesn't seem oppressed, tired, or destitute. At the end the seemingly black train conductor sides with Uncle Aaron against the angry white engineer in front of the stopped train. The conductor says, "How much does you want for de possum?" In response, "Uncle Aaron bow his haid kinda shame faced lack an' say, 'Ah don' know, Ah ain't caught 'im yit.'" This is somewhat like the last part of the text given here, but the two are different in atmosphere. The wish fulfillment of the old man confronting an obvious symbol of white power, both social and technological, which is clearly present in Patton's version, is subdued, if it exists at all, in Atkinson's. Patton's can hardly be categorized as a "carefree tale."

141. Dick the Slave Boy and the Wolves* (1.10.172). After the title on the manuscript is the phrase "a folklore story—True." (*Worker note:* Dick the slave boy, belonged to my grandfather, Harold Pugh. He was a very valuable fellow and grandfather gave 1500 acres of land on Fox Creek for him. This land in part comprises the farms of H. A. and Stonewall Hoffman, at Grant, Virginia. The story told to me by Harold Pugh, my grandfather, now dead.) Motif K551.3.1, "Respite from death while one plays the fiddle. Rescue arrives."

142. Murder at the County Line* (1.2.23). (*Worker note:* The place mentioned is not far from Whippoorwill Mountain and is as described. The facts of the story are well known, although there are but a few of the old people left who can recall the details.) Motifs D1812.1.12.1, "Dog howling as bad omen," E334.1, "Ghost haunts scene of former crime or sin," and F974, "Grass refuses to grow in certain spot." This last is an approximation, since the informant stated that nothing—no trees, shrubs, or grass—would grow at the site of the county line murder. For another case of no vegetation growing at the site of a tragedy, see "Indians Kill a Pioneer Family" (legend 65) in the Indians section.

143. The Woman Dressed in Black (3.3.118). Baughman motifs E402.1.1.3, "Ghost cries and screams," and E574(bc), "Woman in black." Motifs E323, "Dead mother's friendly return," E371, "Return from dead to reveal hidden treasure," and E545.19.2, "Proper means of addressing ghost." These motifs are only applicable if the woman in black is in fact a ghost, but note that in the narrative she is never called a ghost or described to indicate a ghostly nature.

144. The Boy Who Turned Wild in the Woods (5.1.577). Motif F567, "Wild man." Note the theme of the fear of losing civilization and returning to an animal or natural state. For a full discussion of the wild man motif in western art and literature, see Richard Bernheimer's *Wild Men in the Middle Ages: A Study in Art, Sentiment, and Demonology* (New York: Octagon Books, 1970).

145. The Wild Girl (5.1.538). See note for legend 144.

146. The Man Who Ate Live Meat (5.1.580). (*Worker note:* The informant learned the story from his step-mother, Mrs. Josie Morgan Pegram about ten years ago.) Thompson's *Body, Boots, and Britches*, p. 47, refers to a New York legend in which, as a torture, an Indian sliced flesh from the arm and back of a white prisoner and ate it raw. See "Henry Armstrong, de Forgin' Man" (legend 73) for another instance of a person's obsession returning him to jail on the same day he gets out.

147. Roast Cat for Breakfast (5.2.644). Note similarities to the modern legend of the cat in the microwave. See Brunvand's *The Choking Doberman and Other "New" Urban Legends* for two versions of microwaved pet narratives in a chapter on the subject of "Unfortunate Pet Legends," pp. 93–102.

148. The Naked Bull Ride (5.1.576). This tale is similar to such modern legends as "The Nude in the RV" or "The Nude Surprise Party." See Brunvand's *The Vanishing Hitchhiker*, pp. 125–52, for background and interpretation of a whole body of "caught naked" legend narratives.

149. Caught in the Graveyard (3.3.103 and 6.4.886). Type 1676B, "Clothing Caught in Graveyard," Baughman motif N384.2(a). Versions of this legend are in Brown, *North Carolina Folklore*, 1:686; Ray Browne, *A Night with the Hants and Other Alabama Folk Experiences* (Bowling Green, Ohio: Bowling Green Univ.

Popular Press, 1976), p. 53; McNeil, *Ghost Stories*, no. 27, pp. 59–60; Lynwood Montell, *Ghosts along the Cumberland* (Knoxville: Univ. of Tennessee Press, 1975), nos. 458–62, pp. 199–201; J. Russell Reaver, *Florida Folktales* (Gainesville: Univ. Presses of Florida, 1987), no. 82, p. 103; and Randolph, *The Devil's Pretty Daughter*, pp. 65–67.

150. A Man Dies of Earwigs (5.2.696). Note the similarity to the modern "The Girl with the Beehive Hairdo" legend. For other versions and discussion, see Baker, *Hoosier Folk Legends*, pp. 223–25; Brunvand, *The Vanishing Hitchhiker*, pp. 75–81; George Carey, "Some Thoughts on the Modern Legend," *Journal of the Folklore Society of Greater Washington* 2 (Winter 1970–71): 8–9; and Kenneth Clarke, "The Fatal Hairdo and the Emperor's New Clothes Revisited," *Western Folklore* 22 (1964): 249–52. Brunvand mentions a legend very close to the one given here which involves neither vanity nor lack of cleanliness on the victim's part and does not refer to a fashionable hair style. In his paraphrase: "A little boy suffers a headache so severe that in a mad frenzy he jams a fork into his forehead, releasing a stream of ants which had taken over his sinus cavities" (p. 80).

APPENDIX A

VWP WORKERS

WORKER	LEGEND NUMBER
Adams, James Taylor	5, 6, 7, 8, 9, 11, 12, 16, 19, 20, 27, 35, 39, 41, 46, 47, 50, 52, 62, 64, 65, 68, 79, 82, 89, 91, 98, 108, 109, 110, 112, 113, 114, 115, 118, 125, 127, 132, 134, 145, 146, 150
Anderson, Claude W.*	23, 77, 138
Berry, Cornelia	49, 58, 129
Blair, Gertrude	123
Byrd, Susie R. C.*	138
Garrett, John W.	29, 42, 59, 88, 124, 130, 140, 143, 145, 149
Goolrick, John	81
Green, Frances V.	117
Hale, Laura Virginia	120
Hamilton, Emory L.	3, 4, 17, 22, 26, 34, 48, 53, 55, 62, 63, 70, 71, 72, 90, 125, 133, 136, 144
Harris, Louise G.	24
Hylton, James M.	10, 13, 67, 69, 78, 83, 85, 86, 87, 92, 93, 94, 96, 101, 111, 131, 135, 147
Jayne, Lucille B.	43, 95
Lewis, Roscoe E.*	30, 45, 73
Miller, Harriet G.	21, 25
Morrissett, Pearl	2, 33
Morton, Susan R.	44, 51, 56, 57, 60, 61, 99, 100, 102, 103, 104, 105, 106, 107, 116, 142, 148
Scales, Bessie A.	15, 18, 54, 76, 84, 119, 128
Sloan, Raymond	36, 37, 122
Smith, Mary E. W.	80
Sproles, Susie	141
unknown	1, 14, 31, 75, 121, 137, 139
Volley, Isaiah*	32
Warren, I. M.	28, 38, 40, 66, 126
Williams, Grace	97
Williams, Jesse R.*	74
Wilson, Emmy*	23

*African American workers.

APPENDIX B

LEGEND TELLERS

INFORMANT	LEGEND NUMBER
Aunt Sudie	121
Dicy Adams	68, 110, 145
Findlay Adams	27, 112, 113
James Taylor Adams	41
Samuel Simpson Adams	6, 7, 150
Simpson Randolph Adams	19
Spencer Greenfield Adams	62
Patrick Henry Addington	64, 114
Rebecca Ashby	61, 102
Della Barksdale	33
Aunt Fannie Beale	103
Cornelia Berry	58
Mrs. Berry	148
W. Patton Beverly	35, 134
Grant Boles	44
Boyd Bolling	39, 82
Leslie Bolling	117
Elbert J. Bond	64, 98
George Bowden	13, 27, 73
Clara Bozarth	133
Mrs. R. V. Brayhill	29, 124
Henry Bridgett	142
Melviny Brown	25, 119
Mr. Bryant	88
Rev. Richard Buster	32
Mr. Butler	123
Charlie Carter	148
C. Wentz Carter	11, 12
Elizabeth Kilgore Carter	16, 118
Leonard E. Carter	47
Mary Carter	108
Mrs. John Cofer	97
Charlotte Collins	4

APPENDIX B

Minnie Collins	89, 132
Preston Cornett	34
Silas Craft	5, 115
Royce Cress	8
Molly Crews	143
Mrs. Robert Edwards	49, 129
John Elkins, Jr.	92
Miss M. A. Ewell	99
Charles Freeman	101
Willard Freeman	83
Rachell Gardner	46
Miss Lou Garrett	59
Georgiana Gibbs	139
Lee Gilliam	101
John Goolrick	72
Clinton H. Gregory	149
Eliza Gunther	1
Tom Hale	136
Emory L. Hamilton	22
Etta Kilgore Hamilton	70
Goldie Hamilton	144
Judge J. T. Hamilton	20
Lemuel Hamilton	17, 26, 55
Nellie Hamilton	3
Rev. P. L. Harvey	30
Maggie Hensley	105
George Hill	79
Dr. J. M. Hill	48
Joe Hubbard	78
White Coon Hubbard	86
Moses Johnson	60
Mrs. Polly Johnson	63, 72, 93
William Johnson	74
Walter Kennedy	13
Lenore Kilgore	9, 109
Raleigh Kilgore	72
Hector Lane	67
Etta Lawson	71
"Stack" Lee	45, 77
Celia Ann Maggard	52
Molly Mayhew	56, 57

APPENDIX B

APPENDIX C

COUNTIES
WHERE LEGENDS
WERE COLLECTED

COUNTY (OR CITY)	LEGEND NUMBER
Alleghany	80
Amherst	143
Appomattox	30
Augusta	126
Bedford	1
Botetourt	123
Buckingham	42, 88, 92, 130, 140, 149
Carroll	38
Chesterfield	138
Danville (city)	2, 15, 18, 33, 54, 76, 84, 119, 128
Fauquier	56
Floyd	122
Fluvanna	44, 116, 142
Franklin	36, 37
Gloucester	43, 95
Grayson	141
Hampton (city)	45, 73, 77, 138
Hopewell (city)	124
Isle of Wight	97
Loudoun	60
Lynchburg (city)	32, 74
Mathews	21, 25
Nelson	59, 149
Newport News (city)	24
Norfolk (city)	23, 137
Northumberland	49, 58, 129
Page	51, 148
Portsmouth (city)	139

Luray	148
Lynchburg	32, 74
Manteo	42, 140, 149
Newport	126
Newport News	24
Norfolk	23, 137
North	21
Norton	16, 35, 52, 79, 85, 118, 134
Norwood	146
Payne Gap	87, 94
Portsmouth	139
Richmond	14, 75, 117
Roanoke	28, 40
Rocky Mount	36, 37
Smithfield	97
Sword's Creek	47
unknown	1, 25, 29, 30, 31, 47, 48, 53, 60, 80, 88, 121, 122, 143, 146
Waterfall	61, 102, 103, 104, 105, 106, 107
White House	51
Wingina	59
Wise	3, 4, 5, 10, 11, 13, 17, 20, 22, 26, 53, 55, 62, 63, 69, 70, 71, 83, 86, 93, 101, 125, 131, 135, 136, 147

APPENDIX E

VWP WORKERS
AND THE PLACES
WHERE THEY
COLLECTED LEGENDS

WORKER	COUNTY (OR CITY)
Adams, James Taylor	Russell, Tazewell, Wise
Anderson, Claude W.*	Hampton (city), Norfolk (city)
Berry, Cornelia	Northumberland
Blair, Gertrude	Botetourt
Byrd, Susie R. C.*	Chesterfield
Garrett, John W.	Amherst, Buckingham, Hopewell (city), Nelson, Prince George
Goolrick, John	Stafford
Green, Frances V.	Richmond (city)
Hale, Laura Virginia	Warren
Hamilton, Emory L.	Scott, Wise
Harris, Louise G.	Newport News (city)
Hylton, James M.	Wise
Jayne, Lucille B.	Gloucester
Lewis, Roscoe E.*	Appomattox, Hampton (city)
Miller, Harriet G.	Mathews
Morrissett, Pearl	Danville (city)
Morton, Susan R.	Fauquier, Fluvanna, Loudoun, Page, Prince William
Scales, Bessie A.	Danville (city)
Sloan, Raymond	Floyd, Franklin
Smith, Mary E. W.	Alleghany
Sproles, Susie	Grayson
unknown	Bedford, Norfolk (city), Portsmouth (city), Richmond (city), Smyth, Spotsylvania
Volley, Isaiah*	Campbell, Lynchburg (city)
Warren, I. M.	Augusta, Carroll, Roanoke (city), Spotsylvania
Williams, Grace	Isle of Wight
Williams, Jesse R.*	Campbell, Lynchburg (city)
Wilson, Emmy*	Norfolk (city)

*African American workers.